Dreams of Archives Unfolded

CRITICAL CARIBBEAN STUDIES

Series Editors: Yolanda Martínez-San Miguel, Carter Mathes, and Kathleen López

Focused particularly in the twentieth and twenty-first centuries, although attentive to the context of earlier eras, this series encourages interdisciplinary approaches and methods and is open to scholarship in a variety of areas, including anthropology, cultural studies, diaspora and transnational studies, environmental studies, gender and sexuality studies, history, and sociology. The series pays particular attention to the four main research clusters of Critical Caribbean Studies at Rutgers University, where the coeditors serve as members of the executive board: Caribbean Critical Studies Theory and the Disciplines; Archipelagic Studies and Creolization; Caribbean Aesthetics, Poetics, and Politics; and Caribbean Colonialities.

For a list of all the titles in the series, please see the last page of the book.

Dreams of Archives Unfolded

Absence and Caribbean Life Writing

Jocelyn Fenton Stitt

RUTGERS UNIVERSITY PRESS
NEW BRUNSWICK, CAMDEN, AND NEWARK,
NEW JERSEY, AND LONDON

Library of Congress Cataloging-in-Publication Data

Names: Stitt, Jocelyn Fenton, author.
Title: Dreams of archives unfolded : absence and Caribbean life writing / Jocelyn Fenton Stitt.
Description: New Brunswick : Rutgers University Press, [2021] | Series: Critical Caribbean studies | Includes bibliographical references and index.
Identifiers: LCCN 2020043872 | ISBN 9781978806542 (paperback ; alk. paper) | ISBN 9781978806559 (hardcover ; alk. paper) | ISBN 9781978806566 (epub) | ISBN 9781978806573 (mobi) | ISBN 9781978806580 (PDF)
Subjects: LCSH: Caribbean literature (English)—Women authors—History and criticism. | Caribbean literature (English)—21st century—History and criticism. | Women authors, Caribbean—Biography—History and criticism. | Women authors, Caribbean—Historiography. | Caribbean Area—Biography—History and criticism. | Caribbean Area—Historiography. | History in literature.
Classification: LCC PR9205.05 .S75 2021 | DDC 810.9/928709729—dc23
LC record available at https://lccn.loc.gov/2020043872

A British Cataloging-in-Publication record for this book is available from the British Library.

♾ The paper used in this publication meets the requirements of the American National Standard for Information Sciences—Permanence of Paper for Printed Library Materials, ANSI Z39.48–1992.

www.rutgersuniversitypress.org

Manufactured in the United States of America

For Neil, Elizabeth, and Ramsey

Contents

Dreams of Archives Unfolded

Introduction

ARCHIVAL DREAMS AND CARIBBEAN LIFE WRITING

In 1838, twenty-one years after the abolition of the slave trade, four years after emancipation, during the last year of required apprenticeship in the British West Indies, a minor Jamaican newspaper printed a ghostly communiqué from the future. Dated May 2, 1938, the letter described itself as subverting linear European time, instead conforming to the disruptions and disjunctures of temporality in the Caribbean: "The following letter was not received by any of the West India mails. The *post* could not have brought it. It may seem to be antedated, if we compute by the aera [*sic*] of the Old World; but clocks go much faster in the New . . . this certainly rather suspicious forestallment of the European chronology, forbids the announcement of any further particulars."[1] "A Brief Account and Familiar Description of Jamaica in its *Most* Modern Statistics" is arguably the earliest form of utopian and speculative fiction set in a recognizably Caribbean future society.[2] It creates an amalgam of characteristics of European modernity within the supposed Edenic space of the tropics. As important, the narrative uses the autobiographical genre of the travelogue to provide a first-person account of Jamaica in 1938. Arriving in Jamaica, the narrator rhapsodizes that "a den of debasement has been converted into a theatre of glory. . . . It is a paradise of God!" The writer imagines a postslavery Jamaica free of violence and full of respect for the rule of law, where "murder has not been known since the white man forebore to kill the black." Political equality has been established and colorism abolished: "The Assembly comprises a few whites, but the large majority consists of the dark population, through all its shades. . . . Between these exists no rivalry."

After establishing Jamaica as thriving post-emancipation society, the second installment begins by emphasizing that the museum and the archive, technologies of memory, are institutions as important as the church and the legislature. The museum, located presciently in Kingston—the Institute of Jamaica would be founded there in 1879—contains a natural history section with specimens from the Caribbean and Africa. For the narrator, however, the archival preservation of slavery's history draws the most attention:

> Natural curiosities . . . had little attraction to me: *the archives were unfolded, and the history of bondage stood confessed.* There was a model of the slave-ship; the instrument with which they wrenched open the mouth of the poor victims of the middle passage when despair had sealed it; the brands which stamped them; the scourges which tore them; the stocks which distorted them; the thumb screws which racked them! How curdled my blood! How sunk my heart! Horrid insignia of cruelty! . . . *Who shall recall from the grave the bodies ye have been employed to agonize, and from eternity the souls into which your iron entered?* Here is the first order of Elizabeth, authorizing the importation of slaves; and the last proclamation of injustice and bloodshed, signed by the name of Belmore.[3]

These Kingston archives establish and document not just individual acts of violence in the form of instruments of torture but also the historical documents that substantiate state responsibility for slavery and its horrors. The sudden address to the instruments of torture gathered as proof of slavery's violence in this archive of the future is startling. While much can be documented, confessed, and "unfolded" about slavery through historical recovery, the narrator points to the futility of calling forth the bodies and souls of the dead. The enslaved cannot speak, and the material evidence of slavery, such as the stocks, cannot answer for their crimes.

I open with this 1838 newspaper article that combines speculative fiction, time travel, and travel narrative since it eerily predicts tensions and questions central to twentieth- and twenty-first-century Caribbean literature. "A Brief Account" articulates a fantasy of the power of archives—if the horrors of colonization were fully documented and available for examination, then the perpetrators would be held accountable not only in the present but in perpetuity—"a history of bondage stood confessed." The article demonstrates the long-standing association between archival documentation and decolonization, even as it troubles that link by showing that the dead, the marginalized, and the voiceless are absent from archival records of slavery and colonization and thus cannot be recuperated. We experience with the narrator the realization that even in a utopian Caribbean future there is no transcending death or correcting the horrors of the past. The narrative uses the life writing form of the travelogue to describe the limits of the archive and the affects those absences produce.

The presence of this mysterious document from 1838, in an archival newspaper in Jamaica's National Library, raised for me, as perhaps for nineteenth-century readers, the uncanny possibility that it *was* a letter from 1938. Genre has everything to do with my response. The text positions itself as no mere fantasy or prediction but rather as a nonfiction travelogue promising a truthful retelling of what the writer has witnessed. Generic expectations for travel writing encourage readers to see "A Brief Account" as possibly describing a real journey. Reading about the future through a generic form that makes implicit promises of truthfulness creates an illusion that the future described is inevitable. Indeed, the Latin epigraph for the first installment reads, "Look up and rejoice in all the ages that are about to come."[4]

Dreams of archives haunt Caribbean literature. The popularity of historical fiction within Caribbean literature attests to this impulse for recovery in the creation of lost or undocumented stories.[5] Nonfiction writing such as life narrative, in contrast, provides readers what Foucault states is foundational for the archive: a documentary record, which accounts perhaps for its recent upsurge among Caribbean authors.[6] Life writing, much like postcolonial cultural productions generally, promises to provide readers with a previously unknown archive of the past, through memory, interviews, documents, and photographs. The intersection of archival absences and the production of life narrative is revolutionary in the Caribbean context precisely because the colonial project, with its compulsion to name and control, obscured or did not produce documents that could substantiate the lives of the enslaved and indentured from their point of view.[7]

Tracing the shape of this dream in contemporary Caribbean life writing leads me to ask, what happens when we reach the limits of the archives of colonialism, slavery, indenture, independence, and diaspora in the Caribbean? I theorize that the remarkable flowering of autobiographical writing by Caribbean women since 2000 is not an imitation of the "memoir boom" in North America and Europe.[8] Instead, the works of established figures, such as Saidiya Hartman, Dionne Brand, Maryse Condé, Lorna Goodison, Erna Brodber, Ruth Behar, Edwidge Danticat, and M. NourbeSe Philip, and emerging writers, such as Andrea Stuart, Yvonne Shorter Brown, Sonja Boon, and Gaiutra Bahadur, mark a different aesthetic, one born out of encountering holes in archives and ancestral memory that cannot be filled with more research. What do we do, these texts ask, when "the scourges which tore them" and "the grave the bodies ye have been employed to agonize" cannot testify?

By foregrounding the importance of archival absences in these texts, my use of a Caribbean feminist decolonial perspective brings into relief the gendered nature of colonial archival practices, postcolonial masculinist nationalism, and, subsequently, how contemporary women's life writing creates alternative ways of understanding the relationship of the past to the present. My approach, following María Lugones, reveals how contemporary Caribbean writing traces colonial processes of gendering and racialization in order to destabilize and resist these epistemologies.[9] For example, in chapter 1 I discuss Dionne Brand's *A Map to the Door of No Return: Notes on Belonging* (2001), which juxtaposes the erasure of her family's ancestral origin in Africa with the erasure of her experience surviving the U.S. invasion of Grenada and subsequent marginalization as a Black lesbian activist in Canada. Rather than the absences in Brand's family history spurring travel to Africa or a DNA test, she writes of these aporias as an inescapable condition of Black subjectivity in the Americas—one that forms a through line to instances of white supremacy, racialized sexism, and neocolonialism in the present, such as the trauma she experiences in Grenada. Brand's use of life writing to investigate absences in personal and historical narratives represents one mode of decolonial feminist praxis, I argue, in that her work not only describes the effects of the past in the present but makes an epistemological intervention to think in new ways about what those absences mean for Caribbean futures.

In the midst of ongoing debates about relevance of the past to present, known in Caribbean studies as "quarrel with history," and in its North American counterpart as the "question of recovery," I maintain that absence conceptually creates a generative space for Caribbean epistemologies.[10] What interest me are life writing texts grappling with the absence of "evidence" from the past, especially as it relates to women's histories. Absence aesthetics, as I call it, constitutes a new method of understanding contemporary Caribbean women's life writing and, by extension, new movements in Caribbean historiography. The texts treated here engage with and draw from a wide variety of archives, not just official records, and theorize about the power dynamics that produced the absences they find.[11] These writings should be understood differently from traditional uses of autobiography devoted to telling the story of a single life. Autobiography often uses the forward momentum of chronicling a person's life as the engine driving the "plot." In contrast, these texts often take the form of a quest to understand both their own and their family's absence from the historical record and why writing that absence is politically necessary to tell untold stories. The authors of these texts claim epistemic agency in writing history, even as historically women's first-person narratives, especially by African and Asian women from the Caribbean, mark another site of archival absence. The archive as a generative limit rather than the point of scholarship itself is one of the lessons of this body of contemporary Caribbean life writing. By examining the role of Caribbean life writing as a means to elaborate not only what remains of historical memory, but also how historical absence shapes contemporary cultural creation, *Dreams of Archives Unfolded* joins the work of historians Marisa J. Fuentes and Tiya Miles and literary critics Lisa Lowe and Jacqui Alexander in seeking methods to unfold archives while remaining dubious about older methodologies that demand proof from archival materials. Indeed, in the Caribbean context, the archive cannot often function as an originary site, given the absence and silence of written records of the enslaved and indentured.

Absence, Archives, and the Caribbean Quarrel with History

The Caribbean colonial archive may not be able to fulfil the desires of all those who turn to it, but archival dreams continue to haunt Caribbean literature. Caribbean and African diaspora studies takes as a given that cataloguing the past will lead to understanding the present.[12] The archival impulse has long roots; even in 1838 a writer recognized the possibility of the historical record to enable a liberatory dream of the future. Only once "*the archives were unfolded, and the history of bondage stood confessed*" could the utopian Caribbean be achieved. Despite known absences in the archives of the Caribbean, the archive itself retains a special status within Caribbean studies.[13] "Gaining control of their own narratives, telling their story on their own terms are fundamental concerns of decolonized societies," the editors of *Decolonizing the Caribbean Record: An Archives Reader* assert, adding that "decolonizing the archives is one critical manifestation" of that project.[14] Indeed, many of the foundational works in Caribbean studies begin from just such a premise. C. L. R. James's *The Black Jacobins* (1938), for example, provides a corrective to Eurocentric histories of the Haitian Revolution by connecting it to the French Revolution. As important, his work became a model for how archival scholarship could recenter African diaspora peoples as the subjects of history rather than objects of study. Kamau Brathwaite's *The Development of Creole Society in Jamaica* (1972) used archival materials, such as marriage and birth records, for his argument about how interracial families were created and cultural creolization came about. Barbara Bush's pioneering research, in works such as *Slave Women in Caribbean Society, 1650–1838* (1990), led to a reappraisal of issues of gender and agency for enslaved women. More recently Thomas Glave's anthology *Our Caribbean: A Gathering of Lesbian and Gay Writing from the Antilles* (2008) uses other kinds of scholarly techniques, such as collecting first-person narratives and research based on oral histories to document queer lives in the region. In each case, a motivating factor behind these studies is to go back to historical records and reinterpret them as an intellectual method of decolonization. Here I demarcate Caribbean studies' decolonial archival method as a means of radical world making, foundational to its epistemologies, given the region's origin as imagined places: constituted through European fantasies of conquest, populated by people violently imported through the slave trade and indenture, profitable through products such as sugar and coffee, which originated in other parts of the world, and managed through imperial archival practices.

Anthropologist Deborah Thomas argues that gathering, naming, and disseminating historical evidence are central to Caribbean studies, where scholarship across disciplines can be seen as building an alternative archive. "One of the agendas of Caribbean studies," she observes, "has been to create archives—or, more accurately, counter-archives—in order to make claims about the modern world and the significance of the region to the global processes that have shaped it over the past five centuries."[15] Caribbean studies, in Thomas's view, "must think about the process of developing archives as one that creates new possibilities, possibilities for seeing connections previously unexamined and for reordering our ontological taken-for-granteds."[16] Thomas is in accord with David Scott, who in his influential "Archaeologies of Black Memory" postulates that Caribbean criticism itself constitutes archive building.[17] Archive building within Caribbean studies is not simply information gathering; it is rather an epistemological project that shapes knowledge and what can or should be remembered. Archive building is an active intellectual project that provides a way to build community in the present and the future based on the past.

Epistemological questions lie at the heart of Caribbean scholars' and writers' preoccupation about the past's relationship to the present. And while it may be surprising to outsiders, nationalist projects in the Caribbean held literary production as a key to decolonization. The struggle over how literature should engage with the past to write decolonized futures, named the "quarrel with history" by Edward Baugh in 1977, continues to the present. Noting the "specifically Caribbean psychopathology that accretes around history," Laurence Breiner states, "The quarrel is about a relationship with history, but the quarrel itself also constitutes, or plays out, that relationship with history."[18] Embedded within this quarrel are disagreements about what the legacies of history mean. Caribbean literature typically follows two well-worn paths in what is known, following Baugh and later Édouard Glissant, as an omnipresent tension related to historicity and representation.[19] This quarrel surfaces in literary works as either a bent toward an empiricist recovery project or a sense of the past as a nothingness from which modern Caribbean culture can arise. Indeed, it would be hard to name a Caribbean literary text that is not engaged with the force of the past in the present. This impetus to reach back toward the past continues with trends in Caribbean literature such as historical and neo-slave novels that depend on the interest of readers in archival materials, real and imagined.

Writers and critics from across the region from the 1940s to the present have framed this issue as charting a course between the past as abjection and loss that nevertheless can serve as a common cultural touchstone for the future nation.[20] Or, the past is figured as recoverable, translatable, and productive of a direct and even nurturing relationship to the present in the service of establishing postcolonial nations. For example, when Derek Walcott invokes the past as loss, he suggests that the absence of complete cultural legacies from Asia, Africa, Europe, and Indigenous peoples creates a shared basis for "the restoration of our shattered histories, our shards of vocabulary, our archipelago becoming a synonym for pieces broken off from the original continent."[21] In Walcott's case, a full accounting of Caribbean pasts and cultures cannot be restored, but this absence also represents a freedom to create a new and vibrant creolized Caribbean. More commonly, I would assert, the past can be seen as a source of authenticity and cultural continuity. By this I am not suggesting that these scholars and writers see the past in an uncontested relationship to the present but rather that they do not follow strictly a Walcottian framework of seeing their project as creating new cultures from fragmentation.

Recovering the past and writing visions of reparative futures are projects that are intimately bound in Caribbean literature from across the region. Colonialism and its aftermath, slavery and indenture, rightly take center stage in many of the region's preeminent texts. Critics and classroom instructors celebrate genres such as the historical novel, the bildungsroman, and the epic poem not only for their language and form, but for their ability to connect the past and the present. The region's engagement with questions of historicity stems from its status as exploitation colonies controlled by European nations and populated by peoples uprooted from Africa and India by slavery and indenture. Unlike other colonial contexts, the Caribbean did not produce a substantial body of literature before the nineteenth century and did not have a large enough literate population until the mid-twentieth century to constitute a counter public sphere.[22] Much of the population in the Caribbean was illiterate until the decolonization period, allowing for colonial control of information and education. Raphael Dalleo notes in his study of Caribbean literary public spheres that the French, Spanish, and British exerted control over colonial newspapers and presses, so that the life writings that did exist were published in Europe and largely aimed at metropolitan audiences.[23]

During decolonization, and after, there were few indigenous histories or customs to revive—in essence Caribbean people were told to find their own history, in a place where there had been no sources of writing, record keeping, or even a common indigenous language outside of that of the colonizers. In this way, anticolonial movements desired political and economic independence, but also emphasized the necessity of rethinking definitions of Caribbean identity and culture. As David Scott remarks, "(perhaps as a consequence of the distinctive technologies of subjection and cultural erasure that defined plantation slavery) the question of the past—or anyway the past as a question—has been an enduring preoccupation for New World peoples of African descent."[24] The Caribbean is a place long denigrated as having no history or cultures worth remarking on (James Anthony Froude through V. S. Naipaul), and with the only history available taught in colonial schools as a valorization of the European colonizers. In this way, excavating the past and creating texts that represented Caribbean cultures from the people's point of view became a central concern of pre- and postindependence writers.

From a feminist decolonial perspective, it may seem uncontroversial that past social structures and ideologies influence the present. But just what exactly we can learn from the past and how much power it should have over the present constitutes an ongoing debate. For example, Stephen Best suggests that following the publication of Toni Morrison's novel *Beloved* in 1987 the slave past has come to be seen as integral, accessible, and necessary to understand the present in much of African diaspora studies. Best terms this strain of scholarship "the affective history project" and suggests that other intellectual genealogies not requiring a shared sense of unrecoverable loss might inspire more effective social movements.[25] Within African American literary studies, Aida Levy-Hussen argues that two modes of literary thought dominate, leaving little room for other interpretive practices. "Therapeutic reading" sees literary accounts of slavery in the form of the neo-slave novel as important both politically and psychologically, while "prohibitive reading" sees such accounts as potentially harmful returns to the past.[26]

More recently, this binary approach to the past has been theorized by Caribbeanists as an aesthetic as well as epistemological issue. Scholars describe how the mode of midcentury anticolonial romances that demonstrated victory over oppression and the creation of a utopian postcolonial future were used in nationalist projects.[27] More recent literature uses tragic modes to represent the failure to make good on postcolonial promises.[28] David Scott observes that "anticolonial utopias have gradually withered into postcolonial nightmares. I think we live in tragic times."[29] Scott's formulation of the "nightmare" of the present surfaces tragedy as an aesthetic mode replacing the anticolonial romance in postcolonial literature. More specifically concerning the Caribbean, Scott theorizes that tragic modes provide a way to rethink what he characterizes as a regionwide expectation that postindependence nations would create a common culture and set of values, which did not materialize.[30]

Absence aesthetics, I argue, charts a third way of thinking about the past for Caribbean writers and scholars between an insistence on recovery and impossibility of knowing the past. Historian Marisa Fuentes reminds us that the plentiful Caribbean records written by those in power during slavery should not lead to "call[s] to 'find more sources' about people who left few if any of their own" because such a project "reproduces the same erasures and silences they experienced in the eighteenth-century Caribbean world by demanding the impossible."[31] The absences of the lives of the enslaved, indentured, and colonized in archives demonstrate the very power structures that rendered them invisible and disposable. In this vein, Michelle Cliff's works from the 1980s and 1990s can be read as efforts to connect the past and the present as a necessary feminist and decolonial act. However, Cliff does not expect that the methodology of historical recovery will be that of traditional historians. In a much-quoted passage, she argues that even with the knowledge of archival absence, "realizing our knowledge will always be wanting," that "to write as a complete Caribbean woman, or man for that matter, demands of us retracing the African part of ourselves, reclaiming as our own, and as our subject, a history sunk under the sea, or scattered as potash in the canefields, or gone to bush."[32] The political necessity of excavating what can be recovered, rather than building on "shattered histories," mark two versions of the past's relevance to Caribbean futures and constitute an ongoing theoretical debate within Caribbean literary studies.

Gendering Recovery, Gendering the Quarrel

In contrast to Scott's formulation, works such as Saidiya Hartman's *Lose Your Mother: A Journey along the Atlantic Slave Route* (2007) or Sonja Boon's *What the Oceans Remember: Searching for Belonging and Home* (2019) come to the end of evidence to write about archival, cultural, and historical absences without adhering to either the poles of anticolonial romance or the tragic aesthetic that have been proposed to replace it. Boon, a Canadian Dutch Surinamese academic who can trace her ancestry to five continents, challenges the central issue of origins animating the quarrel with history.

> I used to think I came from a family without origins. But perhaps I've been looking at it the wrong way. It's not that I have no origins but that I am the inheritor of a story with multiple origins. There is no logical starting point; I have no single home to return to. Rather, the threads of my past span the globe, reaching across history and geography, through languages and skins and music and memoires. . . . I thought the challenge would be to untangle them. But I was wrong. Instead, it's been to find beauty and wonder in the complex patterns that have resulted.[33]

Boon employs an absence aesthetic to understand her family history, one lacking in the markers of heteropatriarchy (clear lines of descent, land inheritance, and citizenship) that signal the multivalenced "origins" necessary for belonging. Boon neither recovers a heroic story of a foremother, nor tells the tale of her family and contemporary Surinam as a tragedy. Narratives such as Boon's ask readers to question what difference a gendered perspective on historical recovery might make. Appraising Edward Baugh's conception of the quarrel as explicitly masculinist ("The West Indian Writer and His Quarrel with History") and engaged with the preeminent Anglophone Caribbean writers of the time, Derek Walcott, V. S. Naipaul, and George Lamming, Alison Donnell notes that the generation of Caribbean scholars Baugh himself trained "make visible the diversity of women's writing and various forms of theorizing around issues of gender that were always part of West Indian history, even when if they had not always been kept afloat in its rushing waters."[34] The texts considered in this study challenge the idea that because the goals of midcentury nationalism were not achieved, the Caribbean aesthetic mode in the present must be one of melancholy or tragedy, or take up midcentury tropes of anticolonial romance.

The positions of anticolonial romance and tragedy make two assumptions: one, that we can know the past and that it has a direct relationship to the present; two, that we fully understand the "failures" of the postcolonial state. These assertions are gendered since Caribbean women's history is often neither well known nor available for excavation. The potential for "recovery" of Caribbean women's history is limited by their absence from the archive. In her work on eighteenth-century Barbados, Fuentes notes the "historical paradox and methodological challenges produced by the near erasure of enslaved women's own perspectives, in spite and because of the superabundance of words white Europeans wrote about them" confound "historical methods that search for archival veracity, statistical substantiation, and empiricism."[35] Visual representations of enslaved Caribbean women, explored in chapter 3, also testify to their present absence in colonial archives. As important, following Jacqui Alexander and Donette Francis, the impact of state failures to include women as full citizens of the Caribbean is still an ongoing investigation.[36]

Archival dreams, as I am calling them, are the animating force behind much of the recovery project of Caribbean studies, including that of feminist literary scholars and historians. Jenny Sharpe suggests, "Slavery continues to haunt the present because its stories, particularly those of slave women, have been improperly buried. But an improper burial does not mean that they are irretrievably lost."[37] The haunting by the past creates dreams of excavation, honoring the dead with a proper narrative burial, and thus recovering lost stories. Implicit in such methodology is the assumption that the past waits to be found and that experiencing its pain can provide redemptive futures.[38]

Seeing these more recent encounters with the limits of the archive caused me to wonder if during the period of reclamation and creation of new archives there might have been those who, conscious of women's absences from official records, pushed back against what Carolyn Steedman has called the "romance of the archive."[39] The romance of the archive includes ideas of saving the dead or voiceless from obscurity, something that my own scholarship certainly has engaged in. What I found is that concurrent with the ongoing project of historical recovery in the postcolonial Caribbean, there were other voices that were not as confident in positivist scholarly projects. Relying on archival discoveries and the creation of counter-archives as a path toward effective decolonization is not without its dangers. Jamaican sociologist and novelist Erna Brodber warned in 1983 that historiography itself is a court of law in which Caribbean societies will not be able to produce evidence since archival records leave little trace of the "poor African and Asian ex-slaves and indentured labourers."[40] Brodber acknowledges that the political thrust of much of Caribbean studies places an emphasis on recovering the stories of the marginalized and making them subjects of history. Such an effort seeks to displace racist and colonialist discourses that represent the Caribbean as located in an anachronistic state beyond global movements, its peoples positioned as objects of European- or North American–centered history, and its cultures defined as entirely derivative of Europe.[41] However, Brodber cautions, an empiricist approach needs documentation that may not exist. "History, like the judge in the law court, requires evidence. It requires that any event postulated to have occurred, can be demonstrated to other persons to have indeed occurred."[42] Noting the tendency of poets and novelists to create characters in the face of archival absences, Brodber asks, where "will we find the admissible data on the behavior of people who left no memoirs?"[43]

Brodber's concern about the lack of archival evidence of nonelites is well founded: in the partial and fragmented historical record of women in the nineteenth-century Caribbean, there is only one Caribbean slave narrative by a woman, Mary Prince, and no first-person records exist of indentured women in the Caribbean.[44] Women's accounts of their lives constitute an absence in Caribbean archives and literary history. This archival absence, Bridget Brereton argues, is even wider in the Caribbean than in Europe because until the twentieth century, the majority of women were not literate and thus did not leave written records.[45] Most men were illiterate as well, but there are far more extant examples of writing and record keeping produced by men.

Rather than focusing on novels as inventive bridges over silence, I explore the work that life writing, rooted in truth claims, can do in relationship to memory and history. A novelist might reach the end of evidence and move on to creating a narrative, building on the historical foundation important to their story. Historian Martha Jones suggests that the archival gaps that make writing African diaspora history so difficult might be solved through a change in genre. "In the face of silence, fiction might become a source that permits the historian to give voice and even to speak."[46] Caribbean scholars engaged in the quarrel with history have argued that there is either not enough of history, so that it must be reconstructed, recovered, or fictionalized, or so much of it that it threatens to overwhelm.[47] The excess or drought of history in Caribbean studies corresponds to similar concerns over the reliability of life writing as a source of historical material.[48] History and autobiography, then, share dreams of recovery and restoration ("the Archive is also a place of dreams" Steedman tells us) as well as frustrating realizations of the limitations of knowing our own life, family stories, and regional histories ("autobiography reveals the impossibility of its own dream," Shari Benstock writes).[49]

My study explores life writing as having the potential to create a different feminist epistemological space than fiction, concerned with marking the limits of the archive and creating new forms of Caribbean historiography and aesthetics based on women's experiences.[50] I argue that life writing, a more capacious form of autobiography, enables formal innovations in writing about absences in archival, national, family, and personal narratives. Life writing used here, as in much contemporary scholarship, denotes a broad variety of narratives including family histories, personal essays, and travelogues. Many subgenres of life writing, such as collections of letters, travel narratives, and slave narratives, have been used more commonly by colonized subjects and settler women than by male writers of dominant groups.[51] Scholars such as Sidonie Smith and Julia Watson suggest that the term "life writing" allows for a decolonization of the Eurocentric genre of autobiography.[52] Gillian Whitlock notes that "for postcolonial theory, the more expansive category 'life writing' is critical for de/colonizing the subject, as these are the 'minor' genres that flourished in colonialism's literary cultures. The traditional sovereign subject of autobiography and the less exalted or collective subject of life narrative are entangled in western modernity."[53] These "minor" forms were available to writers in colonial contexts as opposed to the prestigious genre of autobiography proper, which was long understood as a European narrative written late in life by an important man for the purposes of educating the reader.[54] Hybrid forms of life writing, such as the combination of family memoir, travelogue, and history written by laypeople, challenge who gets to write the past and who constitutes proper subjects of history.

Caribbean Life Writing and Gender

As the first monograph on pan-Caribbean life writing, *Dreams of Archives Unfolded* focuses on how and why recent personal narratives from across the region share common leitmotifs such as narratives emplotted by absence. Emplotted by absence indicates life writings that structure their narratives around a deliberate facing off with the unknown and unknowable in family and national histories. This formal structure comprises a creative aesthetics related to methods of piecing together narratives that draw on multiple cultural sources but also must encounter the aporias in Caribbean history. The tensions inherent in these texts between truth and fiction, historical accuracy and a good story, and the living and the dead illuminate the limits of the archive simultaneously with the limits of autobiography as a means of entering a related debate about the limits of criticism as it is currently practiced.

Within Caribbean studies, despite the genre's obvious relevance to issues central to the field such as representation and representativeness, authenticity, testimony, and trauma, there is only one monograph each on the Anglophone and Francophone traditions published to date. Sandra Pouchet Paquet's *Caribbean Autobiography: Cultural Identity and Self-Representation* (2002) surveys Anglophone Caribbean texts from the nineteenth century to the late twentieth century, discussing the role of genre in the creation of Caribbean forms of self-making and subjectivity.[55] Louise Hardwick, in *Childhood, Autobiography and the Francophone Caribbean* (2013), the first monograph focused exclusively on life writing in the Francophone Caribbean, confirms the paucity of scholarship within Francophone Caribbean literary studies.[56] Lisa R. Brown argues that given the quantity of life writing produced in the region from colonial times to the present, work such as Paquet's should be seen as a first step that "lays open the gap in criticism that characterizes Caribbean life writing."[57] *Dreams of Archives Unfolded* provides that next step. This project builds on these examples to provide a much-needed theorization of the new aesthetics and strategies in contemporary Caribbean life writing from a variety of linguistic and cultural traditions.

Given these resonances, it is surprising that more attention has not been paid to life writing within postcolonial literary studies. Walter Goebel and Saskia Schabio argue that postcolonial critics' privileging of cultural identity as expressed within the novel has resulted in a lack of attention to issues of aesthetics and formal choices, which can be explored through an examination of literary genres, such as autobiography, the short story, or the folktale.[58] Certainly postcolonial theory from the 1980s and 1990s did not often attend to genre. Widely used theoretical anthologies such as *Colonial Discourse and Postcolonial Theory: A Reader* (1994), *The Postcolonial Studies Reader* (1995), and *Postcolonialisms: An Anthology of Cultural Theory and Criticism* (2005) used themes rather than genre as organizing principles. Perhaps in response to an emerging "generic turn," *Literature for Our Times: Postcolonial Studies for the Twenty-First Century* (2012) includes several essays focused on genre and on life writing. So although I would not confidently proclaim as Philip Holden does that "from the margins of postcolonial literary studies, auto/biography now seems to have travelled to centre stage," I would assert that autobiography studies and postcolonial studies have begun speaking to each other and that *Dreams of Archives Unfolded* contributes to that project.[59]

I did not set out solely to examine women's writing. However, it was this set of life writings by women, containing biography, history, archival research, *and* critiques of racialized and gendered absences in official and unofficial repositories, that is illustrative of a new way of understanding the relationship of the Caribbean present to the past.[60] Indeed, there are many other Caribbean life writings by both men and women published since 2000 that show the vibrancy of this genre and that engage in an examination of how the past impacts the present.[61] In the subset of those texts considered here, I prioritize those that pay attention to gendered historiographical absences and also deploy formal bricolage. I categorize my corpus as "Caribbean" and "women's" life writing, not out of a geographic residency requirement or biological essentialism, but from the commonalities of the questions they ask about identity, history, slavery, and gender. Working through shared themes and questions within the texts, I agree with José Esteban Muñoz that "it seems most useful to me to frame concepts like feminism, queerness, and even race as affective taxonomies—as shared ways of looking and feeling that offer us a different sense of the world."[62] Common questions and tropes, what Muñoz calls "the performative effects of words, objects, and affective states," unite the primary texts composing this study.[63] Their answers, as one might expect, are divergent.

The texts included in this study are distinct from life writing produced by men during this period, not so much in terms of thematic issues, but rather in the way they foreground textual absences. For example, Martiniquan novelist Patrick Chamoiseau's memoirs *School Days* (1997) and *Childhood* (1999) do not invoke historical absences in the telling of his individual story even as they contain thematic parallels with Lorna Goodison's writing of her Caribbean childhood and formidable mother in the 1950s in *From Harvey River: A Memoir of My Mother and Her Island* (2007). Awadh Jaggernath has much in common with Yvonne Shorter Brown, in that they both grew up in the Caribbean, migrated to Canada, and published family memoirs; however, Jaggernath's *Innocence to Impudence: Growing Up in Trinidad, the Story of One Family* (2016) does not self-reflexively examine his positionality in terms of Trinidadian history, or like Gaiutra Bahadur in *Coolie Woman* link his family's story to those of others who have experienced indenture. Well-known Barbadian Canadian autobiographer Austin Clarke's texts and Pablo Medina's *Exiled Memoires: A Cuban Childhood* (2002) are more in the Caribbean literary tradition of recovery and exploration of identity than explorations of the life writing genre itself and its relationship to absence.[64] Dionne Brand, like Clarke, is based in Toronto. However, her subject matter in *A Map to the Door to No Return: Notes to Belonging* (2001), turns from childhood memories to exploring the aporias in African diaspora genealogies that cannot be recovered because records that track individual enslaved persons from Africa to the New World largely do not exist.[65]

For example, In *Dead Woman Pickney: A Memoir of Childhood in Jamaica* (2010), Yvonne Shorter Brown writes, "My body signifies many stories. My female body . . . is marked by the events of the past," using a mixture of personal narrative and critical theory to understand her individual, familial, and national past.[66]

> It is the past of the colony of Jamaica, New World Slavery, plantation economy, and English missionary education, set within the culture of the British Empire as it flourished and faded. . . . My physiognomy is the living record of this terrible linage. My mother is the descendant of a line of Africa enslaved: taken from the Slave Coast, a place unknown in origin, but probably somewhere that would have been known to my paternal descent—English and Scottish colonizers—as the Guineas or Ghana. I cannot be sure because too much of this lineage is lost or hidden.[67]

The broken maternal line described by Brown represents the stories of many descendants of slavery and indenture, which she highlights by stating to the reader her multiple uncertainties ("a place unknown," "I cannot be sure"). The majority of texts considered here involve highlighting the failures of traditional archives to represent the experiences of women, which in turn spurs unusual narrative devices to explain their knowledge. Maryse Condé in *Victoire: My Mother's Mother* (2010) writes of her grandmother's ghost hounding her to write her biography; Lorna Goodison dreams of her deceased mother passing to her the history of her family that would become *From Harvey River: A Memoir of My Mother and Her Island* (2007).[68]

Absence has a relationship to specters, traces, lingering presences, and affect around loss. Absence aesthetics describe the hole in the narrative, the missing, the unrecoverable in ways that clarify what surrounds the absence, and what the cultural stakes are in not naming it. Avery Gordon writes of haunting as a framework for understanding "the paradox of tracking through time and across all those forces that which makes its mark by being there and not being there at the same time."[69] Life writing, above all, signals the presence of the author's story. Yet in these texts that presence is compounded with a specifically Caribbean historiographical issue of what can be recalled only partially and sometimes not at all: women's experiences and perspectives under slavery, the nineteenth- and early twentieth-century postslavery period, and as that brutal system was replaced by Asian indenture and immigration. I read each narrative through a feminist lens attentive to gendered representations of the systemic erasure of lost kin, places, and family histories.

Life writing as a genre and Caribbean historiography invoke uneasy feelings in their writers and readers about absences in memory and historical archives that in turn raise questions of what counts as evidence. Staying off-balance and uneasy about truth claims and archival absences lies at the heart of the primary texts considered here as well as my method for reading them. Reader expectations of life writing still largely include that the author is telling a truthful story about the past.[70] This expectation constitutes what is called the "autobiographical pact."[71] Gillian Whitlock notes, "Life narrative touches the world in distinctive ways, then: it refers to lived experience; it professes subjective truths; and above all it signals to the reader an intended fidelity to history and memory."[72] Life writing is important to the history-obsessed field of Caribbean studies for just this reason: it is a genre grounded in truth claims that contains the possibility of testifying to the destructive nature of the colonial encounter as well as telling personal and communal stories of resistance.[73] However, what happens when we view the self and history through the lens of historical and cultural absences, moments when writers and artists come up against a past that resists memory and choose to center absence through genre?

Patrick Fuery notes, "Absence can be a status measured against other orders. Something is absent because it is not present, but the significant detail is that the absent something is figured as potentially present, that is, held-in-readiness."[74]

Life writing, as practiced by the writers in my corpus, contains formal choices to bridge the sharp distinctions between traditional autobiography, fiction, and historical writing, allowing nuanced presentations of evidence outside of records, such as memory and vernacular traditions and history.[75] This genre allows writers interested in writing an unarchived past access to representing multiple sources of evidence, from the written to the oral, from the interview to the personal memory, to represent the individual's relationship to larger social and historical forces. The absent as held in readiness to be present aptly describes my criterion for selecting the texts examined in this project. In claiming the past as an absence that cannot be fully reconstructed, this corpus refuses anticolonial romance as well as the romance of history that claims that the past can be recovered.

Interpretive Affiliation

Dreams of Archives Unfolded makes a significant contribution to new studies of the Caribbean region by focusing on a genre that both provides interiority for the subaltern and enables the writing of absent narratives that trace a continuum across plantation histories from the nineteenth century to the present. Narratives of the self, I argue, is a genre highly suited to writing the admixture of cultures, forms, and sources present in Caribbean cultures. These texts' sutured genres of first-person narrative, family history, and archival research militate against tidy linear narratives and unbroken lineages of canonical European autobiography as well as efforts to silo linguistic traditions (such as Anglophone vs. Francophone), racial categories (Asian vs. Afro-Caribbean writing), and political and historical differences (independent countries from "overseas departments" such as Guadeloupe).[76] I bridge what Aisha Khan calls the "enclave-ization of Afro- and Indo- (or Asian) diaspora studies" in Caribbean scholarship.[77]

Life writing as a Caribbean historiographical method has not been adequately investigated, to the cost of Caribbean studies as a whole. I am making a more complicated claim than that autobiographical texts are absent from Caribbean scholarship, which is demonstrably not true.[78] Lisa Lowe concludes that although there is a rich body of scholarship on the Atlantic slave trade, there is far less on its connections to indenture and "scarcely any that considers the connections, relations and mixings among the histories of Asian, African, and indigenous peoples in the Americas."[79] What I am claiming is that life writings from across the region, particularly texts that cut across language and race, have not *been read together* as a generically related corpus that can speak with and through each other.

While these texts cumulatively embody commonalities that allow me to identify them as "life writing," I seek a feminist reading practice that goes beyond the theoretical commonplace in literary scholarship of providing historical or cultural context to further explicate the text, or seeking to theorize the texts as a means of claiming authority over their meaning. Instead, I use what I call interpretive affiliation as a curatorial process of putting life writings into conversation with each other in order to draw out their common and conflicting agendas. Affiliating these texts across linguistic, kinship, and national lines remaps the traditional position of women as mothers of the nation, aligning them rather as transnational comrades.[80] This methodology goes against the grain of many Caribbean literary studies focused on monolingual traditions. Thus, it stages a methodological intervention in how to think about life writing aesthetics in a Caribbean context while paying attention to specific colonial legacies, cultural nuances, and differences among the writers' identities. My method here does not follow a hermeneutics of suspicion; these life writings are not mystery narratives with a problem to be solved.[81]

One of the aims of *Dreams of Archives Unfolded* is to identify aesthetic commonalities related to the life writing genre across linguistic and national boundaries, but within the Caribbean region. Françoise Lionnet and Shu-mei Shih observe, "We study the center and the margin but rarely examine the relationships among different margins. The dominant is posited, even by those who resist it, as a powerful and universalizing force that either erases or eventually absorbs cultural particularities. Universalism demands a politics of assimilation, incorporation, or resistance, instituting a structure of vertical struggle for recognition and citizenship."[82] Each chapter seeks to answer three main questions related to Caribbean culture: What archival absence is being written about? What epistemologies about that absence are being created? What formal choices are made by the authors in order to explore absence and knowledge through the genre of life writing? In taking these as the organizing questions for the book, my method allows the texts considered here speak to each other in complex ways across generational, national, and linguistic identities. While all of the texts reflect the viewpoint, summarized so succinctly by Saidiya Hartman, that "narrative may be the only available form of redress for the monumental crime that was the transatlantic slave trade and the terror of enslavement and racism" and, of course, indenture and colonialism, how the narratives are constructed and what archival absence they are engaging with differ.[83] I have chosen to group texts primarily through similarities in formal choices in how to write a life narrative about absence or when differences in how the narratives are structured are so striking that other aspects of archival absence become centralized in intriguing ways.

Chapter 1 contains just such a juxtaposition as it reads the work of Saidiya Hartman, who has roots in Curaçao, and Dionne Brand, Trinidadian Canadian, as representing two poles in the Caribbean quarrel with history, even as both texts center around the aftereffects of slavery as represented by the Door of No Return. While Hartman writes of wishing to recover the histories of the enslaved who are not represented in the archive and uses the methods of a historian to describe her travels to Ghana to do so (echoing at least at first the recovery impulse of midcentury Caribbean intellectuals), Brand's background as a poet and novelist informs her efforts to create a map to the unmappable. Hartman writes her own narrative of return to Ghana but also employs what she calls "critical fabulation" as a new tool for historians to reimagine histories that cannot be recovered. Brand considers "returns" to Africa as useless, much in the way that Caribbean writers before her like Walcott have seen the fractured and incomplete histories of the Caribbean as not something to recover but rather a hallmark of Caribbean culture.

In this chapter and the ones afterward, I refer to the authors by their last names and to the descriptions of their experiences using their first name as a means to distinguish between the writer and the autobiographical "I" present in the narrative. Chapters 2 and 3 are organized by their approaches to the past and the methodologies used in their life writing. They negotiate a path of adhering to a dream of archival recovery necessitating innovative aesthetic practices, as with Hartman's "critical fabulation," or following Brand, writing about the past as fractured and unrecoverable but creating space for the creation of news ways of writing autobiographical texts. Chapter 2 asks who is the proper subject of history and how can the unrepresented be written. This chapter pushes on the long-standing critical conversation within autobiography studies concerning the status of truth in life writing. It does so by bringing the debate over autobiographical veracity into conversation with the similarly venerable and unresolved issue of the Caribbean quarrel with history. Guadeloupean writer Maryse Condé's account of being haunted by her grandmother, whose biography she goes on to write in *Victoire: My Mother's Mother* (2010), challenges the nature of the "proper" subject of Caribbean history. *Victoire* delves into the knotted subject of ancestry in the Caribbean as it contrasts the almost complete archival absence of people like Condé's grandmother, an illiterate non–French speaker born in 1875 in French-controlled Guadeloupe, to the presence of her celebrated grandfather. Thus, Condé uses life writing as a corrective to masculinist history in order to claim a matricentric Guadeloupean heritage.

Chapter 3 builds on the questions raised in the first two chapters about the fraught nature of historical recovery for Caribbean people. It does so through the framework of Erna Brodber's "Blackspace," a term denoting the absence of Caribbean physical and lexical sites of knowledge concerning history and ancestry, and epistemological strategies for filling in those absences to create cultural sovereignty. Brodber enacts her Blackspace epistemology in her hybrid memoir, local history, and genealogical work *Woodside Pear Tree Grove P.O.* (2004), which underlines the importance of land ownership to identity and liberatory politics in the Caribbean. Brodber's intervention allows for a nuanced reading of Lorna Goodison's family memoir, *From Harvey River: A Memoir of My Mother and Her Island* (2007), a microhistory of her family and the landscape in northern Jamaica. In each case, Goodison and Brodber practice what could be termed as an ancestral recovery act, which seeks to link the descendants of slaves to the past of the land they live on. Their work engages with archival presences and absences in order to create alternative epistemologies of Caribbean space and ancestry. This shared project comprises what I call *descendant community life writing*, indicating texts concerned with tracing the relationship between a contemporary group of people and their relationship to the land on which their ancestors were enslaved. Brodber and Goodison center other means of knowledge production than official archives, such as physical evidence in the landscape and oral histories of residents.

The final two chapters focus on texts that use the genre of life writing in order to create and critique counter-archives. Chapter 4 returns to questions raised in the first chapter concerning origins, belonging, and absences in the archive related to violence. Reading Sonja Boon's *What the Oceans Remember: Searching for Belonging and Home* (2019) with Guyanese Gaiutra Bahadur's *Coolie Woman: The Odyssey of Indenture* (2014) illuminates their common methodology of using academic and archival sources to search for their Indo-Caribbean ancestors within the archive of indenture. Both texts document their experience of working with delicate documents related to indenture, frequently coming away with dust or archival debris on their bodies. This experience becomes an absence aesthetic, allowing us to attend to the residue of Caribbean histories of indenture in the present, including high rates of violence against women in Guyana and Suriname.

Chapter 5 begins with the counter-archive created by Dominican American novelist Angie Cruz's Instagram account @dominicanasnyc. Seeking to understand the lives of Dominican women like her mother, who migrated to New York, Cruz finds contemporary archives empty of their transnational experiences. She creates an alternative means of memorializing their stories and images by using social media. This intervention in archival absence sets the tone for the chapter's examination of diasporic identity as expressed through life writing in Cuban American anthropologist Ruth Behar's *An Island Called Home: Returning to Jewish Cuba* (2007), Haitian American writer Edwidge Danticat's memoir *Brother, I'm Dying* (2008) and book of essays *Create Dangerously: The Immigrant Artist at Work* (2010), and Puerto Rican writer Irene Vilar's memoir *The Ladies' Gallery: A Memoir of Family Secrets* (2009). The chapter situates their work as concerned with questions of diasporic documenting, especially those related to visual culture given their common identification of the importance of photographs to write about Caribbean and family history. Using interpretive affiliation to read these dissimilar life writings coming from three different colonial histories, enables a memory-generating praxis in the service of reorienting a central Caribbean epistemological question about how to construct archives relevant to the future.

CHAPTER 1

"Autobiography in a Graveyard"

DOORS OF NO RETURN AND REVOLUTIONARY FAILURES

One might begin a book on Caribbean life writing and historical absences in many places, such as the Jamaican archive discussed in the introduction. Archives are a method of ordering the past and are thus highly resonant with the narratives considered here that combine personal and regional histories. The 1838 *Falmouth Post* article I found in a Jamaican archive invokes another in its imagining of an "archive unfolded" as a reparative act in a postslavery Caribbean society.[1] Such a utopian vision for archives, broadly construed here as official records, oral histories, and family narratives, is a constitutive element of Caribbean studies. Performing archival acts such as gathering memories, documents, and photographs and weaving them into a first-person narrative, what Linda Anderson calls being a "historian of the self," are common elements of life writing.[2] Saidiya Hartman's *Lose Your Mother: A Journey along the Atlantic Slave Route* (2007) and Dionne Brand's *A Map to the Door of No Return: Notes to Belonging* (2001) share these qualities with other life writing texts, but they also center that which cannot be recovered.[3] *Lose Your Mother* and *Map* write of archival dreams while articulating the dangers of looking to archives created by colonial powers as a means of Caribbean self-definition. Most importantly, these texts center absences in familial, regional, and colonial archives as just as important for Caribbean epistemologies as creating counter-archives.

This chapter examines Hartman's and Brand's life writings for how they negotiate the complex issues surrounding the concept of history, the knowability of the past, what is at stake in making or denying connections to the past, and present-day uses of history for African diasporic subjects. The "problem space," as David Scott calls it, of how we should understand the relationship between the past and the present in the Caribbean necessitates frameworks that explore what "history" means for those who would not consider themselves and their ancestors the architects either of the archives or of events like slavery, colonialism, or globalization.[4] My primary aim is to identify Hartman's and Brand's unique methods of feminist epistemology concerned with theorizing the absences in archives of slavery and their relationship to the aftereffects of enslavement. Their texts discuss the limits of archives and traditional academic research for the recovery of Caribbean and African diaspora histories as well as the impact those limits have on contemporary identity. They do so through an examination of the meaning of the Door of No Return, as various slave forts along the west coast of Africa have come to be known.[5] Both texts are concerned with archive making and absence through a focus on sites of death and memory, such as the slave fort and ruins of revolutionary movements. Hartman explores the dream of a free Ghana; Brand writes of the Door of No Return through her memories of surviving the U.S. invasion of Grenada.

I analyze life writings produced Hartman and by Brand as representative strands in Caribbean culture's ongoing quarrel with history. Their differing ways of knowing the past and writing about its absences through the genre of life writing provide a template for the following chapters. *Lose Your Mother* begins with the premise that the aftereffects of slavery related to identity can be ameliorated by a return to Africa. Brand's *Map* repeatedly claims that such returns are ineffective and unnecessary since the dislocations of the African diaspora are part of the structure of Black consciousness. As I argue below, these initial positions, which are recognizable as oppositional epistemological poles related to the quarrel with history (the past as the basis on which Caribbean people need to build their futures vs. the past as irrecoverable), are complicated significantly by the end of their narratives. I begin here with an overview of Hartman's and Brand's differing positions as they relate to a central term in the quarrel with history, "rupture," and then move to separate analyses of *Lose Your Mother* and *Map*.

Édouard Glissant formulates the gap between colonial histories and those that need to be created by Caribbean peoples themselves as the crux of the quarrel with history. This gap, more precisely named by Glissant as a "rupture," is foundational to Caribbean epistemologies. The Caribbean, Glissant explains, "is the site of a history characterized by ruptures and that began with a brutal dislocation, the slave trade. Our historical consciousness could not be deposited gradually and continuously like sediment, as it were, as happened with those peoples who have frequently produced a totalitarian philosophy of history, for instance European peoples, but came together in the context of shock, contraction, painful negation, and explosive forces. This dislocation of the continuum, and the inability of the collective consciousness to absorb it all characterize what I call a nonhistory."[6] The "rupture" central to Glissant's formulation is taken up by Hartman and Brand to describe their own experiences of gendered African diasporic consciousness and their relationship to the unresolvable nature of rootlessness.

Hartman is a U.S. historian with roots in the Dutch Caribbean island of Curaçao. She writes *Lose Your Mother* as an account of the eighteen months she spent living in Ghana searching for the history of those who were sold into slavery. If Brand's text serves as a meditation on its subtitle, *Notes to Belonging*, concerning the psychological conditions of the African diaspora, Hartman's subtitle, *A Journey along the Atlantic Slave Route*, signals a different purpose. Foregrounding an autobiographical experience of attempting to "return" to Africa in the first part of the book makes possible a discussion of other such dreams of Africa as understandable but also subject to critique in the second half. Writing the experience of a "failed" return sets the stage in *Lose Your Mother* for other considerations, such as how to write about a history of those sold into slavery that has left little trace in contemporary Ghana.

In *Map*, Brand recalls a paradoxical event central to her Trinidadian childhood: her grandfather's wish to pass down the name of the African people they are descended from while never quite being able to do so. Her grandfather both knows the name and yet does not remember, stating "he would know it if he heard it" (3).[7] Hungry with genealogical desire, the young Brand prompts her grandfather many times with names of African ethnic groups, but he is unable to remember their family's origin. Their mutual frustration over his inability to recall creates a personal "rift" but also signals a historical "rupture" of the kind described by Glissant.

> That moment between my grandfather and I several decades ago revealed a tear in the world. . . . But the rupture this exchange with my grandfather revealed was greater than the need for familial bonds. It was a rupture in history, a rupture in the quality of being. It was also a physical rupture, a rupture of geography. . . . We were not from the place where we lived and we could not remember where we were from or who we were. My grandfather could not summon up a vision of a landscape or of a people which would add up to a name. And it was profoundly disturbing. (4–5)

In order to tell this particular story of rupture and absence, Brand chooses a hybrid form of life writing combining memoir, travelogue, and theoretical essay to narrate her relationship with her grandfather as it relates more broadly to issues of familial and historical absence and dislocation in the African diaspora. Significantly for her exploration of absence and rupture in this initial story, Brand tells us that her grandfather would not lie to her. A false answer would have satisfied her as a child, Brand tells us, and then she would have "stored it away. Forgotten" (4–5). Instead, her grandfather, and indeed the narrative itself, refuses this easy way out, because to do so would erase the chasm of history. As in many of the texts considered in *Dreams of Archives Unfolded*, Brand's use of her own experience allows her to focus on absence as a structuring element of Caribbean lives. While searching for her origins, Brand insists that appropriating Africa will not resolve the Caribbean crisis of identity and so refuses to visit West African slave ports; her text creates an aesthetics around an uncertainty about origins and history that cannot be resolved.

This lack of resolution, for Brand, has much to do with her social locations as Black, lesbian, and an immigrant to Canada. Familial and historical absences stemming from slavery become a catalyst in *Map* for thinking about what history signifies for those whose identities place them as marginal to mainstream historiography because of race *and* sexual orientation. I read *Map* as a queer text, even though it does not contain the word "lesbian" or "queer" or explicitly depict same-sex desire. This elision of obvious markers of queer identity may seem puzzling, given Brand's long-standing writing and activism around Black, immigrant, and gay rights.[8] However, according to Omise'eke Natasha Tinsley, such absences within Caribbean queer texts are common.[9] As I demonstrate below, it is important to note that a queer text in the Caribbean might reveal its queerness differently than in other places.[10] *Map*, as I read it, has a queer orientation through its exploration of the aftereffects not just of slavery, but of the death of the Grenada vision of collaboration and community and nation building outside of colonial frameworks focused on kinship and hierarchy.

An important context for Brand's and Hartman's work is that travel to specific Doors of No Return, unavailable to previous generations, became more widely possible. Places such as Gorée Island, the Elmina slave fort in Ghana, and other locations in Africa related to the slave trade are now travel destinations for the African diaspora.[11] Of course, "returning" to Africa has an earlier precedent in pan-Africanist circles in the 1960s. Maryse Condé recalls in 1961 the president of Guinea Sékou Touré saying to her, "So you're from Guadeloupe. You're one of the little sisters that Africa once lost and then found again."[12] With Brand's and Hartman's texts published in 2001 and 2007, respectively, their writing can be understood as part of a larger transnational conversation about recovering personal history and African heritage that was sparked in the popular imagination by Alex Haley's *Roots* (1976). Since the late 1990s, access to internet resources about the slave forts, more affordable international travel, and West African nations' support for UNESCO preservation efforts have made possible "heritage travel" for larger numbers of Afro-Caribbeans and African Americans.[13]

In contrast to stories like Alex Haley's in *Roots*, which tells of a triumphant return to Africa and adoption into a clan with a distinguished lineage, Hartman "traveled to Ghana in search of the expendable and the defeated" (7).[14] Of course, these are exactly the populations missing from colonial archives. Hartman knows this from the outset, arguing, "To read the archive is to enter a mortuary; it permits one final viewing and allows for a last glimpse of persons about to disappear into the slave hold" (17). Yet, she persists in looking for that which cannot be found. Hartman writes, "There was nothing exceptional about my journey. Any tourist with the willingness and the cash could retrace as many slave routes as her heart desired. But there was something particular, perhaps even peculiar, about it. My generation was the first that came here with the dungeon as our prime destination, unlike the scores of black tourists who, motivated by Alex Haley's *Roots*, had traveled to Ghana and other parts of West Africa to reclaim their African patrimony. For me, the rupture was the story" (42). The slave dungeon, a graveyard, represents in Hartman's writing a turn away from dreams of African kinship and glorious pasts interrupted by slavery, toward a recognition that the rupture identified by Glissant is her history. Indeed, the rupture is not only related to the dispossession of slavery. It is also the realization that people in Ghana will not welcome her "home." Instead she is called *obruni*, or stranger (3).

The Door of No Return, conceptually, signals how absence functions in the originary moment of the creation of the African diaspora in the Americas. The Door of No Return names sites in West Africa such as in Benin, Ghana, and Senegal where slaves were kept before being forced onto slave ships. The Door, however, signifies more than a place. It is a temporal shift, a before and after of being enslaved. The finality of that shift from being part of a kinship system and hailing from an ancestral place to being enslaved is invoked in the phrase "no return." The Atlantic slave trade, as Orlando Patterson notes, marked a social death for the enslaved who were transformed from kin into property.[15] Slavery hinged on separating people from others who spoke their language, had common customs, or would remember a shared African past. The Efe, Igbo, or Yoruba past was meant to be unrecoverable. Marooning the enslaved linguistically and culturally made them even more vulnerable in a transatlantic economic system that in the Caribbean meant a very short life span and an inability for African-descended populations to reproduce themselves until after emancipation.

Viewing these sites along the west coast of Africa where slaves were held has become a symbolic trip for some members of the African diaspora even if they are *unable* to trace their family's origins.[16] Visitors can be sure that one of their ancestors was held at a slave fort, even if not the one they are currently visiting. The synecdoche of *a place* of enslavement standing in for *enslavement in general* generates productive historical analysis in Hartman's writing and is critiqued in Brand's. As Hartman writes of her visit to Elmina, in Ghana "I was loitering in a slave dungeon less because I hoped to discover what really happened here than because of what lived on from this history. Why else begin an autobiography in a graveyard?" (130). If history is one of the means by which we engage the dead, as Hartman argues, life writing that incorporates history allows us to enter the graveyard of slavery and consider how we are still haunted by it. Graves and memorial sites, then, are another place to begin a book on Caribbean life writing.

Hartman, Historiography, and Absence Aesthetics

Lose Your Mother has become a paradigmatic text related to new critical approaches to colonialism's past and a foundational text in recent work within Caribbean and African American studies concerning genealogy, ancestral returns, the archive, and historiography.[17] *Lose Your Mother*, in conjunction with Hartman's essay "Venus in Two Acts," has been heavily influential in contemporary thinking about archival limits and race, not solely for their content, I argue, but for the formal choices Hartman makes in choosing life writing.[18] Hartman's methodological innovations allow for new ways to think about the urgent projects of representing those made invisible through slavery and colonization not by creating historical fiction, but by attending to the archival fragments or complete absences as a record in and of themselves. Christina Sharpe orients her work around Hartman's, writing of the aftermath of slavery as a "wake," meaning both a ship's trail and the ritual held for the dead: "To encounter people of African descent in the wake both materially and as a problem for thought is to encounter . . . the conditions of Black life and death such as those delineated by Hartman . . . the ways we occupy the 'I' of Hartman's 'I am the afterlife of slavery.'"[19] *Lose Your Mother* has also been theorized as part of a lineage of narratives of Afro-diasporic return. The many imaginative or real "returns" to Africa by the diaspora, including *Lose Your Mother*, are termed "Afro-Atlantic speculation" by Michelle D. Commander for their capacity to imagine Africa as a place of origin and healing.[20]

The idea of the "return" to Africa animates Hartman's text. As Commander notes, "Catharsis, a liberatory act of purging, marks the moment of contact with the past and with the ancestor—it is the most anticipated moment in flights toward imagined Africas and a central force that compels diasporian returns."[21] However, my analysis of Hartman's work in dialogue with Brand's pushes back against critical assumptions about the possibilities of connecting the past and the present, of making "contact" with the African past. The message communicated in many historical novels and taken up in criticism and literature afterward is that engaging with the past is necessary and even therapeutic.[22] In "On Failing to Make the Past Present," Stephen Best challenges what he terms an "unassailable truth" in African diaspora studies: that the past holds the major explanatory power over the present as well as being the source for collective action and solidarity.[23] For Hartman and Brand, encountering the past, whether in a slave fort in Ghana or in an attempt to pass on family history in Trinidad, does not always lead to connection.

Much of *Lose Your Mother* is an exploration of Hartman's first-person experiences related to how the past is not transparently waiting for her. Significantly, Hartman's use of life narrative draws from the genre of the travelogue that, of course, has deep colonial roots.[24] This "quixotic mission" manifests itself in tropes familiar to colonial travel writing. Hartman relates experiences such as panicking and mistaking a routine power cut for a coup. In an instance of cultural misunderstanding, Hartman cannot understand why her Ghanaian colleagues' insistence that contemporary issues such as poverty, lack of education and health care, and threats to sovereignty might seem more important than a search for ancestry by someone whom they perceive to be a wealthy U.S. citizen. The commonality many have hoped to find between the diaspora and contemporary Ghanaians is recounted ruefully by Hartman as a realization that the churchgoing middle-class African Americans who would not want to take a trip of "return" are precisely the people contemporary Ghanaians would probably have most in common with.

One might say that the effort to write a story of "nothing" is what inspires Hartman's travel and her use of the life writing genre. As a historian, Hartman is familiar with the major archives of slavery, which are not located in Ghana, as she emphasizes to the reader (107).[25] Archival absences and the inability of traditional modes of historiography to write those absences are part of what brings her to Ghana. By locating the beginning of the identity of enslaved people as happening in Africa not upon their arrival in the New World, Hartman challenges both *what* and *when* it meant to be a slave, in contrast to many histories that locate the identity of being a slave as starting in the Americas.[26] Her stated purpose is an impossible task—she hopes to connect with what cannot be found in the archive in order to imagine the experience of those taken into slavery.

Hartman writes a travelogue that starts with a deliberately naïve autobiographical voice that longs for a healing return to African roots. Standing in the slave fort Elmina in Ghana, which is essentially a graveyard, and one of the well-known Doors of No Return, Hartman can seemingly find no traces of the enslaved past in the present. The narrative demonstrates that Hartman wants certain affects associated with slavery to manifest again for her in the present, but she cannot will them into being. Hartman returns to Elmina several times but feels nothing in the slave fort.

> I, too, was a failed witness. Reckoning with my inheritance had driven me to the dungeon, but now it all seemed elusive. I struggled to connect the dots between then and now and to chart the trajectory between the Gold Coast and Curaçao and Montgomery and Brooklyn. But I kept fumbling.
>
> I could rattle off all the arguments about the devastating effects of having been property, denied the protection of citizenship, and stripped of rights of equality. The simple fact was that we still lived in a world in which racism sorts the have and have-nots and decides who lives and who dies. (129)

The slave past is not, as Toni Morrison famously wrote in *Beloved*, always present to anyone looking for it. In Hartman's inability to make an affective connection between the history of her enslaved ancestors and the physical location of the slave fort, she at first labels herself a "failed" witness. She can neither feel the echoes of the past nor connect with contemporary Ghanaians.

Hartman's text is simultaneously accessible personal narrative with scholarly paratextual material, pushing the boundaries of academic writing. *Lose Your Mother* contains an unusual citation system, with footnotes in the back of the text providing sources or commentary. Among the many academic studies Hartman cites is an archaeological report from 1973. It describes a dig at the Elmina slave fort. What the researchers find are layers upon layers of human skin, excrement, small beads, cowrie shells used as currency, and the bones of consumed animals that were packed down by the slaves held captive there and became the flooring of the fort. The holding cells were never cleaned but were covered with a layer of sand and then lime, a common practice during a time when it was commonly assumed that clearing the debris of the slave trade in barracoons and on slave ships would lead to infection.[27] Noting that "to the naked eye it looked like soot," Hartman realizes that this floor is the only tangible connection she will be able to make with the dead. "The only part of my past that I could put my hands on was the filth from which I recoiled, layers of organic material pressed hard against a stone floor" (115). Her attempt to "witness" the past by being physically present at sites of enslavement triggers revulsion rather than more noble emotions such as remembrance of the dead or resolve to prevent such atrocities from happening in the future (115). Hartman's archival dreams of connecting to the past through a romantic view of African history fail.

Hartman has an uneasy relationship with what Yogita Goyal calls "the romance of diaspora," the hope of a place, often figured as Africa, where full political and social belonging can take place for the African diaspora.[28] She wrestles with past interpretations of Africa as the "motherland" for those in the African diaspora. As Kelly Baker Josephs notes, "*How* we know the Caribbean" raises questions of related epistemologies of how identity is constructed through language.[29] Hartman's formal choices in moving from the present to fictionalized eighteenth- and nineteenth-century histories along with including historical and sociological writing about the legacies of the history of slavery show both to be equally important for readers' understanding of the aftereffects of slavery.

Another rupture, for Hartman, beyond slavery is a second casting out of paradise, which is the loss of the possibility of a successful Ghana open to the African diaspora and a sense of belonging to it. Hartman draws our attention to the archival dreams manifested in language surrounding Africa. A chapter provocatively titled "Afrotopia" describes how many intellectuals and social change makers in the African diaspora in the 1950s and 1960s flocked to help build a postcolonial Ghana. W. E. B. Du Bois renounced his U.S. citizenship and lived his final years in Ghana. Frantz Fanon, Hartman reminds us, composed much of *The Wretched of the Earth* in Ghana (36). President Kwame

Nkrumah welcomed civil rights leaders such as Martin Luther King Jr. and Malcolm X. Maryse Condé, Hartman states, lived for more than a decade in Guinea, Senegal, and Ghana, teaching French there from 1964 to 1968. Condé ruefully comments that her romantic idealization of Africa as motherland had much in common with others arriving in Africa from the diaspora at the time: "I was going to Africa because I was going to meet *my* people, I was going to find my true home. And when I got there, I discovered that, in fact, I had little in common with the people of Guinea, as I was a French Caribbean."[30] *Lose Your Mother* characterizes such recognitions of African diasporic people's outsider status as simultaneously common but also enviable because "in the sixties it was still possible to believe that the past could be left behind because it appeared as though the future, finally, had arrived; whereas in my age the impress of racism and colonialism seemed nearly indestructible. Mine was not the age of romance. The Eden of Ghana had vanished long before I arrived" (37).

For Hartman, her dispossession represents a transcolonial comparison between the experiences of her Curaçao and African American family. In a reversal of the more common family genealogy that begins with immediate relatives and then turns to African origins, Hartman notes that her residency in Ghana actually sparked her interest in her family's history in Curaçao.[31] Hartman reveals both her family's history and the role the Dutch played in the slave trade. *Lose Your Mother* details Hartman's records of her Caribbean family, the Van Eikers, and includes an image of her grandfather's birth certificate. She retells the family oral history of her father being an illegitimate child of a powerful white man in Curaçao. "The Hartman name, according to my father, was our anchor in the world. It was our sole inheritance; we possessed no wealth but it. So when my grandfather's white cousins tried to buy back the family name from the brown ones in an attempt to erase a history of owners and property they feared would be mistaken for kinship, our clan doggedly held on to it" (82). Like Brand's encounter with her grandfather, Hartman's tale also turns out to include an unsatisfactory origin story. Her grandfather's 1897 birth certificate, written in Dutch and reprinted without translation in the text, contains only his mother's name, Clarita Maduro. Hartman comments, "Four generations were born with a blank space where a father's name should be. In its place was the stroke of a bureaucrat's pen, which had left a line less dramatic than an X and which suggested nothing as harsh as erasure but simply 'not applicable'" (80). Clarita Maduro was an urban woman in the capital of Willemstad making a living as a milliner, a reflection of her status as a multi-racial woman with white parentage.[32] In contrast, Hartman's American family has no record of paternal ancestors beyond her grandfather.

Lose Your Mother contains many such passages about Hartman's family history and of her own experiences growing up. It strategically uses autobiography to foreground the affective limitations of the archive and of traditional methodologies of writing history. While searching for her ancestors in archives, Hartman finds and then loses a record of her U.S.-born great-great-grandmother. "My graduate training hadn't prepared me to tell the stories of those who had left no record of their lives and whose biography consisted of the terrible things said about them or done to them. I was determined to fill in the blank spaces of the historical records and to represent the lives of those deemed unworthy of remembering, but how does one write a story about an encounter with nothing?" (16).

Lose Your Mother, then, is more than a travelogue or meditation on the aftereffects of slavery, as some commentators suggest. Instead, much of its work can be understood as emplotted by absence—as being structured around personal and archival absences related to understanding the past. The social death of slaves is accurately represented in the archives and in scholarship. By that I mean that archives of colonialism and slavery in the Caribbean contain documents related to property—transfer of land and prices and sales of commodities, including the enslaved—but not of the experiences of the enslaved themselves. The presence of European texts when compared to the absence of African and Asian texts demonstrates how archives are shaped by those in power.[33] There is not a single narrative by a woman about the Middle Passage—the journey from the Door of No Return to the Americas. In the Caribbean, there are few slave narratives at all, and only one long-form narrative by a woman, Mary Prince. Nicole N. Aljoe posits that two things characterize the remaining slave narratives in the Caribbean. First, unlike U.S. narratives by Harriet Jacobs and Frederick Douglass, life writing "from multiple languages of the Caribbean are generated from inherently hybrid sources."[34] This means that the surviving narratives are patchworks of personal narrative, historical writing, and articles within newspapers and legal documents. We can see then a link between the corpus considered in this book in which bricolage is a formal choice and earlier texts that resulted in "patchworks" created out of necessity.

Second, Aljoe contends, "The narratives exist as literal fragments in the archive," such as one narrative found on a single crumbling piece of foolscap in a box in the British library.[35] Using traditional historical methods to attempt to find nonexistent sources elides the very thing Hartman and Brand center: the lack of first-person accounts. The absences of the lives of the enslaved in archives demonstrate the very power structures that rendered the lives of the enslaved invisible and disposable.[36] Thus, in Brand's and Hartman's efforts, different as they are, seeking to step outside of the archive can be seen as a direct answer to what is missing: the voices of the enslaved, especially women.

Hartman knows her project is impossible but goes on to create a mode of writing she calls "critical fabulation," which spins us away from the archive as mortuary to a generative place of historical reimagination ("Venus" 11). While the line between autobiography and fiction is always under contention, Hartman's project is a strategy for representing archival absences as unsolvable and central to the narrative, in contrast to texts such as Michelle Cliff's *Abeng* or Jamaica Kincaid's *Autobiography of My Mother* that use fiction to imagine lost pasts. *Lose Your Mother* uses formal techniques to support Hartman's goal of bringing the past into the present, even as it remains an epistemological project that raises questions about how much we can access or understand about the past. Rather than occupying a single subject position of the narrating "I" of many life writings, Hartman moves from being a narrator of her own experience, to being a more disinterested narrator of historical or cultural information, to employing "fabulation" to write from the perspective of those she has found traces of in the archive.

Hartman steps most forcefully outside her training as a historian in the chapter "The Dead Book," where she allows herself to imagine past what archival records can reveal. "The Dead Book" recounts the trial of a ship's captain in England in 1792 for the murder of an enslaved girl on board his ship, the *Recovery*. The chapter title refers to the records kept on board ships such as this of the enslaved who died, a literal book of the dead. Hartman incorporates the testimony of others on the *Recovery* regarding the captain's brutal punishments of his human cargo as well as the sexual violence visited on girls and women by both the captain and the crew. Rather than writing from a historical perspective about the facts of the case, Hartman moves from her own perspective to that of the captain, that of antislavery advocate William Wilberforce, and that of the girl herself. Hartman enters into the space and time of the Door of No Return by imagining it through the eyes of a girl who is not yet a New World slave but has left behind her identity as a free person.

By creating these multiple perspectives, Hartman centers absence through formal choices, such as splicing her historian's interpretation with fragments of the existing archive. This method of writing highlights all that is missing from the archive and all that cannot be written in academic history because of lack of evidence. The girl who was murdered on the *Recovery* does not have a name that survives in the historical record. Hartman writes, "I am unsure if it is possible to salvage an existence from a handful of words: *the supposed murder of a Negro girl*. Hers is a life impossible to reconstruct, not even her name survived" (137). By moving from slave ship captain to Wilberforce and then to the enslaved girl, *Lose Your Mother* shows through decreasing numbers of direct quotes and factual references that what we "know" of the girl's life comes entirely from the testimony of those responsible for her death. The narratives of the ship's captain and of Wilberforce could be from a scholarly biography, but Hartman signals that the girl's narrative has to be an invention because of her status as cargo rather than as a person with a subjectivity, at least as she is recorded in British historical records.[37]

The ship's name, *Recovery*, though a "fact" of the archive, signals also the romance of archival work—the hope of recovery and reanimation of the archival subjects we write about. Carolyn Steedman calls the grandiose vision of the researcher to bring the dead back to "life" one symptom of archive fever.[38] It is not a coincidence that Hartman enters into the consequences of the Door of No Return through court records. Remember Jamaican sociologist and novelist Erna Brodber's warning that Caribbean people may always find themselves short of evidence in a historiographical court of law, since archival records leave little trace of common folk.[39] Hartman's solution to the problem of archival impossibility is to confront the lack directly. "To read the archive is to enter a mortuary," she writes. "It permits one final viewing and allows for a last glimpse of persons about to disappear into the slave hold" (17). And yet, although this pessimism about the archive's possibilities might serve to limit the reader's expectations for how Hartman can achieve her stated goal "to bring the past closer" (17), in this later chapter and subsequently in an essay titled "Venus in Two Acts," about another girl on the *Recovery*, Hartman reads the court testimony against itself.

In writing a narrative from the point of view of the unnamed girl, Hartman uses the historical record to create a "memoir" by someone who could not possibly have written one. That is not hyperbole; there is no existing narrative by a woman who survived the Middle Passage. Hartman deploys what I am calling feminist absence aesthetics to create a text that does not and cannot exist: a woman's life narrative about the Middle Passage. The court documents record the crew's attempt to force-feed the girl. Hartman rewrites this legal "fact" into the one agential act possible for a captive, to purposely refuse food as a means of escape. "She had discovered a way off the ship. It worried her that the ancestors might shun her, or the gods might be angry and punish her by bringing her back as a goat or a dog, or she would roam the earth directionless and never find her way past the sea, but she risked it anyway, it was the only path open" (152). However, Hartman warns the reader that the narrative closure she has invented is only one among many stories. "If the story ended there, I could feel a small measure of comfort. I could hold on to this instant of possibility. I could find a salutary lesson in the girl's suffering and pretend a story was enough to save her from oblivion. I could sigh with relief and say, 'It all happened so long ago.' Then I could wade into the Atlantic and not think of the *dead book*" (153). I distinguish then, Hartman's critical fabulation from historical fiction because it is a strategy for representing what the archive cannot tell by making absence the central story rather than a reparative fiction. Historical fiction in the Caribbean often carries with it the effort to educate readers on the Caribbean past, describing events and people marginalized from traditional accounts.[40] This passage in *Lose Your Mother* does not end with a novelistic recovering of a forgotten figure from history. Instead, it emphasizes that retelling the story using critical fabulation is not "enough to save her from oblivion" (153). Archival dreams in *Lose Your Mother* are not enough to enact historical recovery.

Brand, Queer Absence, and Revolutionary Failures

A Map to the Door of No Return provides a different response to the past than one more typically seen in Caribbean writing, and certainly different from Hartman's archival dreams of recovering those lost in the archives of slavery. While *Lose Your Mother* begins with a genealogical desire to recover lost ancestors as Hartman follows a chain of relatives beyond her family to their ancestral home in Africa, it concludes with finding connections through shared experiences rather than blood kinship. "This give-and-take was not a matter of blood or kinship, but of affiliation. We were the progeny of slaves. We were the children of commoners" (204).[41] Brand also begins with her grandfather's story of the irrecoverability of ancestral origins. In contrast to the many artistic and scholarly works that attempt to reassemble fragmented and hidden histories into a counter-archive, however, Brand refuses archival dreams.

Unlike Hartman's story of "returning" to Africa, there is no need to visit slave forts, Brand asserts, because the diaspora has never left them. The Door is a psychological state internalized by the African diaspora.

> *There are maps to the Door of No Return. The physical door. They are well worn, gone over by cartographer after cartographer, refined from Ptolemy's Geographia to orbital photographs and magnetic field imaging satellites. But to the Door of No Return which is illuminated in the consciousness of Blacks in the Diaspora, there are no maps. The door is not mere physicality. It is a spiritual location. It is also perhaps a psychic destination. Since leaving was never voluntary, return was, and still may be an intention, however deeply buried. There is as it says no way in; no return.* (n.p.)

This epigraph appears on the first page, italicized and standing alone. It describes Brand's approach to her topic. *Map* tells of Brand's life after the Grenada Revolution, but does so through a larger political and historical lens than solely an individual life. This quote illustrates how Brand's project differs from Hartman's, particularly in the use of the phrase "no return." Brand sees the physical places that held enslaved people in captivity on the African continent as evacuated of meaning because they cannot adequately contain the loss represented by their physical structure. The Door, for Brand, is a continuing state of unbelonging, not a place of healing.[42]

Knowledge and memory are thus held in tension from the start of *Map to the Door of No Return*. Indeed, the inability of Brand's grandfather to articulate something he was possibly told as a child but cannot now speak aloud indicates how African diaspora genealogy is more than personal history. Having an untraceable genealogy is a sign of colonial power during enslavement and indenture. Brand describes the absence of family history as a sign of the Door of No Return. "Having no name to call on was having no past; having no past pointed to the fissure between the past and the present. That fissure is represented in the Door of No Return" (5). As Brand notes, "But the rupture this exchange with my grandfather revealed was greater than the need for familial bonds. It was a rupture in history, a rupture in the quality of being" (4). The rupture in history, as Glissant notes and Brand expounds upon in *Map*, is the legacy of enslavement. In conjunction, the absence of family history is related to the removal of enslaved people from one place to another. "It was also a physical rupture, a rupture of geography. . . . We were not from the place where we lived and we could not remember where we were from or who we were. My grandfather could not summon up a vision of a landscape or of a people which would add up to a name. And it was profoundly disturbing" (5). A commonplace of childhood, to ask about the history of one's family, becomes an epistemological crisis. Brand can never know her family's origins.[43] What Brand evokes here is that unlike immigrants who might have some mental image of an ancestral country or a region, such a connection is not possible typically for descendants of the enslaved.[44]

Brand's missing archive begins with many of the same elements as Hartman's such as unknowable family histories and the ruptures of slavery and colonialism, and ends with the missing historical and personal accounts of the Grenada Revolution and the aftermath of the U.S. invasion. However, unlike *Lose Your Mother*, *Map* does not follow the life writing genre of a genealogical quest with a quest's implicit promise of answers. Brand suggests that the Door of No Return will continue to be an organizing feature of many African diaspora archival dreams because it represents a deep desire for connection and the potential to heal historical rupture. The catharsis that Commander notes is an integral part of the hopes of African diaspora visitors to slave forts cannot be accomplished in Brand's view. "Why so compelling? Perhaps it is the Holy Grail of the Diaspora. It is the site of pain which will turn into the site of pleasure. Transform us into full being through its immutable knowledge. Transform us into being" (93). The Door of No Return in Brand's sweeping dismissal represents a place that if revisited could reverse trauma. Brand instead categorizes the Door of No Return as the sign of irreversible trauma.

Brand resists methods that wholeheartedly embrace historical recovery as a means of belonging. In the Caribbean quarrel with history, Brand refuses to align herself with national or cultural origin stories, with what Alison Donnell calls the legitimizing strategies of nationalism or cultural authenticity central to the quarrel with history.[45] Lauren Gantz insightfully comments that while Brand uses methodologies of archiving and historical recovery familiar to those in African diaspora studies, her work also challenges that project. Brand "demonstrates how responses that appear antithetical to remembrance—such as attempting to compartmentalize or forget painful histories are part of the same psychological and historical processes as memory" contribute to the survival of

African peoples in the New World.[46] *Map* engages with resistant archives, while manifesting doubt in the cure-all of historical recovery.

Brand veers away from what might be called a primary function of the archive within Western thought: an empiricist fascination with origins and belonging. Carolyn Steedman describes a central feature of the archive as a repository in which information is readily retrieved, what John Frow calls the "logic of the archive."[47] The "unbelonging" of a Caribbean subject in diaspora is mapped onto the remaking of identity that passing through the Door of No Return made necessary.[48] The Door, in Brand's view, is "the creationplace for Blacks in the New World Diaspora at the same time that it signified the end of traceable beginnings" (5). Brand situates herself within the unknowability of origins, what Stephen Best terms other ways of understanding the past through rubrics such as "unbelonging" and "abandonment," to write about it as the condition for Black subjectivity.

My reading of *Map* centers around resisting the now commonplace idea that knowing the past of slavery is key to Black futurity. It speaks to a newer critical concern among scholars interested in sites of disconnection in contrast to earlier emphases on recovery, resistance, and origins. Seeing the slave past as an explanatory framework for the present of the African diaspora, Best argues, is not inevitable, and is perhaps not even desirable. Best notes, "The project of racial rethinking may well begin with forms of unbelonging, negative sociability, abandonment, and other disruptions that thwart historical recovery . . . invit[ing] contemplation of the gains to be derived from extending the queer acknowledgement of nonrelationality between the past and the present to the racial case."[49] Brand's work also asks the reader to mediate on how little exists of the past, and how unbelonging symbolized by the Door of No Return is a feature of Black subjectivity.

Social belonging, as Nira Yuval-Davis notes, is not simply a matter of possessing documents related to citizenship.[50] Belonging and its opposite, unbelonging, are produced through affiliation, affect, and the policing of boundaries. The ruptures of slavery and colonialism form one major theme in *Map*. A second theme centers around Brand's use of life writing to explore what it might mean as a Black lesbian to reject belonging to the project of the nation-state in the wake of the failure of the revolutionary movement in Grenada in the 1980s. Life writing focalizes the reader's experience as Brand's own. She directs our attention to her quest for answers about origins and belonging and her realization that neither the archive nor returning to present-day Ghana can accomplish her goal of telling the stories of those who left barely a trace in the archive.

Map, like *Lose Your Mother* is also emplotted by absence, but Brand's method is not that of a historian's linear narrative with citations. Brand repeats sources and stories, revealing more as the narrative progresses, much as when the tide goes out it reveals more of the shore, and as the tide comes in it gives new shape to the coast. She also repeats headings over and over, such as the word "Maps," foregrounding absence as a repetition with a difference that structures the narrative. Brand's repeated questionings of issues related to origins, subjectivity, and diaspora are epistemological, but they also reflect an absence aesthetics in that formal aspects of the narrative reflect that there can be no firm conclusion. Brand uses life writing as a means to uncover slowly, for herself and the reader, the ways in which unbelonging is a permanent feature of the psyches of the descendants of the enslaved. As Ann Cvetkovich explains, "Because trauma can be unspeakable and unrepresentable and because it is marked by forgetting and dissociation, it often seems to leave behind no records at all."[51] Just as the slave forts become a synecdoche for enslavement, the dispossession of slavery in Brand's text comes to stand in for the specific dispossession and loss of hope for the future that the end of the Grenada Revolution signaled.

Brand writes of the African diaspora, "Marooned, tenantless, deserted. . . . Cast behind . . . this spirit is no citizen, no national, no one who is christened, no sex. . . . This spirit abandoned by all mothers, fathers, all known progenitors" (213). Although Brand writes here of the orphaned and the ancestorless, kinship and the national as a stand-in for family are not Brand's main concern in *Map*. Christina Sharpe finds Brand's work within the context of African diaspora writing remarkable for its "refusal of nation, country, citizenship."[52] Brand's multiple refusals of normative affiliations coupled with her invocation of Caribbean maroons (settlements created by escaped slaves who were not necessarily kin) allow me to position *Map* as a queer text.[53] Both LGBTQ people in the Caribbean and maroons exist as insiders and outsiders to normative Caribbean national identity and trouble ideas of origins and authenticity.[54] I make this claim not just because of Brand's own identity, but because a queer reading of *Map* allows me to make thematic connections between the aftereffects of slavery and underrecognized elements of *Map* as an elegy to the loss of Brand's women colleagues during the U.S. invasion. The deep grief Brand feels for the women who died and the loss of working together in the movement permeate *Map*. I call these queer affiliations since Brand privileges her chosen same-sex affiliations as her primary affective relationships rather than that of her natal family. Rather than emphasizing ties created through imagined family like African diaspora returnees to Ghana, Brand focuses on creating relation and solidarity not with ancestors or descendants but with those located in the recent past—her comrades in Grenada.

Grenada itself becomes a Door of No Return for Brand in that she sees it as a place that might heal the trauma of slavery's dispossession. Like Hartman's "Eden of Ghana" of the 1960s, many participants in the Grenada Revolution saw it as a chance to create a new postcolonial home. Form is key here, as Brand's repetitions related to the Door of No Return allow her to circle around the unsayable—the trauma of seeing friends killed before her eyes in Grenada, and the exacerbation of that trauma in not being able to communicate her experiences after they happen. Put in linear order, *Map to the Door of No Return* tells of Brand's life when she first arrives in Canada, her participation in the revolutionary government of Grenada in the early 1980s, the aftermath of living through the overthrow of the Grendadan government by the United States, her solitary life in rural Canada in the 1980s and 1990s, and her life in the present in Toronto. In addition, she chronicles her travels to Australia and South Africa. The narrative is not written in this order, however. She returns to themes of Black subjectivity, enslavement, and historical ruptures until the trauma Brand experienced in Grenada is addressed in the last third of the text.

When archives will not unfold, another strategy is to move from the historical record to historical spaces. Hartman notes of both herself and the earlier generations of people who came to Ghana that they held the idea that a return to a place they had never been would heal historical trauma. Brand also writes, "The hope is that *return* could resolve all the old dilemmas, make a victory out of defeat, and engender a new order. And the disappointment is that there is no going back to a former condition. Loss remakes you" (100). Although Brand rejects visiting the sites of the Doors of No Return located in Africa, she does admit to seeking a different kind of relief through location. "This same burning head had led me to this island. I had come here in search of a thought, how to be human, how to live without historical pain" (157). Brand speaks here elliptically of her decision to join the political movement on the island of Grenada. Throughout *Map*, ruminations on losses created by colonialism and slavery are spliced with the more recent occurrence of her personal experiences in Grenada. Brand makes a formal choice to write about centuries-long historical processes in the same paragraph as the days-long events of the U.S. invasion in 1983. This splicing of time periods and events didactically invites the reader to see them as connected, and to see Brand's work as an epistemological project related to a broader understanding of the far-reaching effects of the Door of No Return.

Grenada becomes Brand's Door of No Return in two ways. One, she travels to Grenada in the hope of an origin story, but a specifically *queer* origin story of relationships to others in the movement. Brand's framing of dispossession with a desire for belonging not yet found (or impossible to find) can be read through what Nadia Ellis identifies as a "queered diasporic belonging," a recognition that "the insufficiency of existing modes of belonging is matched by an awareness that new forms remain inspiringly elusive."[55] In *Bread Out of Stone* (1994), Brand writes, "We were born thinking of travelling back. It is our singular preoccupation, we think of nothing else. . . . We are continually uncomfortable where we are. . . . This must be the code written on the lining of my brain, go back, go back, like a fever, a pandemic scourging the Diaspora" (58–59). Being "uncomfortable where we are" and wishing to be someplace else can be seen as the place where diasporic and queer desire for belonging meet. Grenada offered Brand a chance at belonging, buoyed by the hope of an independent revolutionary government, which was shattered with the U.S. invasion.

Brand joined the revolutionary movement in Grenada in the early 1980s. The support of the New Jewel Movement (NJM) for the equality of women's political, military, educational, and workforce participation probably featured in Brand's decision to move to Grenada, as it did for other feminists during the time period.[56] NJM, headed by Maurice Bishop, overthrew the government of Eric Gairy, leading to the Grenada Revolution (1979–1983). Internal political conflicts led to the imprisonment of Bishop and many of his cabinet members in 1983. Bishop and other leaders of the NJM were killed on October 19 of that year. The bodies of Bishop and other NJM leaders were never recovered; they were seized by the U.S. armed forces, and their location remains unknown to this day. David Scott writes that the absence of a grave site in particular for Bishop, who "embodied . . . almost literally" the revolution, has led to an ongoing barrier to grieve the end of the revolution.[57] On October 25 the United States invaded Grenada. This invasion raised fears within Grenada and abroad that the nation's brief period of independence from Britain (which began in 1974) would be replaced less than ten years later by an American neocolonial domination. Perhaps it is not surprising, then, that Brand disavows the possibility of return and belonging for the diaspora in Africa since that could not be achieved within the Caribbean itself.

The Grenada Revolution created a socialist form of government and economy, but as important was its emphasis on decolonizing knowledge and creating new archives through literacy programs and culturally informed textbooks and curricula.[58] All this was lost with the U.S. invasion. The silences and absences related to the fall of the revolutionary movement and the U.S. invasion are profound. The inability to relate to the complexity and damaging nature of this experience, a central feature of trauma, marks the second way Grenada becomes a Door of No Return for Brand. Just as Hartman experiences the failure of the "Eden of Ghana" resulting in her unbelonging in modern-day Ghana as subsequent cultural rupture related to the dislocations of slavery and colonialism, Brand's recounting of the fall of the Grenada government and the loss of her sense of belonging there are another form of the rupture inherent in her grandfather's story. Indeed, a variety of critics note the cultural silences and trauma of the invasion.[59] Grenadian writer Merle Collins observes that even thirty years after the end of the revolution, just what occurred is complicated by the silence of many of the main surviving participants.[60] Shalini Puri suggests that there has been a "massive silencing of the Grenada revolution," with one effect that contemporary Grenadian literature is often set before 1983 rather than after the overthrow of Bishop's government, as if time stopped.[61] This silence and shock, perhaps more common among those not currently living in Grenada, are represented in Brand's writing. Brand does not reveal what it was like to live and work under the NJM government in the immediate years after the U.S. invasion.

The story Brand does tell, however, is a detailed account of October 19, 1983, the day Bishop and many leaders in the party were shot and killed. Brand is not alone in her focus on the events of October; Puri notes that when asked about the Grenada Revolution, many people who were present start by talking about October 1983, rather than the beginning of the revolution in 1979.[62] After unknowable family origins and a lack of social and civic belonging, the third rupture Brand charts is the line marking the before and after of the coup. A section titled "October" describes the death of the leadership of the NJM and the aftermath of the U.S. invasion of Grenada several days later. Brand recounts in detail her memories of October 19, the day she wakes with a fever and goes to Fort Rupert with a friend. There Brand narrowly escapes being shot by the counterrevolutionary forces that kill Bishop. Historical rupture is experienced bodily and is framed by Brand as an illness, a fever, and a pandemic throughout *Map*. Brand is already sick before Bishop is killed but will worsen after his death: "My head was full of a pain and fever. . . . I was awakened instead by the sound of a great crowd. This same burning head had led me to this island. I had come here in search of a thought, how to be human, how to live without historical pain. It seemed to me then that a revolution would do it" (157). In *Map*, the cure for that fever is to move into the revolutionary future promised by the NJM, but the fever is retriggered with the overthrow of the government.

While Hartman's response to archives that will not reveal the subjectivity of women who were enslaved is to work within an absence aesthetics that leads her to critical fabulation as a strategy to deal with the unrecoverable loss, Brand describes different gendered losses—the solidarity she experienced with her friend Marlene, other women in the movement, and the hopes of a revolutionary future. A question posed by Brand to her friend Marlene, "Did we, did you go crazy after?" shows that there is an absence in histories of the Grenada Revolution of the effects on those who survived the invasion. Although in 2002 Brand will memorialize Marlene Green for her "courageous work during the 1983 American invasion of Grenada," *Map* portrays any discussion of that trauma as unspeakable until almost twenty years have passed.[63] If as Jenny Sharpe suggests, and Hartman echoes, the slave past cannot be exorcised because its stories are untold, especially those of women, a similar comparison might be made to the stories of women in the Grenada Revolution.[64]

The question of what happened (i.e., the lasting impacts of the revolution and invasion on Caribbean people) forms the center of an essay published by well-known Grenadian writer Merle Collins in 2013.[65] Collins's response to trauma is one of archival dreams—the hope that stories collected in faraway archives could help her understand her own country's history. "In fact, after the early shock of 1983 had subsided, I kept thinking that I wanted to find out more about how Grenadians and other Caribbean people came to be who they are as a people. One place I wanted to visit was England, where so much of the Caribbean story rests on library shelves and in other archival spaces. How, I wondered, might those neglected stories help me to understand some of the antecedents of this trauma?"[66] The causes of the assassination of the prime minister and his cabinet, the U.S. invasion, and the impact on Caribbean understandings of the possibilities of the future are still unknown and being shaped, Collins writes.[67] For Brand, this question is historical and personal. It encompasses an acknowledgment of the deep wound to Caribbean sovereignty the U.S. invasion caused. It also signals the source of Brand's isolation and anxiety.

When *Map* does address Brand's trauma, the loss of Minister of Education Jacqueline Creft, who was assassinated on October 19, 1993, in the coup, is represented as pivotal. Her loss of the affiliations to other women in the movement, which I am calling a queer affiliation for its emphasis on primary connections outside of marriage and biological family, proves to be the most traumatic. Brand memorializes Jacqueline dressed in yellow and smoking right before her death at Fort Rupert in both *No Language Is Neutral* (1990) and *Map*.[68] Emblematic of Brand's loss of female solidarity that cuts across political lines is her dedication of two poems in *No Language Is Neutral*. One is to Jacqueline; Brand also dedicates a poem to Phyllis Coard, the minister of women's affairs in the revolutionary government who was part of the political faction supporting the coup and was jailed when Brand wrote the poem. Brand's work suggests that an important aspect of the improper burial of the Grenada Revolution is that the women who participated are still unmemorialized.

Brand recounts that on hearing the news that Bishop had been released from house arrest, she joins a crowd walking toward the fort along with a coworker from Carriacou. The text itself gives few clues as to the nature of Brand's work in Grenada, or how close she was to the prime minister and his cabinet. However, the language she uses to describe them, her witnessing the moments before their death, is intimate, using their first names. Frozen in time, Brand's shock at witnessing the deaths of Bishop and other leaders of the party links this text not only to a regionwide sense of political suspension noted above, but to other literary works produced after the invasion.[69] Brand writes of a feeling of time stopping, as though a part of her will always be stuck in the moment of the assassination. Arriving home from the fort in minutes, Brand is in time to look out from her balcony to where she stood just moments before and see Bishop get shot and others in the crowd jump to their deaths on the cliffs below the fort. "We stood on the balcony, she and I, looking to the fort and to the bodies collapsed on the cliff. . . . In any moment like this we might die, too. I was that body draping the cliff. I left myself on the cliff and I stood on the balcony with Marlene spilling a glass of water forever" (166). Formally, this preserved moment of stillness contrasts with the peripatetic travel narratives making up much of the narrative of *Map*. Hartman writes of the slave fort as grave site; for Brand, Fort Rupert becomes a grave.

The overthrow of Bishop and the U.S. invasion are written by Brand in a narrative arc that mimics her writing of the drastic before and after of passing through the Door of No Return as a place that could resolve the trauma of history, but disappointingly will not. Earlier in the text, for those alert to her involvement with the Grenada Revolution, Brand writes of the longing for belonging to the nation in a way that signals that the national homes for the diaspora are precarious. Evoking the trope of the anticolonial romance's fixation on nationalism as a solution, Brand asserts, "Some of us want entry into the home and nation that are signified by these romances. Some of us in the Diaspora long so for nation—some continuous thread of biological or communal association, some bloodline or legacy which will cement our rights in the place we live. The problem of course is that even if those existed—and they certainly do, even if it is in the human contraband which we represent in the romance—they do not guarantee nation for Blacks in the Diaspora" (67). Here Brand speaks doubly, referring to the dream of Africa as home, but also to the knowing reader, referencing how Grenada was for a short time a home, a "nation for Blacks in the Diaspora." She also speaks queerly, in her critique of the belief that finding the right biological lineage or "bloodline" that will bring the diaspora belonging.

The silencing of postrevolutionary disappointment Puri identifies as a historiographical issue emerges in *Map* when Brand summons the courage to ask her friend Marlene, "a woman from whom I learned all I know," if the loss of the promise of the Grenada Revolution drove her crazy (169).[70] Marlene simply answers, "Yes" (169). Brand leaves Grenada after the U.S. invasion, while Marlene decides to return. In the last section of the book, Brand acknowledges her choice to live alone in rural Canada, which represents the retreat of someone who has not dealt with trauma. "My fear," she tells us finally, "has a particular origin" (155). Her fear stems from her previous obliviousness to the politics of location. Location matters, as it does in the repeated theme of maps and cartography throughout the text. Brand is unable to read the signs of a coup and understand where she is, a small Caribbean island about to undergo political violence and invasion. "It's only guns," Brand thinks even as she sees armored trucks driving toward the fort (163). All the maps in the world cannot help her realize that she is on a small island that will soon be bombed by the world's dominant military. Collins writes that that loss of the "country's self-respect was a less tangible casualty of the invasion."[71] The invasion, then, comes as a blow to the psyche of those who survived. Brand's framing of living with the consequences of the invasion as a mental illness shows a bodily response to what her mind cannot process. Trauma as a mental state that lingers is another way the Grenada invasion is spliced with the aftereffects of the Door of No Return on the African diaspora.

Brand ends *Map* by creating a "Ruttier for the Marooned in the Diaspora." A ruttier is map made by sailors that depicts the coastline along which they traveled, rather than an omniscient aerial view of a path on land (213). One has to be on the coastline and familiar with its contours to make sense of the map. There are no directions from one place to another in a ruttier; it is a navigational tool to explain where one is in relation to a stretch of coast. Brand's use of a ruttier turns the reader toward a new understanding of archival impossibility. This ruttier is connected back to one of the first stories told in *Map*: Brand's grandfather's forgetting of his ancestry. Brand suggests for the first time that her grandfather's forgetting of their ancestral location is actually a positive legacy, noting that this lapse in memory "was understandable; after all, when he was born the Door of No Return was hardly closed, forgetting was urgent" (223). Being marooned in history means that her "grandfather's forgetting was not personal. It has been passed on to him by many, most especially the one in my family who stepped through the Door of No Return. It was a gift. Forgetting. The only gift that one, the one bending reluctantly toward the opening, could give" (232).

Carolyn Steedman observes that in contrast to memory, which may contain multitudes, archives are "made from selected and consciously chosen documentation from the past."[72] The dream of a limitless archive unfolded that can be made to answer that which colonialism and slavery has obscured powers Hartman's and Brand's texts, but in different ways. While Hartman's grappling with the Door of No Return involves travel to Ghana and the reimagining of the archive so that the voices of the enslaved can be heard and included in the historical record, even if provisionally, Brand urgently resists common tropes of return and speculation about the past. Hartman suggests that African diasporic people "returned" to Ghana believing that "the past could be left behind because it appeared as though the future, finally, had arrived" (37). Similarly, Grenada offered to Brand the chance to walk through the Door of No Return in reverse. Grenada provided a sense of belonging that was disrupted through the U.S. invasion. In both cases, the epistemological issues raised by the graveyard of Atlantic slavery, unknowable aspects of the past, untraceable family histories, and the absence of subjective accounts by those who survived the Middle Passage and the U.S. invasion of Grenada are written though absence aesthetics that foreground the impossibility of archival recovery.

Although my focus here has been on the divergent nature of *Lose Your Mother* and *Map*'s understandings of the possibility of reconnecting to the past of enslavement and colonialism, I find it remarkable that their endings share a common focus on fugitivity and marronage. Rather than seeing the breakages between the past and the present as indicative of tragedy, Hartman and Brand turn to the symbolism of those who sought to free themselves from slavery. The figure of the fugitive slave in the United States and the maroon in the Caribbean represents those who took flight rather than remain slaves and who created communities based on resistance to white supremacy and colonialism.[73] Hartman ends her narrative by stating her connection to those who struggle to escape oppression, rather than embracing commonality based on ancestry. "For me, returning to the source didn't lead to the great courts and to the regalia of kings and queens. The legacy I chose to claim was articulated in the ongoing struggle to escape, stand down, and defeat slavery in all of its myriad forms. It was the fugitive's legacy" (234). In an interview with Patricia Saunders, Hartman notes that "freedom communities," such as the maroons, allow us to think about home as a space of creation rather than something inherited through biological kinship.[74] The Grenada Revolution, then, can be seen as one such fugitive or maroon endeavor, given its emphasis on creating as society around Caribbean people's needs. Marronage, like Hartman's fugitivity, is an affiliation of necessity and of choice.

Marronage and fugitivity create imaginative possibilities of flight and freedom that allow Hartman's and Brand's readers to imagine the future. The concept of fugitivity is a powerful one, and it is taken up in more detail in chapter 2, "Speculative Autobiography: Ghosts and Feminist Fugitivity." There I analyze Maryse Condé's *Victoire: My Mother's Mother* (2010). Condé describes her grandmother's persistent haunting of her along a demand that her life story be told. Condé works through archival absences in the immediate period after slavery is abolished to tell of her grandmother's life as constrained by *restavek*, the French Caribbean system of unpaid child labor. While most of the work is based on oral histories and archival sources, as we shall see, Condé allows herself to imagine her grandmother exercising erotic autonomy and enacting a feminist fugitivity by fleeing from Guadeloupe to Martinique.

CHAPTER 2

Speculative Autobiography

GHOSTS AND FEMINIST FUGITIVITY

The island on which our story takes place is not well known. It floats, forsaken, in the Gulf of Mexico, and only a few especially meticulous atlases show it. . . . To tell the truth, it is a completely unimportant scrap of earth, and the experts have once and for all dismissed its history as insignificant. And yet it has had its bad times, its past great upsurges, fine copious bloodlettings quite worthy of educated people's attention. But all of that was forgotten long ago.

—*Simone Schwarz-Bart,* Between Two Worlds *(1981)*

"Speculative Autobiography: Ghosts and Feminist Fugitivity" engages with the long-standing critical conversation within autobiography studies concerning the status of truth and veracity in life writing. It does so in an effort not to clarify but to productively muddy the waters by bringing this debate into conversation with the similarly venerable and unresolved issue of the Caribbean quarrel with history.[1] The Caribbean past of slavery and colonialism has been written about as a rupture ("all . . . that was forgotten long ago," as Simone Schwarz-Bart puts it), but also as valuable and necessary to recover in the making of Caribbean futures. Others have posited the chasm between past and present in the Caribbean as a beneficial element allowing contemporary artists and writers to invent cultures anew. Both sides of the quarrel write in resistance to colonial and more recently neoliberal forces that categorize the Caribbean as unimportant and marginal to world history and the rise of modernity.[2] Engaging with the dilemma over how to represent the past, Guadeloupean writer Maryse Condé's absence aesthetics in *Victoire: My Mother's Mother* ([2006] 2010) asks readers to hold two contradictory notions that straddle the quarrel with history and empiricist tendencies in autobiography studies. Condé, this chapter argues, uses life writing as a corrective to masculinist history. She claims a matricentric Guadeloupean heritage, thus participating in the Caribbean feminist recovery strand of the quarrel with history, where the lives of marginal women are brought to the forefront.[3] However, her use of life writing does not imply a transparently true recounting of historical facts or an ethnographic account.

In the first two decades of this century Condé, although a well-known novelist, produced four works of life writing: *Tales from the Heart: True Stories from My Childhood* (2004), *Victoire, What Is Africa to Me? Fragments of a True-to-Life Autobiography* (2017) and *Of Morsels and Marvels* (2020).[4] *Tales from the Heart* chronicles her childhood as a member of an upwardly mobile family in Guadeloupe in the 1930s and 1940s. *What Is Africa to Me?* describes her later education, including attaining a doctorate in France, and then her turbulent twenties and thirties living in France and teaching in Guinea, Senegal, and Ghana, while *Of Morsels and Marvels* describes her love of cooking and food. *Victoire*, a biography of Condé's grandmother inflected with Condé's own memories, engages the question of who should be the subject of history and how that history should be remembered by centering Condé's grandmother, an illegitimate and illiterate woman who was not a hero in the struggle for decolonization. Born twenty-six years after emancipation in 1874, growing up with her family in the slave huts of their grandparents on a former sugar plantation, and dying in 1915, when she and her daughter inhabited a coveted "upstairs-downstairs house" in a fashionable part of the city of Pointe-à-Pitre, Victoire spent her life working unpaid for a white family and preparing her daughter to become educated and enter the Black bourgeoisie.

If the ruptures of slavery and colonization, as Dionne Brand writes in *A Map to the Door of No Return*, are inherent to Black consciousness and manifest themselves through ongoing hauntings—"One enters a room and history follows"—then the history following Condé's family includes Victoire's exclusion from basic rights of citizenship, such as education and paid employment, a social status that continued from slavery (24–25). In one of the central works on Caribbean autobiography, Sandra Pouchet Paquet argues that the genre "constructs multiple spaces where the private and the personal collapse into projections of a public self, where the individual is represented within the context of mutuality and commonality."[5] Condé challenges Paquet's utopian view of the individual writer creating a public self in order to facilitate integration into community, instead often presenting Caribbean publics as individualist and hostile to larger considerations of the common good. As Condé remarks, "Due to the absenteeism and irresponsibility of the fathers, the victimized women are forced to be the breadwinners and assume the education of the children. However, in spite of this sociological reality, we have been fed upon triumphant portrayals of messianic heroes coming back home to revolutionize their societies."[6] Thus, Condé's autobiographical project, we can surmise, is not about establishing a sense of cultural or national belonging by celebrating political leaders. Rather, we should view Victoire's story as documenting women's absence from such modes of belonging. The absence of women from official archives has resulted in Caribbean national stories that misremember or discount the importance of gender and sexuality to understanding emancipation, belonging, and citizenship, as well as feminist responses to those absences.[7]

This chapter focuses on Condé's method for writing about these gendered archival absences and how that method can be understood as a feminist intervention in decolonial historical practices. In *Victoire*, Condé's method involves telling the reader when she reaches an archival limit, a gap or absence in official and personal histories that cannot be overcome because the evidence is absent, and then writing about those absences. Condé writes about these limits by using what I call "speculative autobiography." If speculative fiction writes imagined tales based on historical figures, then speculative autobiography recognizes the "autobiographical pact" that assumes that the author is being truthful and alerts the reader to those moments when the narrative goes beyond what is provable.[8] Carmen Maria Machado, for example, uses what she calls "non-realism" in her work as a means to "tap into aspects of being a woman that can be surreal or somehow liminal—certain experiences that can feel, even, like horror. It allows you to defamiliarize certain topics like sexual violence that some people might unfortunately dismiss as 'oh, just another story about rape.' Non-realism makes room for mythic expressions of the female experience, and I think can be a way to satisfy the hunger for narratives in which women have rich inner lives."[9] Condé's use of speculation in *Victoire* to represent hauntings by maternal figures and mysterious fathers brings a feminist awareness to the reader of the tension between the gendered lack of evidence about women's lives and the political importance of understanding women's role in the history of the Caribbean. Speculative autobiography also allows Condé to deploy the figure of the maroon, the fugitive from slavery known across the Caribbean. Condé describes her grandmother as a maroon in one of the few instances when her grandmother asserts erotic and personal agency. The concept of speculative autobiography allows me to posit that Condé's use of rumor and hearsay functions as a "fugitive" mode of writing about the past that moves outside of accepted historiographical sources.

Before discussing Condé's method of writing her grandmother's life, the political context I believe lies behind Condé's creation of the specific forms of absence aesthetics and feminist epistemologies in *Victoire* should be explored. France traditionally has espoused national identity formation through assimilation to French culture and language. France asks citizens who are not white and native to the country to leave racial or regional allegiances behind to become French.[10] This republican framework has influenced how slavery is remembered: largely through a focus on the state's act of decreeing emancipation.[11] Until very recently, cultural work and historical writing on slavery and its aftermath have been "taboo" in France itself.[12] The lack of French scholarship stands in contrast to work by those in French overseas departments who have attempted to disrupt French notions of national assimilation and a historiography invested in French legislative actions, such as the abolition of slavery, rather than French complicity in the slave trade and colonialism.[13]

Victoire's publication in French in 2006 and in English in 2010 arrived on the heels of a two-decades-long process of France and the French Caribbean reckoning with their past. Condé took a leadership role in these commemorations. The year 1998 marked the 150th anniversary of the abolition of slavery in the French Empire.[14] The date chosen for the national celebration, April 27, when slavery was abolished, was criticized by activists for its self-congratulatory tone in highlighting emancipation rather than the centuries of enslavement that preceded it. After the commemoration in 1998, Christiane Taubira, representative to the French National Assembly from French Guiana, put forward a bill that would recognize slavery and the slave trade as a crime against humanity. The bill became law on May 10, 2001. Consequently, President Chirac created the Committee for the Remembrance of Slavery which comprised historians and writers from French overseas departments impacted by slavery (French Guiana, Martinique, Guadeloupe, and Réunion).[15] The committee, with Condé as its chair, produced a report in 2005. Among its recommendations was an annual Day of Remembrance for the victims of slavery on May 10. Confirming the critique of activists from the 1990s, the committee emphasized that the story of abolition was only one part of a much longer narrative and critiqued French scholarship on slavery as woefully lacking.[16]

While there is no way to know exactly the impact this report had on Condé's creative work, *Victoire* charts how slavery was replaced with other forms of economic exploitation in Guadeloupe in the post-emancipation period. According to Stiina Löytömäki, "The report . . . acknowledged that the memory of slavery was divided into opposing memories that emphasized either abolition or slavery itself, the latter having been marginalised and privatised in the 'national consciousness.' The report encourages recognizing and fostering the complex nature of slavery, of abolition and of their memories, and acknowledges that after abolition new forms of servitude and exclusion continued."[17] Focusing not on "slavery or emancipation itself" but on the post-emancipation period, *Victoire* can be interpreted as responding to the recommendations of the report. Within that context, I show in this chapter that *Victoire* suggests new feminist decolonial epistemologies based not on certainty, but on haunting and fugitivity. Haunting represents the unfinished business of the past that cannot be completely resolved, in this case since archival records of the experiences of the enslaved and their immediate descendants are rare. Fugitivity marks sites of escape from slavery, colonization, and their aftermath in the post-emancipation period, represented in *Victoire* by moments of speculative autobiography.

Haunting Epistemologies

In keeping with Condé's role as a provocateur, *Victoire* departs from traditional epistemologies of the importance of roots in Caribbean life writing: the educated diasporic writer's valuation of their rural origins, featuring a selfless mother who advanced their education and an Afro-Caribbean grandmother who grounded the writer with folk wisdom and a sense of their African heritage.[18] Condé flouts these conventions in chronicling the life of her white-skinned gray-eyed grandmother, Victoire, who alienates her family by working for white Creoles in a city. Condé's mother Jeanne cloaks Victoire's complicated life in a series of platitudes such as "the mainstay of her family, a formidable woman" (4). Condé brushes off these remarks, characterizing them as "worn out clichés of the Antilles that no longer mean anything" (4). In doing so, she resists cultural scripts within life writing where mothers are described as either saintly or monstrous.[19] "I often wonder what would have been my relation to myself, my vision of my island, the Antilles and the world in general, what my writing that expresses all of this would have been if I had been cradled in the lap of a buxom, jovial grandmother, full of the traditional tales" (4). Condé here does not simply regret that her grandmother did not live long enough to have a relationship with her. This passage indicates the immense cultural divide created by Victoire's determination that Jeanne be educated and Jeanne's refusal to let her mother speak Creole or share Creole culture with her grandchildren.[20]

Condé's entry into the life of her grandmother is similar to her project in her novels and essays: to challenge knowledge that is offered as true and to describe other ways of knowing. Cut off from knowledge of Guadeloupean culture, the amputation of Creole language and food creates a phantom limb for Condé. This cultural absence transforms into Condé being haunted as an adult by the ghostly figure of her grandmother, who criticizes the settings of her novels for not being focused on Guadeloupe and its history.

> Sometimes I would wake up at night and see her sitting a corner of the room, like a reproach, so different from what I had become.
>
> What are you doing running around from Segu to Japan to South Africa? What's the point of all of these travels? Can't you realize that the only journey that counts is discovering your inner self. That's the only thing that matters? What are you waiting for to take an interest in me?
>
> Now I have the time to follow her footsteps. (3–4)

Condé is haunted by the unquiet dead, whose story has not been fully told, and whose memory her descendants have not carried on. For Condé, life writing allows her to speak of disenfranchisement in terms of haunting, not as metaphorical, but as fact. The epistemological instability of the supernatural reported as an actual event alerts the reader that fact and truth will be held in tension.

While the facts about someone's life and the truths that emerge through authorial interpretation are always present in composing a biography, the presence of a Victoire's ghost signals that Condé must take steps to remedy her absence from familial and national narratives. At the same time, Condé uses life writing as a means to creatively imagine what Victoire's life might have been like, using speculative autobiography as a narrative method that is not found in traditional historiography.

Condé describes "a kind of silence" around her grandmother and her origins in her family.[21] Condé writes in *Tales from the Heart* as well as in *Victoire* about her parents' reluctance to talk about their family's past and the Guadeloupean past of colonialism and slavery. These historical events would not have been part of Condé's education. Even today, French overseas departments focus on teaching primarily French history and language. Anthropologist Yarimar Bonilla points to the many absences within the colonial system of the French Caribbean departments: "One could argue that the importance of collective histories does not lie in their accuracy or even veracity, and in fact all historical narratives are also inherently 'bundles of silences.' But in the Antilles these sites of muted and confused history, together with the absence of local history in the education system (due to the imposed French national curriculum) and the overpowering presence of a triumphant French national history lead to what anthropologist Christine Chivallon describes as 'a lack of stable narratives about the past.'"[22] Silence about familial and regional history becomes represented as an absent presence in *Victoire* through the motif of haunting when the ghost of Condé's grandmother demands that the story of her life be told even as little evidence of it remains.

Victoire's illiteracy, a central theme in Condé's narrative about the limitations of her grandmother's life, means that she left no direct representations of her inner life or her experiences. Standard documents that aid family members in researching their family's past, such as school records or employment documents, do not exist for Victoire. Her inability to represent herself and leave behind records of her own thoughts through letters or a diary propels Condé's interest, seemingly as a project of recovery. Biographical recovery, however, typically depends on the ability to find documentable facts about that person. Condé's use of a ghost to introduce us to her biographical subject troubles that assumption, showing that empirical facts in the case of her grandmother have been lost or do not exist.

Absences that are unable to be filled by turning to an archive or unofficial records like oral histories or family documents mark a moment I call "archival impossibility."[23] Archival impossibility names the barrier to telling the stories of the colonized and marginalized from their perspective because it has not been documented. It is a sign of their marginalization that these stories do not exist. The lack of historical "recovery" projects related to individual lives in the

Francophone Caribbean, Charles Forsdick suggests, "may be linked in part to the marked emphasis in French historiography on written archives—often European—to the detriment of the more ephemeral cultural traces by which memories of the enslaved are more likely to be freighted."[24] Into this impossibility of recovery, those wishing to write their family's histories must find a methodology to represent absence. Condé writes within the conventions of life writing, but also employs speculative autobiography. Speculative autobiography recognizes that the phantom limb of the past creates dreams of archives unfolded for Caribbean subjects. Speculative autobiography, as I am defining it, allows for formal innovation such as reimagining the past when the writer comes to the limits of evidence, but does so by writing of those limits, rather than fictionalizing them.

Cheryl Wall argues in her work on contemporary African American women's fiction concerned with lineage and history, "It is at those moments when the quest for answers to the genealogical search is thwarted, when the only access to the past comes from what Morrison describes in 'Rootedness' as 'another way of knowing,' that these texts are most likely to subvert the conventions of the literary tradition so that the connection to the past can be forged nonetheless."[25] Creating alternate epistemologies for understanding a family's past links narratives across the African diaspora. Condé slyly points the reader to her own subversion of expectations of autobiographical truthfulness when she begins *Victoire* with an epigraph by French novelist Bernard Pingaud: "What does it matter whether I remember or invent / Whether I borrow or imagine."

Victoire suggests that ancestral haunting is one way of entering into debates about how to write about those who do not write about themselves. The presence of the dead among the living resurrects the Caribbean quarrel with history. The call to write Victoire's life, which Condé heeds, is achieved despite her grandmother having died before she was born, few family stories having been told about her, and her life as an illiterate servant to white Creoles having barely merited any documentation during her lifetime. Archives, Michel-Rolph Trouillot notes, not only reflect the dominant class or culture's ability to gather knowledge but serve as technologies of authorization and believability.[26] Condé's narrative reveals the rupture between her life and her grandmother's by way of a spectral figure who cannot be documented through traditional scholarly methods, just as much of the history of ordinary Guadeloupeans was not documented in the written record. Avery Gordon distinguishes haunting from trauma by virtue of an impetus toward action: "Haunting, unlike trauma, is distinctive for producing a something-to-be-done."[27] When Victoire scolds Condé for her neglect in not writing her life story, this rupture of class and education takes the form of a haunting that allows Condé to create her own absence aesthetics.

As important as haunting is as an intervention from the past, *Victoire* also represents haunting as representing anxieties about how much the past should determine knowledge in the present. Edward Baugh cautions that when history overdetermines the present, Caribbean people are in danger of "becoming the slaves of history."[28] Condé's narrative calls on us to question just what is gained by sticking closely with the "truth," as found in official histories and archives. Victoire's ghost, as a trace of the past intruding on the present, opens up space to question the historical record. Accompanying a haunting, Patricia Yaeger writes, "the trace or remnant introduces a moment of fracture when something unexpected opens up—when insights emerge that may or may not be sayable, when actions emerge that may or may not be actionable."[29] Haunting and the formal innovation of speculative autobiography challenge the authorizing nature of official archives by suggesting that meaning making can occur independently of confirmable historical facts.

The figure of her grandmother's specter sitting in Maryse's room quickly pivots to a description of a photograph.[30] Haunting becomes an epistemic issue through this image of her grandmother as the narrative structure of *Victoire* turns from describing the ghostly apparition experienced by the adult Condé to a description of a photograph that sat on the piano in her childhood home. The strangeness of Victoire's image creates an uncanny figure for the young Maryse. Victoire's light skin startles her, but in contrast to Victoire's lighter skin, which often signaled a higher-class status, she is dressed like a peasant in a headtie and plain dress.

A ghost is perhaps an archetypal source of haunting, but Condé's narrative shows how objects also can be haunted, as when she describes this photograph. The image opens up questions about what we can determine about the past from objects, such as photographs, that are commonly kept in a family as well as in official archives.

> All I have of her is a sepia-colored photo signed by Cattan, the photographer in vogue at the time. . . . The sight of her never failed to make me feel uneasy. My mother's mother had that Australian whiteness for the color of her skin. Her soft-colored eyes like Rimbaud's, set deep in their sockets, were reduced to two Asian slits. She was staring at the lens without the shadow of a smile and without any attempt to appear gracious. Her headtie knotted with two points signified an inferior station. *Kité mouchwa pou chapo* (Swap the headtie for a hat) was the expression of the time that paid homage to a woman's social ascension. In short, she jarred with my world of women in Italian straw bonnets and men necktied in three-piece linen suits, all of them a very black shade of black. She appeared to me doubly strange. (1–2)

From the beginning of the narrative, then, this image of Condé's grandmother Victoire juxtaposes class and racial contradictions: she is light-skinned but poor, dressed like a peasant but with relatives well off enough to have her photograph taken by a fashionable photographer.[31] Victoire's physical appearance is racially ambiguous: her eyes are described as Asian, and her skin, confusingly, is described as white like an Australian, without explanation of what that means. *Kité mouchwa pou chapo*, the Creole saying encouraging women to "swap the headtie for a hat," was also a message about exchanging traditional Creole garb for European fashions (1). The world of upwardly mobile educated Blacks of 1940s Guadeloupe, with women wearing Italian fashions and men wearing suits, such as Maryse's mother and father did, contrasts sharply with the simple cloth headtie of Victoire, emphasizing how dress signifies class in different historical moments.[32] Later in the narrative Condé alludes to Victoire's rejection by her darker relatives. "This color, without money or, failing that, without education, is nothing but a curse" (60). These juxtapositions raise the question of how Victoire's descendants should interpret this image: what kind of knowledge can be gained from a photograph?

A photograph is a liminal object from a historiographical point of view. Photographic images are a source of truth, but one that needs context and provenance to be seen as credible. The image of Victoire as represented by Condé shows another side of the quarrel with history, in which disruptive truths from the past interrupt an established narrative. In this case, Condé's parents' determination to gain class status and success and to forget their origins, which she characterizes many times as a form of alienation, is arrested by the photograph. This second type of haunting represents the eruption into the present from the past of unsettling events, systems, or feelings. Avery Gordon suggests, "Haunting is one way in which abusive systems of power make themselves known and their impacts felt in everyday life, especially when they are supposedly over and done with (slavery for instance). . . . Haunting is not the same as being exploited, traumatized, or oppressed, although it usually involves these experiences or is produced by them. What's distinctive about haunting is that it is an animated state in which a repressed or unresolved social violence is making itself known, sometimes very directly, sometimes more obliquely."[33] The photograph of her grandmother that Condé describes at length is evidence of an "unresolved social violence." The image of Condé's grandmother is present as a physical object, but the story of the violence and oppression she experienced in her lifetime is not a story, following Toni Morrison, that can be passed on. It is an image that marks an absent presence.

These two initial types of hauntings, the eruption of social injustices of the past into the present and the call to action to tell that story, are inseparable in Condé's telling within an epistemological framework of the impossibility of fully recovering that past. While Condé describes her search for the kinds of historical materials we might call "archival," including newspaper articles, as well as her use of ethnographic methods such as collecting the oral histories necessary to write *Victoire*, the photograph of her grandmother stands out in the open in her childhood. The photograph is not a hidden source of history since it is a physical object displayed in Condé's childhood home. However, when Maryse asks her mother Jeanne about the photograph when she is around seven or eight, her mother can bring herself to relate only a few things: that her mother was a cook and a servant. While Maryse is delighted by the idea of cooking, she is "mortified" by her grandmother's lowly job as a servant (2). Her mother refuses to disclose the identity of Maryse's grandfather, banishing Maryse from the room and refusing to talk about the past. We get no sense of Victoire's personality or life experiences in the account told by her daughter Jeanne.

The photograph of Victoire, described but not shown, signals Condé's method of documenting her grandmother's life. Condé writes, "Such as it is, here is the portrait I have managed to trace, whose impartiality or even exactitude I cannot fully guarantee" (4). Condé writes an interwoven autobiography and biography focalized through her own vision of her family and the past. Archival details are presented not as evidence of the truth, but rather as a part of a "reconstitution," as Condé writes in the preface (n.p.). Further, Condé recognizes that what will emerge is just as constructed as a studio portrait. The frame can contain many elements of her grandmother's life but not all.

Genre, Evidence, and Fugitive Speech

Writing from multiple perspectives, Condé asserts, is a hallmark of Caribbean writing. "You have to find the Caribbean technique of telling a story, a polyphonous technique," she argues, defining this method as mixing points of view of people from a variety of social classes, first- and third-person narrative, and men and women.[34] Condé takes what she sees as *the* formal innovation of Caribbean literature and applies the use of multiple perspectives and language to her life writing. Generic classification of Condé's work poses difficulty for scholars, given that she has protested against her novels being interpreted autobiographically. Postcolonial authors are often seen as writing texts that are autobiographical when writing fiction, or of writing fiction when writing autobiography.[35] Since 1997, Condé has produced three texts that she acknowledges as autobiography, while, for example, changing names and other "factual" information without including the kinds of disclaimers in a preface that are common in the genre.[36] In her focus on her own childhood memories in *Tales from the Heart*, then on her grandmother's biography, and then her young adulthood in *What Is Africa to Me?*, Condé weaves biography and autobiography in ways that could be termed auto/biography. These texts are examples of what Sidonie Smith and Julia Watson call "a mode of the autobiographical that inserts biography/ies within an autobiography, or the converse, a personal narrative within a biography."[37] The generic instabilities of Condé's work prompt the question of not just what Condé can achieve using life writing that she could not in fiction, but also what methods she uses to create her life writing works.

The labeling of *Victoire* as "a novel" by its American publisher, despite Condé claiming the text as life writing, proves the possibilities for misrecognition of texts constructed outside the framework of a narrative about a single life. Leigh Gilmore argues that women's life writing may not provide the expected link to a singular identity and authority over a narrative. Instead, "it may, as likely, prompt a profound renegotiation of the terms and forms of self-representation, one result of which is that women's autobiography cannot recognized as 'autobiography' when it is written against the dominant representations of identity and authority as masculine."[38] *Victoire*'s generic indeterminacy allows for the creation of an auto/biography in which its relationship to truth and who should be the subject of history comes under question. The fact that Maryse learned little about her grandmother from her mother and there is scant documentary evidence of her grandmother's life creates an absence aesthetic in *Victoire* as it navigates between first-person narration by Condé and Victoire as well as third-person description. These formal choices lead the reader to wonder how much of what Condé writes can be verified and if quantifying provable historical facts should even be relevant to interpreting a narrative based on oral histories.

In seeking to answer that question I note that unlike Condé's previous life writing, *Victoire* is explicit about her search for sources concerning her grandmother's life, and her failure in some cases to be able to document her story. Condé confirms in the text that there are few documented traces of Victoire's life: "Officially then, Victoire was hired in the service of the Walbergs. Yet there is no document to confirm this" (59). The text is often focalized through Victoire, so much so that it is easy to skim past moments in the narrative that discuss Condé collecting interviews or consulting secondary sources.

Nevertheless, for the attentive reader, *Victoire* foregrounds the labor of crafting such a narrative. Archives and written documents are not mere influences, as in a fictional narrative, but are cited. Condé provides descriptions and the locations of places important to Victoire and Jeanne in Guadeloupe, giving the reader a sense of what they looked like at the turn of the century. These descriptions give a sociological flavor to some of the narrative as it charts the changing possession of the houses and places of business from white Creoles to contemporary Guadeloupeans. Episodes of Victoire's life are typically documented rather than presented as being based on an educated reconstruction, as in Saidiya Hartman's use of critical fabulation to re-create the lives of two enslaved girls who can be known only through their absences in the archives.[39] For example, Condé paraphrases "a confidential note dated May 10, 1890" by a priest in Marie-Galant instructing other priests not to baptize Victoire's illegitimate daughter to document Victoire's status as an outcast within her community (49). *Victoire*'s narrative is further shored up by historical sources such as descriptions of the town of La Pointe by the governor of Guadeloupe (56) and descriptions of the West Indies as found in the travel narrative of Lafcadio Hern, a *Harper's* correspondent who published *Two Years in the West Indies* in 1890. Condé describes not only sources but her labor in trying to locate them. Seven different newspapers from the late nineteenth and early twentieth centuries are cited, along with summaries of relevant information, such as frequent references to *Le Peuple*, a prominent newspaper that existed in Guadeloupe.[40] Dismissing her parents' status as members of "the club of Grands Négres," Condé notes that the two articles written by her mother for *Trait d'Union*, "a pretentious rag," had little merit (156).

In a historiographical move that anticipates historian Marisa J. Fuentes's "reading *along the bias grain*," which involves working with archival material about Caribbean women not for historical veracity but for evidence about how power constructed their archival traces, Condé cites "a history thesis defended at the College for Social Sciences in Paris . . . entitled 'From Plantation Owner to Business Man: A History of the White Creoles in Guadeloupe'" (60).[41] Condé writes that letters by Victoire's employers Anne-Marie and Boniface Walberg quoted in the thesis caught her attention because they mention Victoire's emotional importance to them. "My life would be filled with unhappiness if it weren't constantly illuminated by the devotion of my faithful Victoire," Boniface writes (60). Condé, like a historian, notes that there can be multiple ways to interpret these letters but that she believes they indicate a deep friendship between Victoire and Anne-Marie, and that Boniface and Victoire were lovers (60–61). Quotes from these letters are used throughout the latter half of *Victoire*, which gives the reader an intimate view of Victoire, but only from the perspective of her white employers. Evidence of her interior life remains a mystery. In an interview Condé asserted,

> You know, people will tell you that in places like the Caribbean, West Africa and so on, we have two distinct elements. We have history which is written in books about the white people—how they came to Guadeloupe, how they colonized Guadeloupe, how they became the masters of Guadeloupe—and you have memory, which is the actual facts of the people of Guadeloupe and Martinique—the way they lived, the way they suffered, the way they enjoyed life. We are trained to rely more on our memories and the memories of people around us than on books. So I interviewed people, I asked questions to everybody who knew [Victoire] or knew my mother or my father.[42]

Condé contrasts history as written in books to "memory," which contains "the actual facts of the people." Privileging the oral over the written is surprising for an author such as Condé, who frequently proclaims her love of the French language and of the writing process itself.

Beyond written sources, Condé presents oral histories collected from those who were alive at the time as evidence of Victoire's life. Recollecting Victoire's choice to cut herself off from her family by working for white Creoles, a relative becomes distressed all over again. "Lourdes . . . still lamented 'Victoire, she was my little sister. *Sésé an mwen*. Her child, she was my child. *Ti moun an mwen*. . . . When she turned her back on us like that, I wanted to die'" (54). Put into quotes and containing Creole, such testimony seems constructed to assure the reader that Condé is employing a variety of methods to understand her family history accurately. *Victoire* contains evidence that Condé has cast a wide net to learn about her grandmother, even to the point of including the memories of those who are hostile to her. There are several oral history examples in *Victoire* that read like social science work, including the use of pseudonyms. "I interviewed Léonie X, who has lived all her life in the anchorage district and as a child used to see Victoire" (117). Condé also asks her brother to recount memories of Victoire, who once again is represented as a specter. "Thank goodness for Auguste! He was the only one of us who remembered or thought he remembered Victoire. For all of us, this strange colored grandmother was half imaginary. A spirit. A ghost" (157).

Here Condé uses evidence in a manner that has some commonalities with a work like Barbadian Andrea Stuart's *Sugar in the Blood: A Family's Story of Slavery and Empire* (2012). *Sugar in the Blood*, like *Victoire*, is at once life writing about Stuart's experiences and those of her Barbados family and a historical exploration of her ancestors based on fragmentary archival records. "Ghosts haunt this tale," Stewart writes, "small men whose lives leave only very faint footprints and slaves whose sufferings leave no mark at all."[43] Stuart includes references to the archives she searched, secondary texts consulted, and a bibliography as well as photographs in order to tell the story of her ghosts. These photographs comprise images of oil paintings of white ancestors, locations in Barbados, archival records such as wills, and studio portraits of Stewart's grandparents and parents.

Despite the numerous archival materials that Stuart finds, like Condé, she is prompted to write her story because of its absences. "My family is just one of millions across the globe that were forged by sugar and slavery. . . . Yet despite the ubiquity of this tale, I could not recollect a non-fiction book that tried to tell it; one which explored how the epic forces of sugar, slavery, and settlement made and shaped the life experiences of our ancestors, and our world today. So I have written that book myself."[44] Stuart acknowledges that tracing her ancestors through documentary records of the forces of European settlement and the rise of the sugar trade results in a narrative that begins with her white ancestors and only latterly includes her ancestors of African descent. The absence of records about her enslaved ancestors marks an archival limit that Stuart cannot overcome to tell the entirety of her individual family's story. Archival limits cause her "some heartache" because they center her white ancestors rather than her African ones for much of the text.[45] However, Stuart is able to fill some of the gaps with reference to slave narratives such as Olaudah Equiano's, and other archival sources. Within the Francophone context, however, there are no existing slave narratives, due in part to Code Noir prohibitions on slave literacy.[46] Historian Catherine Reinhardt explains how this archival absence affected her own research methodology in the Francophone Caribbean. "While there is a relative abundance of narratives by North American and to some extent also English Caribbean slaves, relatively few such written traces have been left in Saint Domingue, Guadeloupe, and Martinique. This lack of sources made my original aim of exclusively representing the slaves' viewpoint simply unfeasible."[47] Different archival practices and publishing in the eighteenth and nineteenth centuries in Britain and France result in different historical sources available to the life writer.

Condé's choice to center her grandmother, despite archival absences, creates a narrative describing a different experience of colonialism than Stuart's in the Anglophone Caribbean. A transcolonial analysis of the life of Victoire shows some distinctive elements to post-emancipation life in Guadeloupe. I use the term transcolonial, following Françoise Lionnet, since it describes more accurately that the nations of the Francophone Caribbean are not independent and brings to our attention issues of comparative colonialisms in the Caribbean region.[48] In contrast to Hartman's and Brand's reimagining of slavery and the slave trade, the period in Caribbean history spanning Victoire's life comes much later—beginning several decades after France's declaration of the emancipation of its slaves in 1848, from 1874 to the 1940s. Condé's choice to write about her grandmother's life during the years 1874 to 1915 is significant in that it encompasses a period when Guadeloupeans, as described in *Victoire*, were "emerging from the belly of slavery" (30). This period is called by Guadeloupean historian Micheline Rice-Maximin "the forgotten century" within Caribbean historiography.[49] In contrast to nineteenth-century Anglophone Caribbean and African American life writing, and contemporary historiography on the post-emancipation period, in the Francophone Caribbean the century after emancipation in 1848 has not been as well explored.[50] Although abolition and resistance to slavery were "commemorated in sites, songs, rituals, and movements throughout the hemisphere, fewer people publicly heralded the end of contract labor in subsequent decades," Anne Eller notes of the understudied decades after emancipation in the Caribbean.[51]

Similar to the tension described in chapter 1 between those in African diaspora studies who want to focus on recovery, recuperation, and agency and those who are critical of such an approach, until the 1980s in Francophone Caribbean studies, there was a push for heroic representations of resistance and agency.[52] This was accomplished through figures of rebellion such as Solitude, an enslaved woman who led a resistance movement against Napoleon's reimposition of slavery in 1802. *Victoire* moves in a different direction by addressing the effect of the *restavek* system (the use of "free" child labor in the French Caribbean) on Condé's family. The narrative shows how Condé's grandmother can be understood as complicit with her white Creole employers, the Walbergs, rather than as a resistant heroine as she willingly enters into "employment" and stays with them through most of her adulthood. Complicating this view is that Victoire is also a victim of the *restavek* system of post-emancipation labor. Condé's mother's education, paid for by the Walbergs, paves the way for her family to become educated Grands Négres. This shift in the family's fortunes, one story about a single family, is part of a larger story about the French Caribbean in the early twentieth century. *Victoire* describes a historical shift between the late nineteenth century and early twentieth—from illiteracy and the *restavek* system to the rise of an educated Black bourgeoisie. This historical period is one in which the descendants of the enslaved began to enjoy access to educational and political spheres, but at the cost of assimilation to French language and culture.[53]

Writing from multiple perspectives also means that Victoire's story is centered even as the narrative attends to the mystery of Jeanne's father. When Maryse as a child asks about her mother Jeanne's father, the text describes paternity within the culture of turn of the century Guadeloupe. "Such a conversation might surprise some people. At the time, to have a father, to be recognized by him, to share his daily existence or quite simply bear his name, was the prerogative of rare privilege. It was no shock to me that my parents, like so many others, emerged out of a kind of fog" (3). Recall Hartman's description of her grandfather's birth certificate in 1897 in Curaçao, seven years after Condé's mother's birth: "Four generations were born with a blank space where a father's name should be. In its place was the stroke of a bureaucrat's pen, which had left a line less dramatic than an X and which suggested nothing as harsh as erasure but simply 'not applicable'" (80). Absence of the white father because the children were property or of the Black father because of slavery constitutes what Hortense J. Spillers calls the "common historical ground, the sociopolitical order of the New World," that cuts across continents.[54] Condé notes that her own father did not know his and would alternate between saying he had gone gold digging in Paramaribo or that he had been shipwrecked in Sumatra. "Thanks to him," Condé writes, "from a very early age I understood that you forge an identity" (3).

Condé readily admits that the circumstances of her mother's conception are unknowable even through archival research. Even the kind of relationship between Victoire and the man she names as the father of Jeanne, Dernier Argilius, remains a mystery: "we will never know for certain whether Dernier ever knew about her pregnancy" (47). The question of Jeanne's paternity is addressed through a story that seems to be about Victoire's first unpaid position in the household of members of her extended family, the Jovials. Here Victoire learns to cook, which becomes a major outlet for her creativity. Simultaneously with this thread of the story, we learn that Thérése Jovial, Victoire's godmother, has been carrying on an affair with Dernier Argilius, a protégé of Hégésippe Jean Légitimus. Légitimus was a socialist politician who had the distinction of being the first man of African descent elected to the French Parliament since the late eighteenth century. In 1891 he founded the newspaper *L'Peuple*, a source Condé refers to frequently in *Victoire*. His comrade Argilius is represented as a schoolteacher and an activist for Black rights at a time when whites held most of Guadeloupe's French parliamentary positions and those of mixed race controlled local politics and business.

In a narrative twist, Dernier flees the Jovials' house in December of 1889 when Victoire's pregnancy is discovered and she admits Dernier is the father. Despite referring to an extensive corpus of archival material related to Argilius, Condé acknowledges that intimate details about the relationship between her grandparents are lost to history. Other than Victoire's statement that he was the father of her unborn child, no records such as a birth certificate or letters exist and no observations by those alive at the time survive. "No one will ever know anything about the relations my grandmother had with Dernier Argilius. That story has been erased. Deleted from memory. But I want to know" (34). Such a declaration, in contrast with the many sources Condé refers to in *Victoire*, encourages the reader to want to learn more about this little known but highly accomplished Guadeloupean man.

Even if we want to resist traditional kinds of critique focused on verifying historical sources or adding archival information that goes beyond the text, as I do, Condé leads us into a hermeneutics of suspicion.[55] She provides cues for the reader who wants to learn more about her family, and in particular about their connection to a famous leader. Condé writes, "When he died tragically in 1899, the entire island went into mourning. Ever since then, theses, monographs, and biographies have been written on the subject of the role model and martyr" (30). Condé directs her reader to one source in particular: "There is a photo in a book by Jean-Pierre Sainton, a Guadeloupean historian" (29). As with the photograph of her grandmother, Condé does not reproduce the image in the text but rather describes it for the reader as showing a man with dark skin and curly hair who is "dressed in a tight-fitting frock coat" (28). The inclusion of a description of a photograph but not the photograph itself raises questions about the line between historical fact and narrative fiction. Describing a photograph but not including it in the text is a narrative technique Condé uses in several places in her life writing; *Tales from the Heart* also begins with a description of a family portrait that is not included in the text.[56] Timothy Dow Adams observes, "Just as autobiographies are obviously artificial representations of lives, so photographs are clearly manufactured images: sitters are artificially posed and lighted, made to conform to the laws of perspective and the ideology of the photographic culture, reduced in size, reproduced on a flat plane often without color—and yet there is something undeniably different about a photographic representation as opposed to a painting of that same person."[57] Photographs are artistic representations, and thus constructed as Dow argues, but are also used to document and prove identity, such as one's existence in a legal sense. Condé gestures toward this second documentary sense when she discusses Argilius's photo in a work of history as evidence for the existence of her grandfather.

I suggest that Condé baits her search-engine-ready reader with references to scholarly sources on purpose in her use of speculative autobiography. Although Condé directs the reader to a photograph of her grandfather and mentions his achievements, Argilius is untraceable in scholarly repositories such as the Archives Départmentales de la Guadeloupe or the Bibliothèque nationale de France. A monograph produced by the Guadeloupean archives on print culture in twentieth-century Guadeloupe makes no mention of Argilius or that he or anyone else died in the fire at the press, which did take place. Going directly to the Sainton source, one discovers not only that there is no mention of Argilius but that there is a photograph described in exactly the words Condé uses. However, it is of Légitimus not Argilius. There is almost exact overlap between words attributed to Argilius in *Victoire* that are actually quotations of Légitimus in Sainton. In short, Dernier Argilius does not exist. He is, perhaps, a composite figure of Légitimus himself and other leaders who were exemplary in their public lives but left much to be desired in the private sphere.

By writing about what she cannot substantiate, Condé creates a caesura in the text by pushing her readers to think closely about the contrast between her presumed grandfather and the life of her grandmother. "I would like to ask a question that I deem important. Dernier Argilius has gone down in history like Jean-Hégésippe Légitimus as an ardent defender of the illiterate Negroes emerging from the belly of slavery. When he died in 1899, the entire island went into mourning. Ever since then, theses, monographs, and biographies have been written on the subject of this role model and martyr. My question, then, is what is an exemplary man?" (30). The narrative's exposure of Dernier Argilius / Jean-Hégésippe Légitimus as a womanizing, manipulative liar, who is nevertheless a "hero of the people," challenges the trope of placing anticolonial activists on a moral pedestal.[58] The anger at national "fathers" in *Victoire* echoes Édouard Glissant's searing characterization of the abolition of slavery as a paternalist act that places freed people perpetually in the position of children.[59] The Grands Négres, such as Légitimus and Victoire's daughter Jeanne, then step in as benevolent rulers of Guadeloupean society, in Condé's view. Condé imagines Victoire resenting Dernier for not teaching her to read. "She wondered what her life would have been like if Dernier's passion for the disinherited had materialized into an interest for her own destitution. If this *vayan nèg*, this valiant Negro, who had advocated free schooling for all, had taken her hand to decipher the letters of the alphabet" (81). The powerful juxtaposition between historical hero, whether real or a composite figure, and illiterate woman creates an aesthetic to describe a past that might have been in the absence of archival evidence.

Relying on rumors is not a typical historiographical method. The repeated phrase "I don't know" and use of approximate language such as "at least one" signal to the reader that what is being reported is hearsay. "Dernier Argilius took advantage of I don't know how many people, wrecked the life of at least one of them, and engendered I don't know how many bastards," Condé writes (30). And yet, in relying on tales circulated among common folk in order to bring a larger-than-life political figure to account, Condé ventures outside of the traditional archive, and even of oral history. Lauren Derby argues that rumors are an important source for Caribbean historiography because as "fugitive speech forms" they uncover stories beyond dominant narratives and push scholars to rethink what constitutes an archive.[60] Condé rejects a European model of history focused on the outstanding "great man." Condé's focus on her apolitical grandmother in contrast to her revolutionary "grandfather" or father of the Guadeloupean nation challenges a regional narrative of history, characterized by Donette Francis as "a teleological march from slavery to independence marked by epochal moments of revolution and resistance embodied most often by the accompanying male heroic figure."[61] Traditional notions of citizen as male, educated, free, and property-owning correspond to ideals of the kind of subject that makes history.

A problem space for African diasporic life writing is that more traditional forms of Euro-American biography typically contain stories of overcoming obstacles against the odds or of great achievements, while life narratives of the African diaspora often describe barriers such as structural racism and sexism that are not within their individual ability to overcome.[62] Condé's mixture of realism and nonrealism in *Victoire*, then, may not fit expectations of self-fashioning in traditional Euro-American biography. But it does place her work in a tradition of other African diasporic biographies in which selves are shown as created in spite of forms of captivity. Lack of access to creating life writing after emancipation in the French Caribbean, as Catherine Reinhardt explains, shows how the ability to create a written record of personhood is determined by relative levels of power in a society.[63] Political activists and statesmen like Légitimus have been written about as having interiority and the will to change their circumstances, while the uneducated peasantry has not.[64]

Discovering Condé's subterfuge leads to an epistemological crisis, if we are reading her text as a family memoir girded by evidence such as newspaper articles and oral history. First, given this invention of Argilius, should we read the rest of the text as fiction? Is Condé's absence aesthetic to pretend to create an autobiographical text with reference to historical and verifiable materials but also to dissemble about which of these materials are real? If writing around and through archives that cannot be reconstructed leads to new kinds of epistemologies in life writing, as I am arguing, what are we to do if the formal innovation is to lie about lying? Is Condé is now an unreliable narrator—a purveyor of just enough factual information to obscure the use of fictional aspects? Knowing that she had substituted one identity of a photograph for another made me question if her grandmother's photograph was real.

Recalling the photograph that so obsessed Condé, I searched for more on the photographer. Adolphe Catan, not spelled Cattan as in *Victoire*, is well known for his photographs of Guadeloupe taken after the 1920s when he returned from studying in Paris.[65] Catan did take photographs before left for Paris, but would they have looked like they were produced by a professional studio, when he was only seventeen the year Victoire died? Surveying Catan's photographs made me wonder if I would find an image of another woman similar enough to Condé's description of her grandmother that I would be forced to question the source of Condé's "memory."

In searching for authorizing documents that could verify Condé's work, I found it easy to stray into the territory of privileging historical fact over political narrative. Early in the development of postcolonial autobiographical theory, Gayatri Chakravorty Spivak cautioned, "I am guarded and watchful of the autobiographical impulse within postcoloniality. The line between aesthetics and politics is not necessarily programmed by the authority of the author."[66] Spivak reminds us that acts of postcolonial life writing may be circulated as testimony based on the dominant culture's interpellation of them as sharing a recognizable "truth" that does not challenge existing power structures.[67] I did not find a photograph that matched Condé's description, leaving me in the position of having to trust Condé that her grandmother's photograph is real. In Condé's 2017 memoir *What Is Africa to Me?*, she relates that while being deported from Ghana in 1966 she lost all of her family photographs, including one described in *Tales from the Heart*. The loss of these photographs at least thirty years before the writing of *Tales from the Heart* and forty years before the composition of *Victoire*, including perhaps the one of her grandmother, shows that the images Condé describes are memories as much as tangible pieces of evidence and provides an explanation for why they are not included in her life writing.

Returning to Condé's claim that a major formal quality of Caribbean writing is to write from multiple perspectives, I argue that speculative autobiography is her own version of absence aesthetics. Condé purposefully manipulates her readers by lying *and* telling the truth, by holding the private and public spheres separate and then smashing them together.[68] In this first example, cultural insiders are clued in by references to well-known scholarly works. The trick, then, is played on outsiders. "Like magicians, poker players, or baseball managers, autobiographers must continually claim they have nothing up their sleeves, nothing in the cards, nothing planned for the next pitch, all the while deliberately sending a steady stream of false and true signals, hints and feints to keep the game going," writes Timothy Dow Adams.[69] Blockages to knowing the past, whether through archival absence or family stories, allow Caribbean life writing to generate new questions about historical and autobiographical truths when writing stories about the past. Unlike fiction, life writing depends on the autobiographical pact; we as readers expect the content to be based on experience, memory, family stories, and/or archival records, however loosely. However, life writing also makes allowances for the instability of memory, of "hints and feints," as well as of documentation. Some would argue that signaling doubt within a life writing narrative is actually a feature of the genre. "To complicate matters, autobiographers themselves constitute a principal source of doubt about the validity of the art they practice," Paul John Eakin writes.[70] It is a larger truth we are after when we read life writing—the shaping of a narrative under a framework in which some of what is told is rooted in truth.

Contrasting a reimagined Légitimus with her grandmother's disempowerment allows Condé to tell a true story through a feminist lens about male power and female marginalization and the gendered nature of citizenship and sovereignty within Guadeloupe. Rather than seeing Condé's sleight of hand as a lie, it is more useful to think of this part of the narrative as crossing from realist autobiography into speculative narrative in order to provide a feminist critique of the revered figures of postcolonial history. Condé here uses a feminist framework for interpreting history: she examines closely how binaries such as male/female, Black/mixed race, and educated/illiterate work to construct power relations.[71] *Victoire* as historiography both illuminates these binaries as related to societal power and asks the reader to question their seemingly fixed status. Using nonrealism or speculation in a narrative grounded in actual events allows Condé to write about a past that might have been and probably was the truth: her grandfather was very likely a person of more power and prestige than her grandmother. Condé's mother may have been conceived through rape. While *Victoire* provides no substantial proof that Légitimus is related to Condé, rumors say that he had many illegitimate offspring.[72] Such a power disparity between young women in domestic service and the men surrounding them is hardly an uncommon story. In Condé's hands, it assumes a fairy-tale quality as Victoire goes from rags to enabling her daughter to live in high society, but at a Faustian price of a close mother-daughter relationship.

Autobiographical Freedom Making

My use of the past conditional, "a past that might have been," to describe Condé's move from realist life writing to speculative autobiography gestures toward a theory of how mixing generic modes creates space for seeing how a different past might make possible a different future. I am indebted here to Tina M. Campt's suggestion of a "grammar of black feminist futurity," which describes an event that has yet to take place but must do so.[73] *Victoire*, although set in the past, marks a site of Black feminist futurity by centering Victoire's life as what has made her grandchildren's lives possible. "As for me, I prefer my grandmother to remain secretive, enigmatic, the improper architect of a liberation that we, her descendants, have known how to enjoy to the full" (195). Writing the past, even one that can be only partially understood but that helps imagine a liberated future, is a useful theoretical tool for further understanding Condé's use of nonrealism through the incorporation of fugitive speech acts.

As written by Condé, Victoire does perform a Caribbean act of freedom making—she enacts fugitivity when she refuses to return to Guadeloupe with her employers during a visit to Martinique in 1901. Maryse is first told this story by her mother, in a "watered down version" that emphasizes the dangers to respectability and person for a single woman who leaves home (84). The blandness of the story does not satisfy Maryse, who wonders why her mother repeats this story and what it is supposed to mean. Rather than a narrative about a wayward mother, Condé creates an alternative interpretation of Victoire's yearlong stay in Saint-Pierre, Martinique, while Jeanne remained in high school in Guadeloupe.

In describing Victoire's act as one of fugitivity, Condé resumes writing from her own perspective. In *Tales from the Heart*, Condé recounts her family's failure to inform her of the existence of slavery or the slave trade. In an otherwise realist book of childhood memories, Condé describes meeting a little white girl in a public park. This girl reenacts the violence of slavery by hitting and humiliating Maryse. After Maryse finally refuses to continue this "game," the girl disappears, leaving the adult Condé to wonder if she has been visited by a manifestation from slavery's past in the form of a menacing white child's ghost. With this precursor of a gothic tale in mind, Condé brings up her family's inability to talk about slavery in *Victoire*, not by telling a story from her family's enslaved past, but by commenting on the nature of communal history and her grandmother's brief experience of freedom. Condé remarks, "I have described in *Tales from the Heart* . . . how nobody in my family told me anything about slavery or the slave trade, those initiatory voyages that founded our Caribbean destiny. I had to negotiate on my own the weight of this terrible past. On the other hand, since individual stories have replaced our collective history, my mother on several occasions alluded to a journey my grandmother (whom she seldom mentioned except for a few clichés) made to Martinique in the year 1901" (84). The story of Victoire's temporary refusal to carry on as a servant, an individual story, Condé tells us should be read as having a connection to collective history.

Condé opens this episode of Victoire's life with a one-sentence paragraph: "Here are the facts" (85). The facts include that Victoire and her white employers travel to Martinique for a wedding of elite white Creoles. Victoire is brought to help create the wedding feast. Her employer, Anne-Marie Walberg, publishes Victoire's menus created for special occasions in the local newspaper; these are reprinted in *Victoire*. "Among the papers my mother kept was issue 51 of *L'Echo pointois* . . . the menu lyrically composed like a poem and probably sent to the newspaper by Anne-Marie" (70). Including archival newspaper sources establishes that Victoire's skill is well known, explaining why she would have been asked to help with the wedding food preparation.

As the menu indicates, Victoire was more than a competent household cook.[74] Victoire put together foods both native to the Caribbean and imported in innovative ways, such as combining duck (native to the Caribbean but associated with classical French cooking) with cassava (native to the Caribbean) and lemongrass (brought by Asian migrants). "For her, cooking in no way implied wreaking vengeance on a society that had never made room for her . . . it was a way of expressing herself, which was constantly repressed, prisoner of her illiteracy, her illegitimacy, her gender and her station as a servant. When she invented seasoning or blended flavors her personality was set free and blossomed. Cooking was her Père Labat rum, her ganja, her crack, her ecstasy. She dominated the world. For a time she became God, once again like a writer" (71). Despite these many skills, "for Victoire, who had always worked without possessing anything or ever receiving anything in return, who could neither read nor write, who lived off the goodwill of a white family, the abolition of slavery had changed absolutely nothing" (90). Reading these century-old menus consisting entirely of locally sourced foods from the perspective of today, it is notable that Guadeloupe now imports the majority of its food from France. Indeed, one can read the inclusion of ingredients and menus as Condé's assembling a counter-archive of locally sourced cuisine. Victoire's creations speak to the existence of a local culture worth commemorating and celebrating, in contrast to French directions of assimilation for its citizens and the adoption of French culture and foodways. Despite this, Victoire never received compensation for her work, reflecting the value put on Creole cultural productions during the time period.

After stating what she can substantiate, such as these recipes, Condé turns to "fugitive speech forms." Based on letters, fragments of oral testimony, and gossip, Condé gathers that her grandmother met a man, disappeared from the wedding, and did not send any communication that she was alive to Jeanne. "By way of letters from friends and relatives in Martinique, the affair soon reached the ears of the bourgeois circle of harpies in La Pointe, who gleefully badmouthed Victoire. They let fly at her, calling her *bòbò*, slut . . . and a heartless mother" (91). Victoire ran away with a man named Alexandre Acronte, who was also working at the wedding, and who was also reported missing by his coworkers. Condé hears that Alexandre worked for a wine distribution company, and she is able to confirm the company's existence through finding advertisements in the period's newspapers. However, no record of Alexandre survives.

What connection does Condé's assertion that she "had to negotiate the weight of this terrible past" on her own have with one of her grandmother's few acts of individual agency? What does this have to do with slavery? In the retelling, Victoire's escape, both from her employers and later from the volcanic eruption in Martinique in 1902, becomes an act of resistance rather than irresponsibility. Condé represents Victoire as wondering, "What would happen if she quit her collar? . . . She could become a street seller of popular dishes" (90). The use of the word "collar" summons images of restraints used during slavery, not simply dissatisfaction with employment. Condé writes of this episode in a particularly Caribbean way, bringing together the lenses of marronage and fugitivity to interpret her grandmother's yearlong residence in Martinique. "I can equate her flight with one of those types of marooning of which Victor Schoelcher speaks when the African, tired of the rigors of slavery, dreams of freedom but lacks the determination needed to realize his plans" (85).[75] Marronage was one method of achieving freedom for Caribbean slaves, who would establish settlements in inaccessible places. Within French Caribbean literature, "marronage" stands for acts of cultural resistance to colonialism, first recounted through oral culture and subsequently written about.[76] Successful acts of marronage in the region include temporary leaves, periods of incomplete freedom, in distinction to a North American story of the runaway slave heading for the northern states or Canada to gain absolute freedom.[77] For Victoire, "stealing away" enacts a fugitivity, however temporary, from the assumed subservience and lack of thought expected of enslaved and colonized populations. Fred Moten describes the assumptions her employers have that she would not leave them as a "mythologized" desire to serve and a "pathologized" desire for freedom.[78] Condé represents Victoire's employers as believing that rumored explanations for her disappearance were unlikely. They scoff that there was as little chance of Victoire dying in the woods of a snake bite as leaving them to work for a restaurant owner who had heard of her culinary expertise and offered her a great deal of money to come work for him (91).

In relaying this story, Condé creates a clear demarcation between what is a reconstruction based on evidence and what comes from deploying the nonreal. For example, she notes her frustration that the archives will not unfold when trying to find proof that Alexandre existed, that Victoire was with him, and that they ran a restaurant. "All I could find in the newspapers of that time, archived in the Schoelcher Library in Fort-de-France, were advertisements for wines and liquors by O'Lanyer, father and son. No mention of Alexandre Arconte. . . . My research turned up nothing on Le Gargantua" (93–94). However, through a chance communication with a student related to Alexandre, who relays a family story based on gossip—fugitive speech—Condé confirms that Alexandre did exist and ran a small restaurant called Le Gargantua. Alexandre's descendant had not heard of Victoire. However, two weeks after Victoire leaves, on May 8, 1902, Saint-Pierre is destroyed in a volcanic eruption, which is regarded as the worst volcanic disaster in the first half of the twentieth century.

When faced with archival absence, Condé uses her considerable skill to create a speculative account of what she believes happened. Implicit in her account, perhaps, is the insider knowledge that Saint-Pierre at the time represented a highly sexualized place that also produced high culture. Dominican writer Jean Rhys was eleven during the eruption of Mount Pelée and wrote of it as a defining moment in her life. "Saint-Pierre, they said, was a very wicked city. It had not only a theatre but an opera house, which was probably wickeder still. Companies from Paris performed there. But worse than this was the behavior of the women."[79] Women, Rhys writes, used their headties to signal if they were in love and unavailable or looking for a partner, shockingly to her child self, even if they were married. "You are welcome, I am free." Using fugitive speech herself, Rhys writes of the destruction in Martinique in opposition to the point of view of the pious white Creoles in Dominica. Exercising sexual agency, and choosing to have sex for pleasure, places Victoire outside the boundaries of normative womanhood. The policing of sexual acts, as Jacqui Alexander argues, is not just about sexuality.[80] It is about who belongs to the nation and who poses a challenge to its authority.

Condé re-creates what she believes to be Victoire's attempt to exercise erotic autonomy as well as her right to own her creative powers. Even if this is a fiction, as Condé suggests, such an imagining is important because it connects what could have happened in Victoire's life with what must happen in the future: a prefiguration of Condé's leaving Guadeloupe and becoming a writer. "All that we have left is our imagination. One evening I pushed open the door to Le Gargantua. Not much room. Background music. Beguines. . . . Afterward, amid the rumbling of the volcano they frenziedly make love" (94). Such an invention still lies within the autobiographical contract, in that Condé is clear about the sources for her narrative, such as family oral history and a named source of history about Alexandre. Providing an imaginative re-creation of Le Guargantua and placing Victoire there keeps fact and imagination separate, while providing the kind of speculation that many biographers make when they use known facts to create a retrospective view of their subject's life.

Condé certainly muddies the waters concerning the continuing vexed subject of how to write Caribbean history when the "truth" or at least the kinds of empirical evidence academics use are missing. In writing of herself as haunted and of her grandmother as a disruptive spectral voice from the past, Condé asks her readers to enter into an epistemology of uncertainty about what is real and what can be known for sure about Caribbean history. In the first example of speculative autobiography, the reader's positionality determines how they might interpret the figure of Argilius. Condé is making a pointed critique of the hero worship of great men in Caribbean history—at least for her readers who are knowledgeable about Guadeloupean historiography. For outsiders, *Victoire* does not acknowledge costuming Légitimus as Argilius in its descriptions of his speeches, political actions, and even his appearance in a photograph. In this regard, *Victoire* could be read as an example of speculative history, where actual events are reimagined to theorize about how the future would turn out differently. However, whether Légitimus or a nameless man was the father of Victoire's daughter, her critique of who counts as "exemplary" in mainstream history of the post-emancipation period still stands. Rather than a counterhistory, Condé uses absence as a condition of feminist critique by using what is missing from Caribbean archives, the evidence of daily life of women, to create a biography that along the way skewers historiography written through the lens of the singular individual.

In Condé's second use of speculation, all readers are made aware of her use of imagination to "one night enter Le Gargantua" and observe Victoire and Alexandre running their restaurant. In this case, Condé's archival dreams can be fulfilled only through meticulous research *and* imagination. Condé must further speculate about what her grandmother might have felt after leaving Martinique. Victoire's marronage is tinged by her second escape—she leaves Martinique two weeks before the eruption of Mount Pelée. Close to thirty thousand people died and the city was entirely covered with lava. The wedding party and the guests in Martinique all died. "Boniface and Anne-Marie had trouble getting over the fact that a year earlier they had danced with a group of *morituri*, whereas Victoire got the impression of having escaped the arms of a cadaver" (93). But, of course, Condé has also been dancing with the dead.

In writing the eruption of Mount Pelée as a central event in her grandmother's life, one that Victoire narrowly avoids being erased by, and the ruination of Saint-Pierre by lava where "the wicked fairy turned the pearl of the Antilles into the ghost town visited today by tourists and souvenir hunters" (93), we can see a parallel for the writing of Caribbean history and biography with an absence aesthetic. Saint-Pierre is now destroyed by fire and covered in lava, rendering its contents inaccessible, just as are many of documents related to the everyday lives of Caribbean people. Victoire's decision to leave Martinique just two weeks before the eruption meant that her life was not lost among the thirty thousand. Perhaps just as improbable, her life as an illiterate domestic has been recovered from history. Condé's use of speculative fiction to bridge archival gaps means that Victoire's life story will not be lost.

CHAPTER 3

Repicturing the Picturesque

GENEALOGICAL DESIRE, ARCHIVES, AND DESCENDANT COMMUNITY AUTOBIOGRAPHY

One of the largest archival gaps in the record of Atlantic slavery and its aftermath is the connection between the enslaved, *their place of enslavement*, and what happened to these communities post-emancipation. Surviving the Middle Passage from Africa or crossing the *kala pani* (black waters) from India to the Caribbean to clear fields and plant them with sugar and coffee meant not just radical cultural disruption. The plantation system forcibly rerouted and rerooted indentured and enslaved peoples, tying them to specific locales while undermining kinship. The relationship between land, history, and ancestry remains highly charged in the Caribbean. Colonizing the Caribbean entailed a long process of mapping, claiming, and agricultural colonization to turn it into the paradise of European imaginations. The labor of the enslaved and indentured altered the landscape. Caribbean colonization, then, was a conquest of not just people but also environments in the founding of agricultural exploitation colonies.[1]

European colonialism produced a corresponding archive of records of land and the enslaved, but one that is often incomplete or inadequate for use by the formerly colonized who wish to know how their personal and family histories are tied to specific locations. In addition to the expected and yet always shocking written archives of the enslaved (registers of births, deaths, purchases, sales), visual representations such as maps, portraits of the enslaved, and landscape paintings constitute another repository of information. Landscapes painted in the picturesque mode in the early nineteenth century, in particular, framed the Caribbean in ways legible to European viewers. Picturesque images constitute an important archive of European views of the relationship between the enslaved and the land they worked especially since, as Krista Thompson notes, no photographs of slavery in the British Caribbean exist; daguerreotype photography only became available in 1839 after emancipation.[2] Scholars such as Thompson, Charmaine A. Nelson, and Elizabeth A. Bohls suggest that European picturesque representations of the Caribbean promoted colonization in the region through visual stories that framed slavery as desirable and inevitable. The colonial picturesque as a body of visual images remains important to understanding contemporary modes of decolonial feminist resistance to the legacy of colonial ideologies concerning the value of the lives of the enslaved and the land they worked. Considering picturesque imagery as relevant to the present brings into focus specific interventions into a decolonized epistemology of Caribbean belonging and the environment. For these reasons, I bring this archive into conversation with Caribbean life writing by Jamaican authors Erna Brodber and Lorna Goodison. This chapter investigates Brodber's and Goodison's use of life writing to articulate a different relationship between the land and the people than that of an exploitation colony in response to the colonial picturesque archive.

Countering the existing archive of colonial representations of the Caribbean, Brodber and Goodison create alternative epistemologies of Caribbean space. Their writing centers other means of knowledge production than official archives, such as physical evidence in the landscape and oral histories of residents. This chapter provides a framework for understanding location, slavery, and community history in their work. Brodber's nonfiction publications span many of the genres of life writing: autobiography, autoethnography, biography, and recording of testimonials of the marginalized. Important in its own right, Brodber's work also serves as a means to dig deeper into a similar epistemology of understanding the past and historical absences in the work of Jamaican poet and memoirist Lorna Goodison. Brodber's and Goodison's writings demonstrate that for those interested in place-based historiography, whether for genealogical, scholarly, or life writing purposes, the effort to recover complete records of the enslaved and their descendants connected to sites of enslavement is a project marked with difficulty. The "question of recovery," as it is known in Atlantic slavery studies, consists of a dialogic approach to the related issues of the political necessity of investigating the past and "the impossibility of recovery when engaged with archives whose very assembly and organization occlude certain historical subjects."[3] Archival dreams of connecting contemporary Jamaicans to the land their ancestors worked are fraught and continue to be marked by absence.

Sandra Pouchet Paquet argues that autobiography works as a strategy to assert agency in a number of different Caribbean genres. "Autobiographical narrative is used to lend authority, immediacy, and integrity to other discourses like ethnography, politics, and government, and literary and cultural criticism."[4] In Brodber's case, life writing legitimizes her work and signals her embeddedness in the community that has encouraged and authorized her to write their story. I discuss Brodber's methodology of historical place-based recovery using life writing, which she calls "Blackspace." Her creative use of traditional archives, oral histories, and the natural and built environment of Woodside Jamaica directly engages with the main themes of this project: ancestry, absence, and the relationship of the past to the present. In telling Woodside's history through the stories of both men and women, Brodber offers a still necessary account of the gendered nature of enslavement and its aftermath.[5] In addition, her rerouting of the colonial gaze in order to create a vision of Woodside stands in contrast to a dominant theme in colonial representations of people and landscapes in the Caribbean: the picturesque.

Finally, an understanding of Brodber's Blackspace epistemology as a form of resistance to the picturesque provides a framework for interpreting another Jamaican work of life writing, Lorna Goodison's *From Harvey River: A Memoir of My Mother and Her Island* (2007). Goodison uses life writing as an authorizing strategy to write Jamaican history, in the vein of what Carolyn Steedman calls the process of "imagining and remembering" rather than the "stuff" of the archive.[6] *From Harvey River* begins where Brodber's work leaves off in the mid-nineteenth century, in what I see as a shared project of uncovering the lives of Jamaicans post-emancipation. The post-emancipation period in the Anglophone Caribbean, just as in the French Caribbean as discussed in the chapter 2 in Condé's *Victoire*, has received less attention from creative writers and scholars. Nevertheless, this period is of interest to everyday Jamaicans, as the conclusion of the chapter discusses.

Brodber and Goodison use the rhetorics of autobiography to authorize their narratives about the function of land, time, and ancestry. I call this descendant community life writing, indicating a genre of autobiography concerned with tracing the relationship between a contemporary group of people and their relationship to land on which their ancestors were enslaved. The term "descendant communities" can apply to any group with a relationship to an archaeological or historical site. While used in anthropology to refer to Indigenous people's relationship with land, it is also used to describe descendants of the enslaved who wish to know more about their family's past.[7] Brodber and Goodison seek to relate the experiences of Jamaicans in the period after slavery as they occurred in two very specific locations.

Fraser Neiman, the director of archaeology at Thomas Jefferson's plantation Monticello, states that being able to connect a known enslaved person with a specific workplace is highly unusual.[8] The archival absence relating enslaved persons and their place of enslavement cannot be overcome with more research because records of the enslaved that would allow them to be traced, such as their surnames or points of arrival in the Americas, do not exist. This is a source of frustration for the descendants of the enslaved. The questions raised by working with "descendant communities," groups who can or wish to trace their ancestry to those enslaved at specific locations, frame this chapter's investigation into epistemological alternatives to relying on repositories of materials (and the inevitable absences within them) created by those in power. In the British

Caribbean, slave owners were not required to list the names of their slaves on the "slave returns" related to taxation until 1817, making tracing ancestors and where they were enslaved before then almost impossible.[9] Impulses to recover the links between spaces of enslavement and the present speak to a central predicament of contemporary postslavery societies: How and why should the past be remembered? What is necessary to recover from the past to envision decolonized futures? Such questions lie at the heart of the impulse to create counter-archives and new histories by postcolonial subjects, given that archives played a central role in imperial governance.

Even when post-emancipation records exist, writing from the point of view of "descendant communities" is not a typical method of historiography.[10] In 2018, the United States' National Trust for Historic Preservation (NTHP), working with the African American Cultural Heritage Action Fund, issued a set of best practices for how historians should work with descendant communities. Recognizing the absences in the archive of slavery, they note, "A perceived lack of primary documentary sources is sometimes used as a justification for minimal slavery interpretation at museums and historic sites with the argument that 'we simply don't know enough.' But even in the absence of documents written by or about enslaved people at a particular site, a creative and expansive approach to primary source analysis can ensure that interpreters incorporate stories of the enslaved. . . . Although sources have to be used and interpreted with care, this information is not hidden."[11] Traditional recovery projects reflect the reification of the material archive. NTHP is correct to recommend a "creative and expansive approach" to engaging with the past of enslavement, even if the methodology of such projects is not detailed.

While the two previous chapters explored archival absences, the gaps in colonial histories related to the enslaved as in Hartman's and Brand's writing, and of the post-emancipation period as in Condé's writing, this chapter deals as much with archival misdirection, a colonial sleight of hand, as it does with archival absence. For in the British Caribbean, an archive of sorts of the enslaved does exist, and is certainly not hidden, but rather than written records it is a visual archive that renders slavery as a natural occurrence within a tropical landscape. As this chapter reveals, slaveholders conceptualized Jamaican space through the boundaries of plantations, places of profit, rather than towns built for citizens. Nineteenth-century paintings of Caribbean landscapes rendered in the style of the picturesque naturalized the brutality of slavery and the mirrored the mapping of Caribbean colonies through their possession by individual slave owners. The picturesque made the artificial, the colonization of the environment through the use of foreign flora to turn a profit, seem natural and beautiful.

Colonial discourses about Jamaican families, agricultural labor, and land used the aesthetic mode of the picturesque to represent the righteousness of colonial rule to those in the colonies and back in Europe. The picturesque began as a visual mode for representing nature and the European countryside in order to create the impression of bounty, leisure, and a union of manmade buildings with nature. English artist William Gilpin wrote that the observer of a natural scene could create the picturesque through framing it properly, much like creating scenery for a stage, by creating an appropriate backdrop, "side screens" such as the banks of a river, and a central "front-screen" such as a depiction of a river.[12] Further, Gilpin instructed that while scenes of agriculture such as laborers or "furrowed-lands" might be suitable for poetry, they are "ill-accommodated to painting," while pastures and cattle "present an agreeable surface."[13] The picturesque as a mode of representing natural scenery was transported to the New World, where it was used by key figures in eighteenth- and nineteenth-century Anglo-Caribbean writing such as Edward Long in his *History of Jamaica* (1774), William Beckford in *A Descriptive Account of the Island of Jamaica* (1790), and Bryan Edwards in *History, Civil and Commercial, or the British Colonies in the West Indies* (1793). British colonial governments commissioned artists such as George Robertson and (1778) and James Hakewill (1825) to use the picturesque as a technology to describe the Caribbean for European audiences.

Hakewill is just one of a number of writers and artists to deploy the picturesque in this time period. However, in pursuing the relationship of the colonial visual archive to the present-day writings of Brodber and Goodison, when I reviewed Hakewill's *A Picturesque Tour* I was surprised to find direct connections the places and people Brodber and Goodison write about. *A Picturesque Tour* is a form of life writing meant to convey personal experience as evidence of a social setting: the colonial travel narrative. Hakewill catalogues his visit to Jamaica with illustrations as well as commentary on the people he meets and a moral justification of slavery. He lists a visit to Point Estate, Hanover, the place where Goodison's great-grandmother was enslaved, as part of his itinerary, although he does not create an image of this particular plantation. He does, however, create a number of images of plantations in St. Mary's parish, where Brodber's hometown of Woodside is located (see fig. 1). The images contained within James Hakewill's *A Picturesque Tour of the Island of Jamaica from Drawings Made in the Years 1820 and 1821* (1825) are particularly instructive of the power of the picturesque to shape Caribbean landscapes and the enslaved portrayed in them into consumable orderly tableaus for European viewers. [14] Elizabeth A. Bohls frames Hakewill's *Tour* as central to understanding how the planter picturesque allowed British readers to imagine slavery as beneficial for both the enslaved and their nation. "Reimagining Jamaican land according to a metropolitan aesthetic paradigm, the planter picturesque thus completes a circuit of commodification and exchange between colony and metropole: picturesquely packaged plantations circulated for British consumption along with refined West Indian sugar."[15] The enslaved are a present absence in these images and archival records—locatable within the gaze of the artist or plantation scribe

Figure 1. James Hakewill, *Trinity Estate, St. Mary's*. From *A Picturesque Tour of the Island of Jamaica*, 1825.

but missing a sense of individuality or personhood. Many of these images depict enslaved people as part of the environment and their labor as no different than the grazing of animals.

The rising antislavery movement during this period represented a crisis for British imperialism. Topographic and picturesque visual representations arose at the same time the British slave trade was being called into question, making it a likely medium to allow British people at home and in the colonies to make sense of unfamiliar landscapes and to validate colonial rule.[16] As Édouard Glissant notes, the planter class used artistic expression to "fantasize legitimacy" through depictions and descriptions of Caribbean landscape that "pushed [it] to extremes—the gentleness and beauty of it."[17] British and colonial visual art produced during this period reflects struggles over imperial power and representation. Their aesthetic choices were anything but innocent depictions of the natural world: they framed sociopolitical institutions such as plantation slavery as part of the West Indies "natural" landscape and so presented slavery as timeless and inevitable to a European audience.

Hakewill presents an orderly and cultivated landscape without depicting the labor behind it. The image shows cattle and sheep and their shepherds in the foreground and in the middle distance a group of workers walking with their hoes casually thrown across their shoulders. The faces of the cows and sheep are more readily distinguishable than that of the people. Charmaine A. Nelson interprets the figure of a slave in one of the images in Hakewill's *A Picturesque Tour* as a deliberate blank, reflecting Hakewill's larger erasure of slaves and their back breaking work. "The slave, although directly facing the viewer, is literally faceless, the blackness of the skin creating a flat field against the blue and white clothing," which mirrors "the absenting of (laboring) slave bodies" generally in his work.[18] Hakewill's artistic depictions of the Jamaican landscape cannot be separated from questions of history and social conditions. He quotes with no apparent irony the slavery apologist Bryan Edward's inscription on his uncle's tomb in St. Andrews, Jamaica, describing the plantation owner's work as difficult but honorable, and one that recognized all people as kinfolk. "He added Industry, which, without Genius, might/Have commanded Fortune. He acquired Wealth with Honour,/And seemed to possess it only to be Liberal . . . He considered Individuals as Brethren, And his Country as a Parent." Writing generally about some of the strongest British objections to slavery, Hakewill expounds upon the probability that freed slaves would no longer want to work for wages and claims that the Caribbean enslaved are better off than the English working classes. Landscapes such as these that included laboring Black bodies as scenery, naturalizing their enslaved labor, were created in the colonies and then recirculated in Europe. The Caribbean picturesque functioned as a type of advertising of the profitability of Caribbean colonies, an affirmation of the necessity of enslaved labor, and an inducement for European men to attempt to make their fortunes through plantation slavery.[19]

The Imperial Gaze and Brodber's "Blackspace"

Erna Brodber has employed her training as a sociologist by gathering oral histories related to her home in northeastern Jamaica since 1980.[20] She is perhaps best known for her novels *Myal* (1988), *Louisiana* (1994), and *Nothing's Mat* (2014), winning the prestigious Yale University Windham Campbell Prize in 2017. Brodber's confident articulation of the necessity of local history, through her life writing and the community development organization Blackspace, is what interests me here. After obtaining her doctorate in sociology at the University of the West Indies in Mona, Jamaica, Brodber began her work in rural Woodside. She writes, when "the university decided that it no longer needed my teaching and research skills I decided to practice them in my village. Out of this determination came a theory of community development that had as its central motif the giving of information concerning themselves to the people of the community" (*Woodside* vii). Located in rural Jamaica, the Blackspace project celebrates and reenacts Emancipation Day, collects data, and transmits history to local people in both written and oral forms.[21] This work has resulted in numerous interdisciplinary publications related to excavating the roots of the community of Woodside, which include Brodber's personal history, oral histories of the inhabitants of her village, and references to archival documents and photographs.

Brodber's publications focused on in this chapter, *The People of My Jamaican Village 1817–1948* (1999) and *Woodside Pear Tree Grove P.O.* (2004), articulate Caribbean genealogical desire as a radical project of recovery that is very much concerned with what she terms the "full emancipation" of her community.[22] In *The People of My Jamaican Village*, Brodber creates a pamphlet for her community that traces the ancestry of local people through the use of slave registers on the coffee plantation of Woodside. Difficult to obtain outside of Jamaica, the pamphlet is clearly a work intended for a local audience of general readers. The chapters are shorter, the language used is plain and direct, and it contains no footnotes or citations. Photographs of current residents of Woodside are placed next to Brodber's own personal recollections, oral histories of the area, and genealogical information. *Woodside Pear Tree Grove P.O.* was published by the University of the West Indies Press and includes archival location information, references to other scholarly works, and footnotes. In distinction to many academic book authors who hope for a wide readership, Brodber states that she intends *Woodside* to be converted back into oral history and passed on to the community's children via their teachers (viii).

Brodber theorizes in her 1997 essay "Re-engineering Blackspace" that mapping and the claiming of space are of the utmost importance in "completing the task of emancipation" and creating fully vested citizens: "The 311,070 persons of African ancestry emancipated in Jamaica in 1834 and fully so in 1838, owned no land and were outside of the political system—they had no vote. Few had family power—mates, children; few owned livestock. They owned no space. They had no army, no ships, no compass, no respected organised grouping. All they had was their individual minds and souls with which to create a viable space for themselves and their progeny in Jamaica and eventually to weld themselves in a nation or a respected part of a nation."[23] Assessing the condition of the newly freed people of Jamaica, Brodber emphasizes their lack of space, "no land" and "no space." For Brodber "space" means the land ownership necessary to be self-sustaining, but also personal and community space in which to create a post-emancipation future. "Real emancipation," Brodber writes, "clearly has to eventuate in some accepted claim on space (physical or otherwise) in these countries to which our forefathers were brought and into which we were legally emancipated."[24] Claiming Blackspace means being able to locate one's history as happening in particular places. Brodber's project is more than a strategy for telling the local history of the people of her hometown. Blackspace marks an act of cultural sovereignty in wresting away colonial representation of faceless enslaved people merged into the landscape in order to articulate a genealogy of their descendants embedded in claimed space.

Brodber's archival dreams concern not just her biological lineage, but a larger project of descendant community life writing that seeks to understand her community's ties to their ancestors' place of enslavement.[25] By prioritizing local and regional histories over the broad histories of the British empire taught in colonial schools, Brodber's work joins a larger postindependence movement of archival recovery and self-definition by Jamaican writers and scholars such as Kamau Brathwaite, Rex Nettleford, and Barbara Bush.[26] In this sense, Brodber's project can be read through postindependence frameworks of archival recovery as necessary for the creation of postcolonial selfhood.[27] Antonia MacDonald sees Brodber's fiction and life writing as belonging to a "sub-category within Caribbean poetics: a literature of reparation that returns the precolonized person to a former condition of wholeness and provides metaphorical and spiritual compensation for damages suffered because of slavery."[28] I agree with MacDonald that Brodber's works contain a satisfying sense of historical recovery since, after all, they do locate archival evidence of the ancestors of the residents of her village. However, Brodber does not situate her narrative of the aftermath of slavery as offering wholeness *or* as beginning in a graveyard, as Saidiya Hartman does in *Lose Your Mother*.[29]

Brodber's pioneering work within her community of Woodside provides a way to think though tensions between records, oral history, and place. In the ongoing Caribbean quarrel with history, Brodber stakes her claim that local stories should count as "History" and that the records of women's enslavement constitute importance evidence of the community's past. The archival materials she uses include "maps, deeds and titles, registers of births, deaths and marriages, and inscriptions on tombs" (*Woodside* viii). These are traditional materials for a historian or biographer to consult, but Brodber's point in listing them in the preface to *Woodside* is pedagogical, so that community members reading her work know the provenance of the documents cited and sometimes reproduced within it. In *Woodside*, Brodber anchors the narrative in the location of her town and then tells the story of the place through the "socio/physical past," moving chapter by chapter through those who owned the land, the whites who lived upon it, the enslaved who worked it, the freed people, and then post-emancipation educational and religious institutions within the town.

Although she is of an earlier generation, Brodber prefigures many of the concerns of the fourth wave of Caribbean writers born after 1970 who have divested themselves of national paradigms. Instead, their texts are concerned with moments of personal and cultural agency or sovereignty, as Sheri-Marie Harrison convincingly writes, rather than the nation-state.[30] In this vein, Brodber takes care to frame Blackspace as a work in process rather than a recovery project completed—from refusing to romanticize enslaved people as proto-revolutionaries ("enslaved people did not spend all their time in conscious reaction to slavery") to portraying their descendants complexly, writing critically of those who have chosen to leave rural Jamaica (*Woodside* vii, 74).

The importance of Brodber's work, I argue, for those interested in life writing and the African diaspora, comes from her ability to use data that still carry the histories of racism and colonization but re-create them in order to deliver that past to present-day inhabitants of Woodside. Understanding land and ancestry, Brodber theorizes, is central to a teleology of full emancipation for the citizens of Woodside. Her method of writing Woodside underscores how absence emplots this project: not even the location of Woodside can be taken for granted. First, Brodber has to decide where Woodside is. For outsiders, locating Woodside on a map is difficult. Brodber notes that it is not found on "signposts or consistently on roadmaps or official survey maps of the parish of St Mary," something that has not changed with the advent of Google Maps or detailed road maps of Jamaica (*Woodside* 1). Even on a highly detailed Collins Jamaica road map, I can locate Woodside only by triangulating between three towns, Palmetto Grove, Windsor Castle, and Pear Tree Grove, that are on the 1952 survey map Brodber includes in the text.

Although Woodside is labeled on the map in the text, Brodber consults an elder in the village born in 1912 for guidance on how to understand Woodside as a space constructed through human interaction. He instructs her to think of Woodside as a "social space, a place in which people interact with each other in the pursuit of the necessities of life, as well as a physical space" largely based on the location of the school for area children as well as the Woodside Anglican church (2). Brodber then hand draws a circle on the second image of the survey map to educate readers about the social space of Woodside, which includes the towns mentioned above. The 1952 map, Brodber shares, hangs on the wall of her house and had to be photographed there by a friend or it might "disintegrate" if moved (x). The map's fragility underscores the metaphorical and real precarity of Brodber's archive. Such personal details show that although Brodber takes pains to present her research professionally, she maintains a long-standing personal connection to Woodside.

The next maps presented in the text are from the early 1800s and are credited as coming from the National Library of Scotland, not Brodber's home. These maps show that rather than the names of towns, indicating social and civic life, maps of the area that would become Woodside were labeled with the names of the owners of plantations, such as Neilson's and Burrow's. Before exploring records related to the enslaved workers in Woodside, the text makes clear that this is a society structured around the business dealings of Europeans relying on plantation labor. John A. Aarons and Sharon Alexander-Gooding suggest in their research concerning which records were selected to be kept in Caribbean archives during the colonial period, "As far as Britain was concerned, the [Caribbean] colonies were plantations and not settled communities that needed to preserve records for their own use and identification."[31] Viewing the Caribbean as spaces of economic enterprise rather than as communities of citizens influenced how the landscape was recorded on colonial maps. In the countryside of St. Mary parish, plantation ownership orders the landscape with plantation owners' names marking spaces, rather than the names of towns. The landscape being described by its possession by slave owners is a distinctive aspect of Caribbean cartography. "The Caribbean area is the classic plantation area," Sylvia Wynter observes, "since many of its units were 'planted' with people, not in order to form societies, but to carry on plantations whose aim was to produce single crops for the market."[32] As exploitation colonies, the British West Indies were not settled with towns and civic structures, as in the United States and Canada. They were cleared for plantation labor. The labeling of areas by the names of their British owners creates a sleight of hand reinforced by picturesque paintings, suggesting that such ways or ordering and naming the landscape were unremarkable.

To return to what is most relevant to Brodber's audience, however, the question remains of how to trace the linage of those who currently live in Woodside. Brodber writes of the lack of evidence of the ancestors of present-day Jamaicans, asking where "will we find the admissible data on the behavior of people who left no memoirs?"[33] A text such as Mary Prince's narrative and post-emancipation oral histories such as *A Narrative of Events, since the First of August, 1834, by James Williams* can tell us something of the inner lives of enslaved and newly freed West Indians.[34] They rebut narratives propagated by men like Hakewill, who declared that Jamaican women were mercenary and did not have affective ties to their white lovers. The failure of Afro-Jamaicans to properly enter into two markets, the labor market and the marriage market, or perhaps their inability to participate in these institutions without the close supervision and control of colonial elites, occupies Hakewill, as it did other commentators during the period.[35] "Notoriously good mothers, he soon sees himself surrounded by a family on which his best feelings may be placed; and whenever the moment shall arrive which shall see him so far master of his fortunes as to allow him to form a more honourable connexion, his partner sees no duplicity in his conduct, nor considers it a desertion of principle, expecting only a proper provision for herself and family."[36] Representing Jamaican women as defective in their affections and focused on material gain is, of course, a reversal of the actual situation, where whites made money through enforcing the reproduction of the enslaved. Hakewill represents those who could not defend themselves from his characterizations.

What cannot be recaptured, as Brodber notes, are the thoughts and desires of those who did not have access to someone to record their life narrative or who remained illiterate post-emancipation. The people of Woodside's links to the land around Woodside, however, can be traced back to the granting of provision ground rights. Provision grounds, Trevor Burnard notes, were often a key component in community solidarity for Caribbean slaves and created a sense of belonging that linked slaves to land, even as they lost their rights to claim each other as kin.[37] Land becomes evidence of family survival in Brodber's vision, with the sons and daughters of a particular enslaved woman, Mary Ann Drew, becoming key to the establishment of farms post-emancipation.

Before the creation of online archives related to slave owners and the enslaved and their places of origin (which are still emerging), Brodber pioneered a descendant community life writing methodology to link present-day inhabitants of Woodside to those who were enslaved there. Indeed, it is Brodber's research that is cited in University College London's Legacies of British Slave-Ownership database related to the area of Woodside.[38] However, aggregating data from archival materials such as lists of enslaved people into searchable databases, while seemingly advancing the fields of African diaspora and slavery studies, may replicate structures of violence and dehumanization such as racist nomenclature. Jessica Marie Johnson argues that when "left unattended, these devastations reproduce themselves in digital architecture, even where and when digital humanists believe they advocate for social justice."[39] For example, racist biometric categories of the enslaved, such as *quadroon*, now reappear in online searchable databases without comment or reference to the history of resistance to these terms.[40] As another example of the pitfall of moving from analyzing data to engaging people, when "Engaging Descendant Communities" urges historians to consider that "descendants can be your greatest resource—use this as a tremendous opportunity to learn," it is clear that they do not conceive of descendants as historians and that rather than co-creators of history, descendants are a resource to be accessed.[41] They are the keepers of memory who can help make historical interpretations of places of enslavement more accurate, rather than the drivers of historical interpretation.

Woodside takes a different approach to existing archival data than that of traditional historiography. Brodber uses the only official archival evidence remaining, that of enslaved people's names on slave registers. However, she does so in a way that seeks to avoid re-creating trauma for their descendants. In 1817 the "registration" or reporting for tax reasons the number of enslaved people on an estate began to be required by law, which gave Brodber a paper trail for her community's origins. In a move that transforms the narrative from a regional history into an archival resource, Brodber publishes the slave returns for Woodside in 1817 in their entirety in both *My Jamaican Village* and *Woodside*. All of the data from a slave return are listed: name, racial categorization (e.g., mulatto), age, origin (e.g., Africa), and relationship to others on the estate (e.g., son of Nancy). Reflecting that bringing captured Africans to the Caribbean ended only in 1807, Brodber puts herself in the place of the enslaved to underscore that there must have been people who remembered their homeland and their given names in the years for which records exist between 1811 and 1832. *Woodside* narrativizes a string of data, the same kind that Johnson cautions us can reinscribe harm. She lists "Quiano(?) alias Charlotte Downs Negro 30 African" by noting that African-born Quiano loses her birthname to become Charlotte but is able to name her son Quaco, an Akan day name for a child born on Wednesday (64). Commenting that on one estate 21 percent of the enslaved were described as African-born and old enough to remember their names, Brodber asks, "Where were those names? Through Jamaica they disappeared into ones reflecting the perceptions the masters had of them—Congo Jack, Chamba Hack; into the names of Greek and Roman figures" (57). Another woman enslaved on John Neilson's estate at the same time as Quiano is listed as "Fanny alias Mary Ann Drew Negro 23 African" (60). The slave registers show that Mary Ann Drew had four children while enslaved: Edward John Marshall born in 1813, Billy Ferguson born in 1817, Kenneth Forbes in 1824, and Annie Forbes in 1828. Ferguson and Forbes are surnames held by enslaved men also owned by Neilson. In this way, the text enters into a conversation with the archive and seeks to restore humanity, cultural context, and the erased paternity of enslaved children from the bare facts of a listed name, origin, age, and racist categorization "Negro." In many cases the enslaved people listed cannot be traced to people still living in Woodside. Brodber does not gloss over these absences in order to create a positivist account. She instead gives these absences the same attention as those who have a traceable linage.

Descendants of Mary Ann Drew through her Ferguson and Forbes children still live in Woodside. "Old Ferguson and Old Forbes have the one mother," a descendant notes, information that Brodber is able to confirm archivally (*People* 23). Brodber uses tax and church records to trace these oral histories of the descendants and to link them to landholdings. After emancipation, it appears that Mrs. Neilson gave her emancipated slaves rights to the village spring still in use today, and acres of land to the Marshall and Ferguson families (*Woodside* 114). Brodber links her family to Mary Ann Drew, noting that her father's sister married the son of Annie Forbes. Brodber's own aunt and uncle, then, are two generations away from Mary Ann Drew born in Africa.

Brodber ends *The People* with a lyrical description of this ancestry.

> Ernest Brodber's sister, Gladys to whom this volume is dedicated, married Thomas Walker, the son of Annie Forbes, the daughter of Mary Ann Drew a woman who was born in Africa in about 1794, was captured, sold, crossed the dreaded middle passage to Jamaica and eventually to slavery on Dr Neilson's Woodside estate, and who in 1813 at age 19, began to give sons who have helped to develop free Woodside.
>
> These are the people of my village, Woodside, living here between 1817 and 1948. (31–32)

Thus, Brodber's descendant community approach to life writing proves a genealogical connection between the formerly enslaved in Woodside and the residents living there in the early twenty-first century with Mary Ann Drew as a founding mother. The residents of Woodside, now, can see their family and community histories stretching back before emancipation to realize they are rooted in the land of Woodside and have contributed to the development of its agricultural, religious, and educational resources. The picturesque mode of foregrounding the landscape and erasing the individual identities of slaves working on it is repictured by Brodber's painstaking work. Instead of faceless slaves, we are presented with the names of those enslaved in Woodside. Rather than figures of humans blurred into the landscape making their presence there seem natural, Brodber reconstructs the roots-ripping journey of people such as Mary Ann Drew, African. Brodber emphasizes the political agency of the enslaved and their descendants over the passivity depicted in the colonial picturesque.

"Where Is Here" and Jamaican Life Writing

Brodber invites us to consider Caribbean identity as inseparable from land. Land, Brodber tells us, is the very foundation of Caribbean identity. "No one—but no one—sells his land. Weeds may grow on it; the grass may die; you may plant nothing viable on it; but you do not sell your land. It is the evidence that your forebears lived; to sell it is to sell not just yourself but your dead."[42] Brodber's work provides a critical framework for interpreting Lorna Goodison's *From Harvey River: A Memoir of My Mother and Her Island* (2007).[43] *From Harvey River* explores questions about how to create an archive of the intertwining of place and people through the lens of the author's mixed-race Jamaican family in the years between emancipation in 1834 and the 1960s. Brodber's work, containing more oral and archival history than personal narrative, helps clarify the feminist epistemology of Goodison's project, which has been misread by critics partially because it contains more personal narrative than oral or archival history.

Born in Jamaica in 1947, Goodison is an accomplished author of twelve books of poems and two collections of short stories. She has been awarded Jamaica's Musgrave Medal and the Commonwealth Poetry Prize for the Americas. Her turn to family memoir in *From Harvey River* creates a creolized life narrative drawing on the genres of oral history, folklore, European history, genealogy, and her own poetry. Goodison reshapes themes central to her poetry, such as maternal strength, Jamaican history and culture, and the natural world, in order to generate an immersive experience for the reader as she tells the story of her family and their relationship to the environs surrounding Harvey River in northern Jamaica.[44] Like *Woodside Pear Tree Grove P.O.*, *From Harvey River* examines in detail a small area within Jamaica, rather than attempting to write a national history.[45] *From Harvey River* satisfies a genealogical desire possessed by many contemporary Caribbean subjects who deeply wish to know "where is here," as Goodison characterizes her project, a connection to place through the prism of their family history.[46] *From Harvey River*'s richness of ancestral memory and connection with familial homesteads stands in contrast to the losses of ancestry and land experienced by most African and Asian diaspora people in the New World. Goodison writes of her knowledge of her family tree dating back to the mid-nineteenth century and her family's ability to own and keep land as rooting her deep within Jamaican history. *From Harvey River*'s achievement in this remapping is best understood within the rhetorics of feminist Caribbean decolonial practices. *From Harvey River* documents the efforts of Goodison's grandparents in creating a viable space for themselves and their family in the century after emancipation. In turn, it suggests a mode of identity and knowledge formation possible for contemporary citizens of the Caribbean, especially women, through their own family histories and ancestral locales.

From Harvey River begins by praising Goodison's mother's double consciousness as a survival strategy to cope with the "hard life" of the present by drawing sustenance from memories of her family's land in Hanover Parish. "Throughout her life my mother lived in two places at once: Kingston, Jamaica where she raised a family of nine children, and Harvey River, in the parish of Hanover, where she was born and grew up. Harvey River had been settled by her grandfather William Harvey, who gave his name to the river, and the river in turn gave its name to the village. I do not think that there was ever a day in my childhood where the river or the village was not mentioned in our house" (1). Life in rural Harvey River is contrasted with the "hard life" of Kingston, where Goodison's parents moved after the beginning of World War II (183). Doris and Marcus Goodison's loss of their garage business due to wartime shortages in car parts and gasoline invokes the earlier memory of Marcus's mother losing her home "in the same way that thousands of poor Jamaicans have lost their land for nearly two hundred years," a legal system of property set up to benefit the ruling elite (158). Telling even this small sliver of Goodison's family history from a woman's perspective would be a departure within Caribbean literature, since according to Omise'eke Natasha Tinsley, "When the story of World War II in the tropics is told, West Indian scholars and novelists focus on its impact on male bodies and masculinist nationalisms."[47] In contrast, Goodison depicts Doris drawing on her memories of childhood in the country and her ancestors to give her the strength to cope with the demands of nine children, the privations of wartime life in Jamaica, and the "roughness" of postwar yard life in Kingston. Doris's ability to return mentally to Harvey River in times of stress, such as when her son goes missing, is a form of cultural sovereignty that grounds her and her children in a specific place.[48]

Contemporary Caribbean life writing such as Goodison's offers alternative ways to re-represent the colonial sleight of hand of picturesque paintings. For example, Goodison describes her great-grandmother Nana Francis Duhaney as having "jet-black skin" and as being descended from an African man who was enslaved on the Point Estate plantation by the Dutch family Duhaney in Hanover Parish. This plantation is among those Hakewill lists in "views taken in Jamaica," noting that he visits "Mrs. Dehany" of Point View estate. While the experiences of the enslaved are left out of Hakewill's account, Nana Duhaney is mapped by Goodison into space—descending from enslaved people in Hanover Parish—as well as in time in the 1840s and through her connections with her descendants in the present. Goodison describes Nana Francis as refusing to wear shoes indoors, "as if she needed her soles to always be in touch with the powerful work energy issuing from the Hanover ground through the floorboards, the same energy that enabled labourers to perform the ferocious, back-breaking tasks involved in the production of sugar cane; an endless cycle of digging, planting, weeding, cutting, grinding, and boiling under the ninety-six-degrees-in-the-shade sun, and the cut of the whip" (36). Describing her grandmother as drawing power from the Jamaican landscape may seem at first glance to be simply a poetic tribute to the labor of feeding and clothing a large family. However, something deeper is at work here when Goodison claims a connection between the Hanover ground and her great-grandmother's labors. By highlighting the work done by women such as Nana Francis, Goodison shows the labor extracted from Jamaicans by the British during colonization—an exploitation colony consists of not just extracting raw materials and produce such as sugar cane, but also human work. In "Trinity Estate, St., Mary's," (see fig. 1) for example, Hakewill elides plantation labor in his portrayal of slaves walking leisurely with their work implements, implying but not portraying their work. As I have argued, picturesque paintings deliberately obscure the work performed by the enslaved by depicting them as simply existing in the landscape.

Goodison relates her genealogy through place, splicing her family with the river itself as "as source of life" of the village. "How Harvey River became Harvey River. For all we know, the village of Harvey River used to have another name, but when my mother's paternal grandfather and his brother founded it in 1840, the old name was lost forever. The Harvey River was a source of life to everyone in the village. It was named by David's father, William Harvey, and his brother John, two of five brothers named Harvey who had come from England sometime during the early half of the nineteenth century" (29). Goodison, unlike many in the African diaspora, has access to a family tree, no doubt because her white ancestors were landholders and kept records.

The Harvey brothers' delight in the abundance and natural beauty of the Jamaican landscape is echoed roughly a hundred years later by young Lorna, who feels a sense of safety and homecoming when she leaves Kingston for a summer, returning to the village and river where her mother grew up. Even in this short section concerning Lorna's introduction to Harvey River, Goodison does not simply recount a nurturing childhood experience but links identity to a specific place in Jamaica. Lorna's first visit to her mother's ancestral land figures as a religious rite, with "hot toasted cassava bammies spread with yellow salt butter—cocoa like rich wine, and bammy like fresh host, a pure country communion after my river baptism" (213). Lorna's initial immersion in Harvey River as well as in the abundance of country life in Hanover Parish seems idyllic indeed.[49] "For the first time I saw the river that was named for my mother's people. Then, it seemed like a huge wide green sea with the cleanest swift moving water . . . I was so happy. I felt somehow that I would never come to any harm as long as I was immersed in that water named for my family" (212). In contrast to the many unknowns Brodber investigates about the relationship between the people of Woodside and their ancestors in the nineteenth century, Goodison is able to reproduce a complete family tree in the front pages of the text and link those people and herself to locations around Harvey River. In distinction to the erasure of African ancestry more commonly found in mixed-race families during the 1950s and 1960s, as depicted, for example, in Jamaican Michelle Cliff's life writing and novels, Goodison's mother passes on stories of her great-grandmothers and their African ancestry. The family tree beginning in the 1840s, placed at the beginning of *From Harvey River*, shows four generations of Goodison's family.

However, Goodison's aesthetic choice to focus on rural Jamaica and the rich cultures of those who populate it places her out of step with contemporary literary criticism that highlights migration and cultural fragmentation. *From Harvey River*'s method of writing history through landscape and genealogy offers a substantial rebuke to colonial and neocolonial methods of depicting Jamaica (as well as postcolonial privileging of diaspora) but also becomes unreadable within dominant critical approaches within Caribbean literary studies. *From Harvey River* asks us to reconsider the separation of identity and location popularized in much of contemporary diasporic theory.[50] Instead, we might think of Caribbean family history and origins as located not in an African past, as did many midcentury writers as discussed in chapter 1, but in the century after emancipation in the region itself.

Given the type of language that Goodison uses, it is easy to see why critics would identify *From Harvey River* as a romance. The romance genre is focused on pleasure, in contrast to the more typical antiromance narratives found in recent Caribbean literature, as Donette Francis notes, which is a genre appropriate for addressing the many problems facing the region.[51] This makes *From Harvey River* seem out of step in the context of more politically charged life writing also published during the same period by Jamaicans, such as Staceyann Chin's *The Other Side of Paradise: A Memoir* (2009) and Yvonne Shorter Brown's *Dead Woman Pickney: A Memoir of Childhood in Jamaica* (2010). Chin and Shorter Brown detail worsening economic and social conditions in Jamaica in the 1950s through the 1970s, which are mirrored in their dysfunctional families.

Thus, *From Harvey River* presents certain challenges to critics of life writing. Chief among these are the focus on the domestic life of Goodison's ancestors from the 1840s to the late twentieth century rather than a story of Goodison's own life and work as a poet, and the cursory treatment of obviously political topics such as labor unrest during the late 1930s or independence from Britain in 1962. Even though *From Harvey River* was published during a period of high interest in life writing's ability to critique divisions between public and private, it has largely been read as a domestic memoir. "A . . . conventional picture of aspiring middle-class domestic fiction, while also showing the complexities of its location" is how Supriya M. Nair describes *From Harvey River.*[52] Nair's assessment reflects a larger critical uncertainty of the political nature of Goodison's writing in general; Alison Donnell notes that Goodison's poetry might not have been deemed "Caribbean" enough by nationalist critics demanding validation of Caribbean rural folk and the suitability of Caribbean Creole for poetic language.[53]

In writing a family history that is twinned with detailed descriptions of the environment of Harvey River, Goodison goes against the grain of stories of displacement, which form a central theme within Caribbean literature, and within African diaspora studies generally. Critical movements within Caribbean literary studies, such as a midcentury desire for texts with positive representations of the folk and "authentic" representations of Creole, have a bearing not only on which texts receive critical treatment, but also on which texts are considered legible and are passed down to younger generations.[54] Alison Donnell cautions against an overvalorization of the possibilities of self-expression by diasporic writers: "The displacement of 'geographical location' by 'cultural construction' further shifts debates away from the demands of hereness and of Caribbean place," and in doing so risks homogenizing the Caribbean to the point "that the region almost slips off the world map as culturalism offers the new way of mapping the globe."[55] Caribbean literary archives and canons foreground diasporic experiences, which helps explain the wider critical treatment of authors such as Jamaica Kincaid, Edwidge Danticat, and Caryl Phillips, in distinction to the tepid critical engagement with Goodison's *From Harvey River.*[56] As I explore below, an analysis of generic expectations helps to clarify the ambivalent responses of critics to *From Harvey River.* A focus on genre also makes visible Goodison's innovation in rewriting the Caribbean as Eden script, not as tragedy or antiromance.[57]

In 2010 the Caribbean studies journal *Small Axe* commissioned several essays on *From Harvey River* and invited Goodison to reply. In their essays Sandra Pouchet Paquet, an authority on Caribbean autobiography, and Donette Francis, a leading scholar on Caribbean women's literature, share a sense of confusion about how to interpret the book. Francis approaches *From Harvey River* doubtfully, pointing to recent Caribbean life writing showcasing the region's high rates of violence, stigma around HIV/AIDS, and homophobia, which "underscore that neither familial home, national homeland, nor immigrant nation function as safe spaces of belonging" and belong to the antiromance genre.[58] In turn, Paquet confesses to being bewildered by the absence of Lorna's voice. "*Where is Lorna?* was the question that came most frequently to mind."[59] Francis and Paquet conclude that Goodison's loving portrayal of her mother is not simply saccharine or hagiographic but instead can be seen within larger themes of nation-building and postcolonial self-making. However, they acknowledge that Goodison's text does not do so in ways they might expect within their understanding of Caribbean literature. Their responses might be related to generic expectations of the memoir, as well as, perhaps, a lack of cross-pollination between the fields of visual and literary Caribbean studies, as I explore below.

Generic expectations of life writing, as Julie Rak has argued, structure not just our pleasure in reading memoirs but also the meaning we take from them.[60] Generic expectations can cause us to lose sight of the singularity of Goodison's work. Goodison's text takes neither the path of anticolonial romance nor that of tragedy. If *From Harvey River* frustrates our desire for Goodison to produce a portrait of herself as an artist, it also uneasily conforms to expectations of a maternal memoir.[61] Instead, Goodison presents place and people, land and genealogy, as having intertwined histories that must be mapped together. Responding to Paquet's essay, Goodison pushes back on the expectation of the centrality of individual identity in life writing. "The questions 'Who am I?' and 'Where am I?' that Paquet poses are certainly those that engage all of us. But in some ways I like to think that '*Where is here?*'—the question that the Canadian critic Northrop Frye once asked—is the one that my book explores on behalf of all Caribbean people who were taught history and geography from books and maps that barely acknowledged our existence."[62] In her response to Paquet's and Francis's essays, Goodison redirects their critiques from the individual-centered traditional memoir to the historical and geographical.

"Where is here?" is a primary question in the Caribbean quarrel with history because embedded in that question are the related issues of how the Caribbean came to be and how we should interpret that history. What constitutes the Caribbean and how we talk about it is a central question in Caribbean epistemologies because of the nature of European conquest and the remaking of the Caribbean through enslavement, indenture, and the terraforming of the landscape through imported plants and animals.[63] Absences in colonial archives and what I am calling the sleight of hand of picturesque representations of the Caribbean work to hide the what and how of the creation the region. This larger project is what I would like to attend to since what is remarkable about *From Harvey River* is not just the admirable figure of Goodison's mother, but Goodison's detailed knowledge of her ancestry and their labor and her ability to "map home" across space and time.

Critical figurations of *From Harvey River* as Edenic unwittingly play into a long-standing colonial discourse that seeks to depopulate and depoliticize the landscape in imperial possessions. Goodison redirects our vision from the Western male gaze's ordering of the Jamaica landscape as an aesthetic object to an interwoven relationship between place, culture, and people. While Goodison reconfigures Harvey River in distinction to colonialist depictions like Hakewill's, it is worth noting that she also seems to anticipate contemporary interpretations of Jamaican nature by metropolitan readers as a surface to be viewed rather than as an interactive landscape. Shortly after the beginning of *From Harvey River*, Goodison gives us the view of her great-uncle Edmund, who challenges his father David's naming of Jamaica as Edenic because of the lack of "fierce animals or poisonous snakes" (21). This is obviously a very different version of a tropical Eden than the colonial view of the landscape as one in which Afro-Caribbean people would not have to work to sustain themselves, as David, a farmer and part-time solicitor, would have been well aware. Even so, "Edmund used to kiss his teeth when he heard it. Yes, but what about all those blasted insects, what about the thick darkness? He particularly hated the peenie wallies, fireflies, damn stupid little flies with that weak on and off light coming out of their backsides. He craved real lights. Street lights. . . . From the first time that his father had took him to Kingston when he was ten years old, he knew the city was the place for him" (21). Edmund's viewpoint quickly dismisses the idea that the residents of Harvey River would not have been aware of the lack of development and privations of living in a rural area and, in contrast, the delights of the urban landscape.

Despite the centrality of visual representations to the British imperial project in the Caribbean, John E. Crowley notes, "Caribbeanists have no strong tradition of studying eighteenth-century traditions of their region in contrast to the many studies of elsewhere in the eighteenth-century British Empire."[64] I speculate that a lack of familiarity with the picturesque mode of visual expression and its role in maintaining colonial rule and the plantation economy in the West Indies might further explain the lack of a critical language among reviewers and scholars of Goodison's work to understand her revision of this mode of colonial representation. Goodison's depiction of the Jamaican landscape is not a neo-picturesque mode of representing Jamaica as Edenic, as claimed by critics. Instead, Goodison works against some of the key modes of racist/colonial picturesque representation, including (1) a Caribbean landscape devoid of laborers, (2) a masculinist view of the land and people as interchangeable and exploitable, (3) the depiction of Afro-Caribbean people living off the land without cultivation on their part, (4) the naturalization of a white plantocracy's ownership of land, and (5) the inevitability of European means of mapping, understanding, and controlling land.

Hakewill's *Bridge, over the White River, St. Mary's* (1824) (see fig. 2) exemplifies many of the key aspects of colonial depictions of the Caribbean landscape. It depicts a white stone bridge crossing a river, screened on each side by tall trees

Figure 2. James Hakewill, *Bridge, over the White River, St. Mary's*. From *A Picturesque Tour of the Island of Jamaica*, 1825.

that curve at the top, described by Hakewill as an "elegant frame of bamboos." This imagery replicates Gilpin's ideal of a natural view set up as if on a stage, with natural objects enclosing the view on each side like curtains. The bridge is set at middle distance, with a solitary Black figure walking away from the river. In the foreground two women are caring for a child, and one woman is in the river washing clothes. Two baskets, presumably for laundry, are placed in the lower corners of each side of the painting. The retreating figure as well as the laundresses are figured as part of the landscape, unaware of the painter, and seemingly unconcerned (in the case of the woman in the water who doesn't appear to be wearing clothes) about being observed. In addition, no white overseer or male figure of authority is represented, leaving open the interpretation that the women are at leisure, or at the very least carrying out these domestic activities in a way that makes the coercion of slavery markedly absent.[65]

Hakewill's depiction of the White River in terms of its aesthetic qualities as well as its utility to European colonizers is consistent with his portrayal in *A Picturesque Tour* of other natural resources, such as *Waterfall on the Windward Road, Near Kingston*. In this drawing, Hakewill once again depicts Afro-Jamaican women making their way down to a river, presumably carrying laundry. In his description, however, Hakewill focuses on the waterfall's ability to supply water to places like Up Park and Kingston. Potential anxieties provoked by this landscape, powerful and unfamiliar to European readers, are resolved by insisting that a viewing subject would see this landscape as a smaller version of one already existing in the views of the Simplon Pass in Switzerland: "The rocks have been in two instances pierced (one of which is seen in the annexed Plate), and give a good miniature resemblance of the celebrated galleries of the Simplon." As with the White River drawing, enslaved labor is naturalized through the depiction of women making their way down an incline to the river and erased through the description of the modified landscape: "The road is tolerably good, having been formed with much labour for the traffic of the mules, for the supply and convenience of the estates and coffee mountains, which abound in its neighbourhood." Who performed the labor to create the road, lead the mules, and work the estates and coffee plantations is not specified.

As in Hakewill's depictions of the White River, the Harvey River is also a place for doing laundry, but in Goodison's reimagining, this is a space claimed by the women of the village who also have rules about the use of the river and the proper way to do laundry. How to scrub clothes, where to dry them, and where to wash are all part of the ecoculture of the women of Harvey River. Echoing the framing bamboo of Hakewill's drawing, Goodison describes this as a highly private space for washing menstrual cloths: "This washing was done in pails of water drawn from the river, off to the side, under the shade of the bamboo which screened the river. Young women were told not to pour this 'small clothes' water back in the river, so they used it to water the roots of the flowers growing on the riverbank" (59). Rather than a picturesque view of the Jamaican landscape where human interactions with the natural are made opaque, Goodison describes an interdependent relationship between the women of Harvey River and this particular plant. The women water the plant, which in turn grows beautiful red flowers that can be used as shoe blackener or by schoolchildren who cannot afford to buy ink.

Within the context of this mutuality between residents and nature, Goodison presents a story of her mother swimming in the river and being rudely disturbed by a visiting boy who does not know the rules for using this landscape. Doris decides to bathe in the river by herself one day. Spied upon by a boy visiting a Harvey River family, Doris tells him to leave her alone. "He had to be a stranger, for normal river protocol dictated that if a village boy came across a Harvey girl bathing, he would leave immediately. Instead, this one stood on the riverbank, big and bold, staring at my mother" (59). Claiming her right to bathe undisturbed, Doris violates norms for polite female behavior during the early twentieth century and starts shouting every curse word she knows to drive the boy away. It works, and Doris finds herself praised by her parents for defending her honor. Important for my analysis here, Doris is not punished for swimming alone—her autonomy within the Harvey River landscape is not questioned. Her brothers are sent on a mission to find the boy who disturbed her and to explain to him that women swimming in the river are to be undisturbed.

While Doris's actions and the river itself are given aesthetic qualities and cultural context by Goodison, a number of differences exist between this representation and Hakewill's. Goodison's absence aesthetics map Doris into the landscape and show her belonging to it. The landscape is also shown to belong to her. The narrative demonstrates Doris's subjectivity and knowledge of communal norms for using this natural resource. Goodison reframes what Mary Louise Pratt calls an imperial eye on Jamaican women bathing and washing clothes, one that would see European vantage points and occupation of colonized space as the central if not the only story to tell. Rather than simply appearing as an aesthetic element, as the Afro-Jamaican women in Hakewill's drawing meant for European viewers, Doris and the other women of Harvey River are shown as exerting agency in their occupation of the river environment. Finally, the narrative presumes Doris's right to privacy and the inappropriateness of the male gaze on her as she is bathing. Notably, this entire scene takes place without reference to white colonial elites. Even the intrusion on Doris's bathing is not by a white viewer. In reworking and re-representing her mother's memory, Goodison creates a map of the river space of Harvey River that represents a local culture invisible to the colonial picturesque gaze.

Goodison does not only remap Jamaica's past. In mapping Harvey River, Goodison provides her readers in the present with an imaginative place of sanctuary that defies colonial representations of Caribbean spaces by showing the labor attached to farming in the Caribbean and Caribbean people as having an intersubjective relationship with their land. The picturesque mode of European control and mapping of land, presented as inevitable and natural in nineteenth-century representations, is challenged by Goodison's text, which provides its own counter-map showing Jamaicans as exerting agency and stewardship in their environs.[66] Goodison depicts Harvey River as a site of memory, belonging, and pleasure for the Jamaicans living there. Her memories of her family members returning to Harvey River (both psychically and in person) mark it as a form of "family land." "Family land" in the Caribbean denotes a space that all descendants have a right to return to and live on, even if not all of them own the land in practice.[67] Framing *From Harvey River* within the context of family land links Goodison's text to Brodber's and shows that it is a form of descendant community life writing.

Genealogical Desire in a Black Space

I like this site. My mother is Noret Harvey daughter of flavious harvey who is the son of one of the original Harvey brothers David Harvey that came to Ja. setled in Hanover. 2 brothers stayed in Hanover, 1 westmoreland and 1 in St James the others I don't know where they went but David married a half white so heis descendants are fair Tom married a free slave so his descendants were dark. I would like to know about all the Harvey especially those in Jamaica as

I know we are family. The Harvey men had a way of being wild so there are lots of us out there around the place. —*Rhonda Ferguson, May 18, 2008*

Rhonda Ferguson posted this on an American genealogical website, Harvey Family History, set up by a white American woman, Susan Harvey, who wished to trace her British ancestry. The Harvey Family website, established to meet the needs of white North Americans, found itself flooded with messages from the descendants of five English Harvey brothers who settled in Jamaica in the late 1830s. Ferguson and other Jamaican Harvey descendants filled the comments section with posts about their desire to know more about their family, despite there being no evidence that these two Harvey families are related.[68] These Harvey family members, "branches without roots" as Zora Neale Hurston described members of the African diaspora, demonstrate the desire of everyday Caribbean people to know their ancestry and to connect with their larger family.[69] Put another way, Hurston signals a post-emancipation condition for African diaspora families, where branches of the family tree are legible, while their roots in the past are not. Ferguson's post echoes this loss, when she can simultaneously state of other Harveys, "I know we are family," without knowing where or when these connections happened. She knows the names of her father and her father's father as well as that "David married a half white." This "half white" was Margaret, Lorna Goodison's grandmother. Ferguson's grandfather Flavius is Goodison's uncle, making Rhonda her first cousin once removed.

Jana Evans Braziel suggests that genealogy and the genre of autobiography connect in the Caribbean through their negotiation of a history encompassing imperial exploration, colonization, the slave trade, and genocide.[70] Goodison's family tree, then, is not a simple listing of ancestors but an archive of people placed within a historical time period and a geographic location. This archive is both unusual and valuable. The genealogical desire Rhonda Ferguson articulates on the Harvey family website is one that Brodber also recognizes as existing in her community. Impetus for the publication of *My Jamaican Village* and *Woodside* came from observing a visiting scholar holding the community of Woodside "transfixed" in a lecture on Jamaican post-emancipation history (*Woodside* ix). "'When my history is being discussed I don't move'" (*Woodside* ix), one audience member said, explaining why she preferred to walk three miles home rather than accept a ride that left before the talk was over. Acknowledging her community's historical and genealogical desire as a legitimate basis for development work, Brodber writes of Blackspace not simply promoting knowledge of local and personal history but helping to create new modes of belonging. "It is my hope that linking the present inhabitants of Woodside with their enslaved ancestors who lived and worked on the Neilson's Woodside coffee plantation in the early nineteenth century, as this work does, will give us, the new generation, a sense that we are part of a process from slavery to freedom and will lend us a greater measure of responsibility" (*People* n.p.). In *Woodside Pear Tree Grove P.O.*, Brodber rearticulates her decolonial project with the hopes that readers of her texts will recognize their genealogies of both ancestry *and* landscape, prompting a return to the land: "It is hoped that the many people from Woodside who have left the area will read this, the memories will flood back and that they will be moved to creative use of the vast acreage of land which they have left to the mosquitoes and the grass lice, ticks and the very dangerous duck ants" (viii). Writing Blackspace reclaims not just genealogy but also family land in the present.

In the epilogue to *From Harvey River*, Lorna describes surfacing from sleep into a dark, tomb-like place that "smells like the rusting interior of a trunk" (277). She cannot find light switches and does not know where she is. Countering this epistemic crisis reminiscent of the hold of a slave ship, Lorna invokes her mother's practice of imaginatively returning to Harvey River in times of crisis. She claims her ancestry and connection as to the Harvey River as a means of connecting herself to the present. "My name is Lorna Goodison. I was born on the first of August, which is celebrated as Emancipation Day in Jamaica. . . . My mother's name is Doris Louise Goodison; she was born a Harvey, of Harvey River. Harvey River is in Hanover; Hanover is the smallest of the fourteen parishes of Jamaica, which is 345 square miles. . . . I can turn this darkness into the river at night. My mind like the riverbed will become cool and still. I dive and under the surface of the water, I know what I'll find. Evidence of my generations" (277–278). Doris has given Lorna a family tree that is also a map, allowing her daughter to know her family as belonging to a space as well as to a chronology. This map is something Lorna can submerge herself in and find family, "Evidence of my generations." This is not an Edenic space; dangers lurk there as well as shards of broken-heart history. "There are lost pearls and hopeless cases and the bones of runaway Africans down there as well as wedges of iron-hard brown soap which the women of Harvey River used to wash acres of clothes in this same river. As long as I swim in it I will be borne to safety" (278). Although Goodison did not grow up as a full-time resident of Harvey River, her mother's storytelling allows her to access this locale as a refuge in times of crisis.

By representing the history of a place as linked to the descendant communities of the formerly enslaved, "born a Harvey of Harvey River," or descended from "Mary Ann Drew, African," Brodber and Goodison use life writing as a method of creating community accountable history. Their accounts do not just chronicle what they are able to recover but also detail the limits of official archives—its inability to fully answer the questions they pose to it. Goodison must rely on family and community oral history to write of her mother's Harvey River. Brodber uses official archives, but notes their limitations in conveying information before enslavement—the designation "African," for example, leaves so much unsaid about the origins and possible histories of those that lived in Woodside. In acknowledging these archival absences, their works stand in contrast to more official histories that have ignored the history of the enslaved, whitewashed it, or replicated racist biometrics or terms without a full consideration of their potential for harm in the present day. Brodber and Goodison's writings are particularly cogent in helping us understand the harms of not knowing the past, or living with accounts that are partial and written by those in power. The next chapter shares similar concerns with the fragmentary nature of the colonial archive, but Gaiutra Bahadur and Sonja Boon investigate archival impossibility as descendants of indentured Indians in the Caribbean. As we shall see, questions in their life writing concerning how archival absences impact notions of home and ancestry link Bahadur's and Boon's writing with Brodber's and Goodison's representations of genealogical desire.

CHAPTER 4

Ashes to Ashes, Dust to Dust

INDO-CARIBBEAN ARCHIVAL IMPOSSIBILITY

While the concept of "the archive" functions in a number of ways in contemporary cultural criticism, such as José Esteban Muñoz's archives of ephemera or Ann Cvetkovich's archives of feeling, this chapter thinks through the material conditions and affects archival work produces.[1] Before digitization, in order to come into contact with the archive one had to literally come into contact with it. Researchers physically handled rare documents, often required to wear cotton gloves in order to prevent the oils on their hands or salt from their sweat from contaminating paper. In the Caribbean context, contact between people and often fragile archival records are complicated by a lack of funding for preservation and by challenging climatic conditions such as humidity and heat.[2] Records meant by colonial administrators to be permanent that are now used as evidence of the aftereffects of colonial rule, such as slave registers or indentured workers' emigration passes, can crumble to dust if not handled carefully. The Caribbean quarrel with history over what should be remembered and how, it turns out, is not just about ideas but about the resources and priorities of governments and universities related to safekeeping the past.

Coolie Woman: The Odyssey of Indenture (2014) by Gaiutra Bahadur and *What the Oceans Remember: Searching for Belonging and Home* (2019) by Sonja Boon prompt us to think more expansively about what the quarrel with history means for contemporary Indo-Caribbean women.[3] This chapter marks a shift to analyzing texts by a younger generation of Caribbean writers born in the 1950s and later who moved to North America as children. As I proposed in the introduction, reading Caribbean women's texts together in an act of interpretive affiliation allows us to see epistemological innovations produced by a cohort of writers whose works create generative influence on the field. *What the Oceans Remember*, one of the most recently published texts considered here, documents the influence of Saidiya Hartman's *Lose Your Mother*, Dionne Brand's *A Map to the*

Door of No Return, and Bahadur's *Coolie Woman* as making possible a method of combining life writing and family history with critical feminist perspectives on race and colonialism. Reading Boon and Bahadur together in this chapter enables a practice of comparative reading of the afterlives of slavery, following Hartman, and thinking through the afterlives of indenture. Such a project feels especially urgent after Lisa Lowe's groundbreaking *The Intimacies of Four Continents* (2015), which notes the absence of studies on the interrelated histories of Indigenous people, immigrants, and the formerly indentured and enslaved.[4] As previous chapters explored, contemporary Caribbean writers employ life writing as a means of thinking through archival absences related to enslaved women. "Slavery continues to haunt the present because its stories, particularly those of slave women, have been improperly buried. But an improper burial does not mean that they are irretrievably lost," Jenny Sharpe observes.[5] But what about the descendants of indentured Indo-Caribbean women? How do their histories haunt the present, and what aesthetic modes are necessary to write them?

In one sense, both Bahadur's and Boon's texts describe entering archives of the state in order to claim an ancestral body. Bahadur writes of the search for archival traces of her great-grandmother Sujaria, who left Calcutta in 1903 to become an indentured plantation worker in what was then British Guiana and is now known as Guyana. Boon looks for her great-great-grandmother Joorayee Radha, who departed India in 1874 on the sixth ship bound for Suriname carrying indentured laborers. Both their ancestors arrived in British Guiana as single mothers, with Sujaria giving birth on board ship and Joorayee traveling with her young son Sahatoo. In their search for Sujaria and Joorayee, Bahadur and Boon find themselves surrounded by the afterlives of imperialism in the forms of disintegrating archives, which are a physical symptom of the archival absences related to indentured women's lives in the Caribbean. In a move that flips the modern-day neoliberal strategy that creates what Cynthia Enloe calls "labor made cheap" by locating factories in developing countries, planters in the Caribbean imported labor that was made cheap through indentureship.[6] Needing more workers after previously enslaved people refused to return to plantation work, British Guiana received close to 240,000 Indians between 1838 and 1917.[7] The Dutch brought 35,000 indentured workers from India as well as smaller numbers from China and Java to Suriname.[8] Writing on historiographies of the Caribbean family, D. Alissa Trotz argues, "The bulk of the literature has tended to focus on the English-speaking Caribbean, and on the experiences of Black Caribbeans, the descendents [*sic*] of slaves transplanted from Africa. . . . There is far less material on, for example the descendents of indentured laborers from India who have settled in such countries as Trinidad, Guyana, Martinique, Suriname, and Jamaica."[9] If existing scholarship on the family has not focused on Indo-Caribbean lives, that which does tends to recycle the debate over whether emigration created specific gendered dangers for sexual and economic exploitation (it did) or if it allowed some women a measure of sexual agency and financial independence that they otherwise might never have experienced (that happened too). *Coolie Woman* and *What the Oceans Remember* engage with this debate, but they also address issues of subjectivity and the sexual agency of women outside of familial frameworks.

Indo-Caribbean women's experiences of indenture are an important example of why feminist interventions in studies of the family and sexual relationships are necessary. Rather than being personal decisions taking place in the private sphere, sexual and domestic arrangements for emigrants required transnational cooperation. Feminist analysis of government promotion of heterosexual marriage through legislation has been well known in the literature for more than fifty years. Gayle Rubin's "The Traffic in Women: Notes on the 'Political Economy' of Sex" (1975) provides an analysis of how men who are peers cement social and economic bonds through the circulation of women within a social class as marriage partners. "Mama's Baby, Papa's Maybe: An American Grammar Book" (1987) by Hortense Spillers provides a corrective to the universality implied in Rubin's essay, demonstrating how those who trafficked in slaves refused to recognize paternity and legal unions for the African diaspora, which would have radically disrupted the logics of enslavement and white supremacy. The case of Indo-Caribbean women workers, in contrast to Rubin and Spillers, demonstrates how governments trafficked women to the Caribbean in order to support the plantation economy. Women were not exchanged between equals but supplied to Indo-Caribbean plantation and plantation workers by those who needed to extract labor from them. The British, Dutch, and French governments set up extensive bureaucracies dedicated to the management of the gender ratio among the bonded labor populations in the Caribbean.

Going beyond the framework of the family, and wondering about the sexual lives of Sujaria and her shipmates, Bahadur writes, "Could she possibly have foreseen me someday asking such impertinent questions? What would she have made of my pouring over *The Clyde*'s passenger manifest with gloved hands, examining the emigration passes of 207 of the 225 females on aboard, afterwards brushing away the *ash* from the quiet cataclysm of turning century-old pages?" (47, emphasis added). Boon expresses frustration with how Dutch archives obscure what they purport to record of the emigration of Indians to Suriname in the nineteenth and twentieth centuries. "Even after all my reading and thinking, my great-great-grandmother remained almost completely hidden. All I had left of her was some biostatistical data—her name, age, height, birthplace and skin colour—and annotations about her reproductive and conjugal history. . . . The more I read, the less I seemed to know. The fragments wouldn't arrange themselves. Some of the materials related to the immigration depot had crumbled to *dust* as soon as I touched them. I had too much information and nothing at all. I couldn't see Joorayee and Sahatoo" (213, emphasis added). "Ash" for Bahadur causes a cataclysm of emotion over the many stories that can never be known, while Boon's archive "crumbles to dust," leaving her wanting more substantial information about her ancestor.[10]

Dust and ash connect Bahadur's and Boon's experiences in the archive just as transnational movement from India to the Caribbean across the *kala pani* connects their ancestors. Asian and African diasporas in the Caribbean share a history of transatlantic crossings, European colonial rule, and current neocolonial exploitation, even as enslavement and indenture cannot be considered coterminous.[11] The unity between Caribbean spaces and peoples, as Kamau Brathwaite teaches, is submarine.[12] The Caribbean Sea connects the archipelago, Belize on the Central American isthmus, and countries in South America such as Guyana and Suriname. I want to suggest another point of unity between Caribbean identities and places—archival dreams and archival dust. This chapter proposes that the "ash" and "dust" Bahadur and Boon find in the archive and detail in their life writing constitute an absence aesthetic, a method of creating a narrative attentive to the residue of Caribbean histories in present-day lives. Archival dust and ash represent a present absence—when archival knowledge consists of partial or fragmented information or is so infused with the perspectives of colonial powers that seeing women's agency becomes difficult. The materiality of the archive becomes part of the story they tell of their genealogical search. Archival absences, as I have argued, can be fertile grounds for creating new feminist epistemologies about gender and Caribbean historiography. "Dust" represents evidence of women's lives in the archive of Caribbean indenture and slavery that survives, even as the concept of dust invokes its fragility. Archival dust clings to Bahadur and Boon's narratives, becoming embedded in their aesthetic choices about how to represent historical absences and familial silences in life writing, as well as posing ethical challenges about how to responsibly tell the stories of others in the continuing afterlife of indenture.

Coolie Woman and *What the Oceans Remember* reroute inherited epistemologies of history and the archive, showing how North American and European beliefs about quantification and permanence of archives do not translate easily to the Caribbean or to many other non-European sites of preservation. In *Dust: The Archive and Cultural History*, Carolyn Steedman contends that contemporary historiography inherits nineteenth-century European structures of knowledge, particularly related to the assumed permanence and importance of official archives, which she calls "Dust."[13] Steedman identifies how state and other official archives came to represent the potential to access the past: "To enter that place where the past lives, where ink on parchment can be made to speak, still remains the social historian's dream."[14] However, colonial archival materials represented a means of control over peoples, economies, and landscapes.[15] "Dust," as I am using it, carries the connotation of the archival past in the present, but differs from Steedman's use because the Caribbean quarrel with history places the fallibility and impermanence of archives at the center of the debate. This is why creating counter-archives remains central to decolonizing projects in the region. As Bahadur and Boon discover, traces of an ancestor in archival materials do not reveal knowledge about their subjectivity, their experiences, or their story from their own perspective, and so they must access different sources outside the official archive in order to write their life narratives.

Dreams and Dust, Bodies and Origins

> *Documents that are dusty and dirty may be lightly dusted with a clean, soft brush of the same type recommended for dusting photographs. . . . Dusting should begin at the center of a document and extend out across its edges. . . . Documents that are brittle or torn should not be subjected even to light surface dusting, since this action could cause or aggravate existing damage. Dusting only removes loose surface dirt and debris that have not become embedded in the paper; records with embedded dirt or stains that are obscuring textual information should be brought to the attention of a conservator.*
>
> —*U.S. National Archives and Records Administration, "Dusting"*[16]

Begin at the center, the U.S. National Archives and Records Administration advises, and move toward the edges to remove debris from archival materials. Documents brittle to the touch should not be dusted at all. Dirt might prevent archival documents' legibility. However, these instructions about dusting do not address documents that are almost dust to begin with. Bahadur and Boon describe the fragility of passenger manifests and emigration passes as giving off ash and dust that settle on their bodies as they read them. Documents that can turn to dust at a touch might reflect their age, but given that many of the records of indenture are less than one hundred fifty years old, their brittleness also reflects their assumed lack of importance as documents to be kept for the future. The British government removed Caribbean colonial archives to London in the 1960s and destroyed many of these records either because they were seen as unimportant or because they could cause national embarrassment. As John A. Aarons and Sharon Alexander-Gooding note, "The tragic result of the removal/destruction of these files was that the archival institutions of the newly independent countries were denied valuable records which should have been in their custody and therefore left gaps in their history."[17] Suriname experienced a similar removal of records to The Hague and a subsequent fight over relocating materials after independence in 1975.[18] The movement Bahadur and Boon document between archives in the Caribbean and those in Europe reflect how political power determines what will be archived and where it will be housed. Boon writes approvingly of everyday people using the National Archives of Suriname, while European archives carefully monitor access through requests for identification and academic credentials. I see the centering of the experience of finding and handling materials related to indenture and enslavement in *Coolie Woman* and *What the Oceans Remember* as signifying an epistemological shift, where the ephemeral and the previously unimportant become central to the narratives these texts tell. In doing so, they articulate a Caribbean feminist move, following Erna Brodber, of challenging what counts as evidence in the court of history. Brodber presciently noted in 1983 that dominant archives contain few records of "poor African and Asian ex-slaves and indentured labourers" and that other methods would have to be discovered to document Caribbean history.[19]

Still, at the beginning of both of their narratives Bahadur and Boon write of Caribbean archival dreams containing the possibility that excavating the past might lead to emancipated futures. They describe archives as sources of untapped riches, places that might lead to wonderous discoveries, including an understanding of their origins. "Archives are my childhood dreams of locked trunks and dusty attics realized," Boon observes. "They are the mysteries that filled both my imagination and the books I devoured. That day in The Hague was my first experience with the tactility of the archives, with the idea that the work I was touching was created by hand, and that hands, present and past, could somehow touch one another through time" (26). The family history Boon hopes to research is complicated. Her great-grandparents include Aldophina, a descendant of slaves born ten years after emancipation in Suriname in 1865, Theodor, an immigrant from Germany, and Sahatoo, the son of an indentured woman from India who took his Chinese stepfather's last name U-A-Sai. Boon initially experiences archives as a form of time travel—a way to go back to the past and make an emotional connection with her ancestors. For Boon, born outside the Caribbean and with many threads to trace to her family's Indian, African, Chinese, and European ancestors, Suriname marks the place of "return" without having been there before. Bahadur descends from Indo-Caribbean indentured workers on both sides of her family. Her great-grandmother Sujaria's emigration pass provides details of the very things many Caribbean people researching their family histories want to know: Where did my family originate before enslavement, indenture, immigration? Bahadur characterizes the location of Sujaria's birthplace in India as a treasure map. "Though my great-grandmother claimed no husband, she did list coordinates for home. The pass pointed to it precisely, almost like a map to some mythic location with hidden riches. X marks the spot" (18). Bahadur's archival dream, then, is to return to this village in order to learn more about Sujaria's origins.

Before talking jointly about Boon's and Bahadur's projects, I want to pause for a moment to consider a distinctive quality of the composition of *Coolie Woman*. While archival dreams animate many of the texts considered in this book, the weight of the responsibility of representing Indo-Caribbean women runs throughout *Coolie Woman*.[20] Although other authors discussed here, such as Saidiya Hartman, Ruth Behar in the next chapter, and indeed Boon herself, are accomplished scholars, Bahadur's training and experience as an investigative journalist result in densely cited prose and foregrounding of her archival research and bibliography (including archival call numbers). *Coolie Woman* communicates to an attentive reader an urgency to document archival, scholarly, and oral history sources in one place as if they are in danger of being lost. Given the precarious nature of Caribbean archival materials, this may well be the case.[21] We can see the need for documentation and contextualization of Indo-Caribbean women's lives in Bahadur's description of perceptions of Sujaria by colonial officials and plantation overseers: "The power of her colonizers to name and misname her formed a key part of her story. To them, she was a coolie woman, a stock character possessing stereotyped qualities, which shaped who she was by limiting who she could ever be. The word coolie, in keeping with one of its original meanings, carries the baggage of colonialism on its back. It bears the burdens of history" (xxi). Bahadur draws on her experience as a journalist in her pursuit of Sujaria's and other women's stories. *Coolie Woman* bears the demand for representation of women who were otherwise left out of historical records, as even their stories were not passed down to family members, and of the family members who perhaps did not think their journey was worth asking about. It is not so much a trail of bread crumbs for those who come after Bahadur but a full road map to scholarship on Indo-Caribbean indentureship in the Anglophone Caribbean.

Despite the profound effect the large-scale movement of people from India had on the Caribbean, Indo-Caribbean histories and culture often are often marginalized within Caribbean historiographies and literary history. This marginalization accounts for why *Coolie Woman*, as its title suggests, takes a much broader scope than the single life of Sujaria. Joy Mahabir and Mariam Pirbhai suggest not only that Indo-Caribbean cultural productions are understudied, but that when Indo-Caribbean women are represented they take on stereotypical traits of the mainstays of their family, or as "unthinking objects of abuse and violence."[22] Further, scholars debate the contours of indenture for Indo-Caribbean women, noting their shared status as exploited laborers with Indo-Caribbean men as well as the unique forms of sexual exploitation they experienced. Women experienced sexual exploitation at the hands of plantation managers and overseers, in common with Afro-Caribbean women in the post-emancipation period. However, the stark gender imbalance between Indo-Caribbean women and men, with Indo-Caribbean women making up only 10 to 25 percent of the population, created opportunities for women's sexual agency as well as increased risk for intimate partner violence. The weight and complexity of this history inform *Coolie Woman*'s structure.

The narrative of *Coolie Woman* could have been constructed in many ways, such as recounting the family's oral histories of Sujaria or using family photographs as a source of evidence, like Maryse Condé does in *Victoire: My Mother's Mother* (2010), as I discussed in chapter 2. Although *Coolie Woman* contains multiple oral histories as well as family photographs, Bahadur instead begins by recounting her attempts to find her great-grandmother's ancestral village in India through the existing archival evidence. Bahadur repeats several times in the narrative the fact that the geographic locations could have been transcribed incorrectly by colonial administrators or that Sujaria may have lied about her origins. Such a textual move centers the instability of the evidence and creates an absence aesthetic. *Coolie Woman* alerts us to its project of emphatically not retelling of triumphant historical recovery of verifiable facts, like a reality television program of a celebrity's genealogical search.

Gaiutra's impulse to "return" to someplace she has never been propels the first section of the narrative.[23] *Coolie Woman* contains a photograph of Sujaria's emigration pass as well as detailing its text in the narrative: "the state of Bihar, the province of Chhapra, the police district of Majhi and the village of Bhurahupur." While the reader first encounters Gaiutra in the present as she attempts to travel to Sujaria's home in India, we first see Sujaria through her presence in Guyana's national archives, documented on her "Woman's Emigration Pass" issued in Calcutta in 1903. The pass states that Sujaria arrived in Calcutta from the village of Bhurahupur in the state of Bihar, and goes on to provide a full accounting of her body. "Catalogued on this brittle artifact, sepia and crumbling with age, was everything about Immigrant #96153 that the imperial bureaucracy had considered worth recording. 'Name: Sheojari.' 'Age: 27.' 'Height: five-feet, four-and-a-half inches.' 'Caste: Brahman.' Here was colonial officialdom's cold summary of an indentured laborer's life. Yet, it included strokes of unsettling intimacy. The emigration pass told me that my great-grandmother had a scar on her left foot, a burn mark. Someone had scribbled 'Pregnant 4 mos' in pencil at the document's edge. On the line for husband's name there was only a dash" (17–18). Bahadur describes her careful interaction with Sujaria's fragile emigration pass, which is "crumbling with age." Crumbs accurately captures this particular form of dust, the biostatistical markers that provide evidence of Sujaria's passage from India. For Bahadur the pass represents a "cold summary" of her great-grandmother's bodily information, which carries twinges of an "unsettling intimacy" in describing her pregnancy and scars.

Searching for where Sujaria is "really from" through archival materials replicates Western understandings of the archive as "origin." Desiring to recover the past and find the origins of knowledge, Derrida writes, constitutes a form of archive fever.[24] Indeed, the political impulse for historical recovery by Asian and African diasporas in the Americas often has its roots in the search for origins. While the gesture toward recovery may stem from European exclusionary nationalist ideas that privilege lineage and origins, Bahadur's inability to confirm Sujaria's natal village listed on her emigration pass marks *Coolie Woman* as a particularly Caribbean narrative. *Coolie Woman*'s narrative arc is Caribbean, not so much for its failure to find Sujaria's village and descendants, but for the hope that the colonial archive can provide a source of restitution for the losses of colonization, and for the centrality Bahadur makes of the limits of the archive. Indo-Caribbean archival absences related to origins haunt the present in the form of imagined homelands and ghostly ties to India, both of which are revived as forms of archival dust. Bahadur writes that "many Indo-Caribbeans I know suffer from a kind of phantom leg syndrome. Dismembered from our imaginary homeland, we have felt the severed limb of India for generations" (176). Indenture contracts promised passage back to India, although the majority of the formerly indentured did not return. Bahadur learns from family oral histories that Sujaria never returned to India but would cry with longing to see her homeland (172). While not equating enslavement and indenture, Dionne Brand suggests these transoceanic journeys that make ancestral origins unknowable connect the Asian and African diasporas in the Caribbean. "We have no ancestry except the water and the Door of No Return. They signify space and not land. . . . It is not India which is beyond imagination; it is the black water" (*Map* 24–25). What Caribbean peoples' ancestors experienced in the dislocations and violence of enslavement and indenture is precisely what cannot be known, and yet is precisely what both Bahadur and Boon desire.

Writing such narratives of the marginalized requires a different methodology, one that can draw on multiple sources. Choosing life writing as a medium, Bahadur explains, was a daring act that came after the realization that conventional historiography would not allow her to tell her family's history fully. Her choice exposed her to family and community pushback for using the word "coolie" in her title, revealing her grandfather's status as an illegitimate child, and airing the dirty laundry of how the unequal gender balance of indentured workers led to men and women having multiple partners outside of marriage. Bahadur experiences what I call autobiographical harm, which occurs when discoveries related to family history can reactivate past traumas in the present for the author and/or her family. "How could I locate myself in my homeland's [Guyana] history of hate? For answers to my questions about identity, I had to look elsewhere, in the personal rather than the political" (11). Writing about indentured women and their sexuality, and subsequently herself, crosses over into dangerous territory for Bahadur.

When the trail goes cold in Bahadur's search for her great-grandmother's Indian origins, that absence precipitates another kind of reckoning with the archive. Bahadur could have written historical fiction incorporating the facts she learned, or a history unrelated to her family. Instead, she uses life writing to tell her own story as an immigrant to the United States and her great-grandmother's story as an indentured worker. Bahadur turns to multiple genres and sources as a method to describe the absence of women's experiences of indenture in the Caribbean as well as in an attempt to reconstruct their lives:

> How could I write about women whose very existence the official sources barely acknowledged? To enter their unknown and to some extent unknowable history, I had to turn to alternative, unofficial sources. I looked for clues in visual traces and the oral tradition: folk songs, oral histories, photographs and colonial-era postcards, even a traditional tattoo on the forearms of elderly Indo-Caribbean women. Perhaps most daringly, I turned to the self and wrote about my own journeys: to India, to visit my great-grandmother's native village in order to uncover why she left; and back to Guyana, where I was born.[25]

Bahadur examines the lives of other indentured women to create a narrative that is simultaneously personal and national. This long-buried and fragmented archive creates space for Bahadur to write about the lingering effects gendered relationships under indenture have on violence against women in Guyana today, as I discuss in the next section. For now, I want to think about origin stories, archival dreams, and dust.

Bahadur describes her family's immigration to the United States from Guyana as a "magician's box," a process that cut her in half with few clues about how she might be pieced together. In the United States, her family's creolized religious practices and food are deemed inauthentic by other immigrants newly arrived from India, while their Caribbean cultural identity is negated in favor of their Asian heritage by white Americans. Bahadur remembers how in 1987 a racist group calling themselves the Dot Busters attacked anyone perceived to be Indian:

> We did feel solidarity with Indians in our neighborhood because of the attacks. . . . But the embrace offered to Indo-Caribbeans by immigrants directly from the subcontinent often has a subtle edge. Indeed, they are eager to tell us our own story—what part of India we probably came from, what dialect of Hindi our ancestors probably spoke, how our singers inevitably garble those dialects when they perform chutney, the hybrid dance music indigenous to the Caribbean but rooted in India. I doubt they meant to offend, or to hold us to the light like an artifact, a fascinating shard of pottery. (8)

Gaiutra's account of Indo-Caribbean identity, in the context of the United States, leaves her outside of Indian communities in New Jersey. She imagines Guyana as "a place of imagined wholeness" (9) but finds when she returns in 1997 that being Indo-Caribbean does not make for automatic belonging in a nation divided by race, just as her American assumptions about gender equality make her seem odd to her relatives. "The deepest alienation came from the unspoken rules about what women should not and could not do" (12). While in

India, Gaiutra surprises herself by asserting her freedom as an American to associate with men and travel by herself, an identity she had not previously claimed so forthrightly. In the United States, Indo-Caribbean people are positioned as an "artifact," a historical relic belonging to another time and place. The description of her family's inability to name their origins precisely creates an example of archival dust, in that evidence of her origins exists, but to locate it precisely is impossible. The absence of information about her family's origins animates her search and points to how the narrative is structured through an archival quest. This moment is linked in the text to another as Bahadur also uses "artifact" to describe Sujaria's emigration pass, her state-sponsored permission to travel. The crumbs of the archive are not enough to establish Gaiutra as an authentic Indian or even Guyanese subject, just as her great-grandmother's pass cannot establish her origins. Gaiutra's interpellation as a stranger throughout her travels might have caused postcolonial melancholy, as it does for Saidiya Hartman in *Lose Your Mother* when she is repeated called *obruni*, or stranger, by people in the streets of Ghana (3). Instead, Gaiutra reflects that her ability to travel may be a positive consequence of her family's leaving Guyana, and wonders if her great-grandmother experienced a similar "liberation" in leaving India (15). Indeed, Sujaria experienced a degree of sexual autonomy in British Guiana and the ability to earn a wage. But like her great-granddaughter she experienced cultural dislocation because of emigration.

Like Bahadur, Boon writes of the dislocation caused by her family's movements around the globe. "I've spent my life on the outside, looking in. I've never lived in a place that I could fully call 'home.' I am rootless, my selves spreading across three continents, my histories spanning five" (7). Boon was born in the United Kingdom to a Surinamese mother and a Dutch father. Her family moved to Venezuela for several years before settling in Canada. Recounting her family's travels, Boon realizes that facts such as the passports she holds or records of where she has lived, which will be available in archives of the future, cannot explain what it feels like for everyone in her family to be born on a different continent. The interiority Boon knows her own archival trail will not reveal is what she hopes to find about her ancestors. Her genealogical desire is sparked by her experience as a racialized person with dark skin, but one who cannot be easily placed in the immigration landscape of Canada.

Similarly to Bahadur's pursuit of her family's past, Boon searches for knowledge about her ancestors' lives, but what she finds instead is evidence of her great-great-grandmother's body in the Dutch National Archives in The Hague. Translating from the Dutch, Boon notes, "Joorayee's immigration record states that she was 1.513 meters tall, and *donker bruin*—dark brown—in complexion. She was Hindu, and according to the transcribed records, she hailed from the village of Aburpore in the district of Faizbad, in the North of India" (199). Colonial administrators documented and colonial archives collected only the most important data needed to run an empire. In the case of women workers recruited from India, emigration passes documented their bodies—their height, bodily marks, and reproductive status. Emigration depot surgeons certified a woman's fitness for the voyage and the labor that would follow, ensuring that "she is free from all bodily and mental disease."[26] Male plantation workers, the colonial regime assumed, required women's bodies. Although women were outwardly recruited as labor, the British, and later the Dutch via treaty with the British in 1872, strove to increase Indian women's emigration because of the social turmoil an imbalanced sex ratio caused, including labor unrest and high rates of violence toward women. In other words, the presumed heterosexual needs of Indian men already working on plantations had to be met.[27]

Boon finds Joorayee in three archival sources: her emigration pass; a map of de Resolutie, the Surinamese plantation where she served her indenture; and her 1880 documentation allowing her to stay permanently in Suriname. Joorayee did not leave any record of her experience from her point of view. Arriving with a child to Suriname, Joorayee had additional children while she was indentured and later married a Chinese man. She may have experienced freedom to choose her partners in Suriname, but the records cannot reveal her perspective on these choices, if indeed they were choices. Bahadur observes, "The archives leave gaps. Missing, with few exceptions, are the voices of the women themselves. They did not leave behind diaries or letters. The vast majority wasn't literate, in English or in any Indian language. They did not tell their own stories, except indirectly, through the often-biased prism of government investigators and court officials who occasionally took their testimonies. The relative silence of coolie women in the sum total of history reflects their lack of power. But could it also reflect a strategy by women who had secrets to keep?" (32). Both Bahadur and Boon's works share historian Marisa Fuentes's methodology of "reading against the bias grain" using gaps in the archive not as barriers to interpreting the past but as indicative of the forces shaping indentured women's lives.[28] Boon begins *What the Oceans Remember* by cautioning against the seductive nature of archival dreams. "Archives are seductive spaces. In their vaults, they hold the dreams and longings of those who come before us. Their reading rooms, meanwhile, gather the hopes of all the researchers who have ever come through their doors in search of the fleeting truths of the past. Archives are places where a seeker's dreams can come true, but where they can also be shattered" (1). As a scholar of eighteenth-century European culture and life writing, Boon is forthright about her long-standing fascination with archival materials. Researching her own family history proves more challenging as she confronts the limitations of official archives for telling a complete story of her family's origins.

Beginning her research in the Netherlands, perhaps logical for Boon as someone fluent in Dutch with a father from that country, she struggles to explain to her Dutch family how her research is different from composing a family tree. Arguing that genealogy, with its fixation on "marriages and legitimate offspring," does not fit her "messy family" (3), Boon signals that *What the Oceans Remember* will not be a linear recounting of her family's history. Lineage as determined by official documentable "facts," Julia Watson argues, works outside the logics of life writing.[29] Life writing as Watson and Boon understand it articulates the writer's embodied experience rather than rehearsing a list of verifiable facts. Critiques of genealogical projects as privileging the legitimate biological family are not necessarily valid in the Caribbean, as I argued in chapter 3. In that chapter I characterized Lorna Goodison and Erna Brodber's life writing as "resistance genealogies" that are meant to serve as resources to their Jamaican communities. In her resource-rich text that invites others to use it as an archive, Bahadur's work comes closer to resistance genealogy than Boon's. Boon engages more strongly with the European historical record. Her family's history becomes a counter-archive to modes of heteropatriarchal genealogy. For example, rather than the family tree found in some family life writing, such as Lorna Goodison's in *From Harvey River* (2007), Boon creates a timeline in a ladder format. World events such as the end of the Dutch slave trade in 1814 are listed in one column and family history, such as the approximate 1798 birth date of Frederick Noa, the oldest enslaved ancestor Boon can document, is given in the other. This allows the reader to see Boon's family events such as births and deaths as being related to global history, instead of related only to previous births, deaths, and marriages as in a biological family tree.

I suggest that rather than providing a traditional genealogy through a family tree, *What the Oceans Remember* meditates on histories located in the body. The stories the body can tell are one way to engage an absence aesthetic in Boon's work, as she writes about what cannot be known. "There was a much more complicated story waiting to be told, and that story was always within me. It's a story written on my skin, moulded in the shape of my face. It's in the range of bodies and voices and colours and flavours that make up my family. It's also in the many and varied identities that others have ascribed to me, in the reasons why so many people continue to feel compelled to ask me where I am from, even though I have called Canada home since 1975" (37). Sonja recognizes, as a child immigrant like Gaiutra, that her claim to citizenship in her new home will be questioned as a racialized subject with multiple origins. Both realize that to have a hyphenated identity implies having a single origin and a new home, rather than, as Boon puts it, "the complexity of multiple belonging" (21). The idea that race and origins can be assigned with certainty, what Lorgia García-Peña calls a "diction" that is "projected and performed on racialized bodies to sustain the exclusionary nation," finds itself challenged by Boon's counter-epistemology of how an identity may contain multiple origins.[30] Similarly to Gaiutra's experience of being seen as Indian in India until her speech, dress, or behavior gives her away as American, while Sonja is in Suriname, she is hailed as both an insider and a foreigner depending on the situation. In Sranan, the Creole language of Suriname, the word for a white person is *bakra*. *Bakra* appears linguistically similar to *buckra/bakra*, commonly used in English-language Creoles across the Caribbean and also meaning white person or boss. Sonja learns that after a lifetime as a racialized brown person in white-majority Canada, she is often perceived as *bakra* by Surinamese people, something her multiracial family warns her about before she returns (114).[31]

These multiple origins mean that Sonja's body becomes a troubling presence for archival attachments—affects about historical subjects based on shared identity—given that her ancestors include the enslaved, the indentured, and their masters. Her previous experience as an archival researcher fails her when faced with a ship's log quantifying each enslaved person taken on board with a number, and then a skull and crossbones next to the deceased. The reach of the trade overwhelms Sonja, as she realizes that these forms of archival dust—receipts for hardtack, beer, plates, fabric, and other goods to provision the slave ship with—were made by local businesses, which were then complicit in the slave trade. "In these documents I could trace the inner workings of the slave trade. I could measure its economic impact with breathtaking clarity. I told myself that I would remain objective, that I would take notes on exactly what I saw before me. . . . *But I can see the captain purchase slaves*, I protested silently" (46). Her mind and body react with shock to the evidence of the buying and selling of people. Sonja's experiences in the archive recall Hartman's account of the difficulty of researching lives of the enslaved despite her academic qualifications. "My graduate training hadn't prepared me to tell the stories of those who had left no record of their lives and whose biography consisted of the terrible things said about them or done to them" (16). With her "professional research shell firmly in place," Sonja combs through records of the Sarah plantation in Suriname on which fourteen of her ancestors were enslaved, most of them listed as *veld*, or field slaves (81). This shell, however, impedes her full ability to process and write about what she finds in these records. Like her emotions, Sonja shuts the archival box she is working on. "Closed it. Tied the ribbon. Put everything back in the box. All around me, a light brown dust from the crumbling edges of nineteenth-century paper. *Ashes to ashes*, I thought, *dust to dust*" (79). Ash and dust surround Sonja's body, and become inescapable reminders of the materiality of slavery in the present.

Afterlives of Indenture

Archival dreams, bodies, and origins make up only one aspect of Bahadur's and Boon's narratives. For both of them, life writing demands an ethics of accountability. Boon's and Bahadur's search for the words to describe their families' multiple displacements and their similarly multiple origins resonates with the concept of "post-indentureship feminism" offered by Gabrielle Jamela Hosein and Lisa Outar.[32] Post-indentureship feminism names the creation of new knowledge about the afterlives of indentureship, especially by those who are triply diasporic—Indo-Caribbean outside of the Caribbean. In this final section of the chapter, I explore how Boon and Bahadur articulate their ethical responsibilities in the present, following what they learned about the past through their archival journey.

Boon ends *What the Oceans Remember* by relating how she was called to account as she begins to take a photograph of one of the large wooden clapboard houses in Paramaribo, with a sprawling veranda and picturesquely peeling yellow paint. As she attempts to take a picture, a man stops her. "This is my grandparents' house . . . it's one hundred and fifty years old" (243). In this moment Sonja realizes that her anthropological impulse to collect and document interferes with her ability to see the people in front of her. The man refuses her documentation process and claims space in Paramaribo as rightfully his family's but not hers. The presence of tourists ready to take in the history of Suriname marks another form of archival ash, the continuing presence of the gaze of European and North American tourists. They come to gaze at the remnants of a former colonial capitol whose architecture has been recognized as a UNESCO World Heritage Site, without offering reparations for colonial enslaved and indentured labor that enriched their countries. Within this context, the man asserts that Sonja does not have the right to capture images of his family's home and to later display and tell stories about them. The residents of the home and its history are his, not hers, to share. Boon self-reflexively understands her impulse to document as part of her training as an academic. She refers to work by Eve Tuck and K. Wayne Yang that seeks to decolonize research methods that assume that every fact, image, and story collected by researchers should be shared. Tuck and Yang argue that in the social sciences, researchers demand narratives of pain and trauma without concern about aftermath of telling those stories for individuals and communities: "The subaltern can speak, but is only invited to speak her/our pain."[33] Literary and scholarly productions can reproduce this model by figuring Indo-Caribbean women as victims whose stories are interesting because of the trauma of indenture.[34] Deciding what stories relate to indenture and enslavement, for Boon, becomes part of an ethics of life writing: "I didn't know that this would be the hardest work I'd ever done, and that it would demand more from me—ethically, personally, and emotionally—than any work in which I'd previously engaged" (27–28). As Boon acknowledges, archives by their very definition impose limitations on what can be discovered. Since *What the Oceans Remember* is not an academic book, the reader cannot evaluate the sources Boon chooses to include. We must share her epistemological uncertainty if the stories she chooses to tell are inclusive or accurate.

Key among the issues Boon faces is the inadequacy of data. In her quest to learn about the interiority of her ancestors, "A family tree was only the beginning. I wanted passion, desire, longing, grief, rage, sorrow, joy" (25–26), Boon realizes that the colonial archive cannot supply that. The archive can reproduce dehumanization and trauma.[35] Boon sees this, as noted earlier, in the lists of registries of those making the Middle Passage. She can most readily access her grandfather's life. Leonard, born in 1905, the child of an enslaved woman and a German man, was a professional musician who performed in the Netherlands. The family saved his music and concert bills, which Boon studies. Noting that most family histories are not contained within official records, Boon learns that her grandfather could be tracked through "concert announcements. Reviews. Interviews. The stuff of a musician's life is written for public consumption" (68). Boon was a professional flutist before becoming an academic, and her training allows her to interpret Leonard's musical choices such as compositions he chose to play and the concerts he performed in order to gain at least a partial understanding of his life.

However, the inner lives of the generations before him remain opaque. Grappling with *slavenregisters* in Paramaribo, Boon insists on the ethical imperative of entering into her family's past. "If I wanted to understand this history, my family's place in it, and how these pasts continued to affect contemporary realities, then I needed to enter that history, no matter how uncomfortable or how angry it made me" (157). Unlike Hartman in her practice of critical fabulation in "Venus in Two Acts," Boon does not attempt to represent the point of view of an enslaved person. Archival records do allow Sonja to realize that while her life has been marked by travel, over three generations of her ancestors were enslaved at Sarah plantation, living their entire lives within the same 500 acres (166). Sonja's discomfort stems from the contradictory realization that these places of forced labor also became people's homes. The plantation under slavery or indenture, as Bahadur explores in more detail, was a space of intimacy, even if the conditions of those intimacies are not always available through traditional archival records.

For the Indo-Caribbean side of her family, Boon wants to re-create an inner life for Joorayee to rescue her from merely being an indentured number in an archive. In considering the still debated issue of the benefits for women of indenture, Boon proposes that macro-level analysis will always be found wanting, because it can't satisfy an ethical imperative of archival dust which accounts for weight of the past in the present. She writes of Pieter Emmer's positive assessment of indenture as an avenue for women's agency: "The problem with this vision is that things are always much more complicated than they seem. Emmer's data sets are invaluable in revealing large patterns, but they can't get below the surface; they can't reveal the nitty-gritty of lived experience. And they certainly can't get at what interested me most: what happened in the century that followed, and what remains for those of us who have inherited these histories" (211). Reading the archive against the grain concerning Joorayee, as well as oral histories of other indentured people, Boon writes of their continuing "sense of surprise" in finding themselves in Suriname and the continuing longing for India.

In recognizing the shock of the formerly indentured, Boon echoes V. S. Naipaul's observations in 1962 in *The Middle Passage.* Naipaul wrote of Indo-Caribbean people as misplaced in an alien landscape forty-five years after the end of indenture. Naipaul, born in Trinidad, is often rightly critiqued for his dismissive and often disparaging attitude toward the Caribbean. I share reservations about Naipaul's outlook, but find his view helpful here in identifying a strain of Caribbean thought that recognizes how the formerly enslaved and indentured become the majority populations but do not follow the logics of settler colonialism because they are not colonizers. Consider Naipaul's description of meeting a man in the remote rural interior of Suriname: "A derelict man in a derelict land; a man discovering himself, with surprise and resignation, lost in a landscape which had never ceased to be unreal because the scene of an enforced and always temporary residence; the slaves kidnapped from one continent and abandoned on the unprofitable plantations of another, from which there could never be more escape: I was glad to leave Coronie . . . it held the full desolation that came to those that made the middle passage."[36] Naipaul's is a fundamentally tragic view of the Indo-Caribbeans, brought to labor in exploitation colonies and then abandoned.

Naipaul reproduces the anthropological and colonizer's gaze that Boon critiques. Boon calls this "gawkery," the right of those in power to gaze upon those who are marginalized. Naipaul also focuses on men as marooned in the Caribbean without their rightful culture, with little attention to gendered dynamics of power. Boon's ethical stance, then, involves integrating for the reader the gendered power dynamics of the indentured and enslaved family past with the present of Suriname. Unlike some of the texts considered in this study, Boon's does not claim that stories of the indentured or enslaved are unknown in Suriname. Instead, her ethical intervention consists of the importance of the past in the present. For Boon, with ancestry from Africa and India, a comparative study of the colonial processes results in disbelief over how little changed between the inauguration of the slave trade in the 1600s and mid-nineteenth-century colonial practices.

> It's not like I hadn't encountered archival silences before. As devastating as my journey though the accounting declarations and slave registers had been, I had, in some ways, anticipated silence there. This is, after all, what slavery does. It tears families apart. It erases kinship. It dehumanizes the enslaved, turning them into property, numbers. But I expected something different from stories

> of indenture. And somehow, I expected more from events that took place less than 150 years ago. I thought that things might have improved, that colonial authorities might have learned something. I thought wrong. (202)

Realizing the legacies of colonial rule on Suriname from postindependence mismanagement, the political instabilities that caused her grandparents to immigrate to the Netherlands and neocolonial struggles over the nation's gas and gold reserves, perhaps incongruently allows Boon to focus on Suriname as a country in process rather than stuck in the past.

> It had taken me too long to figure out that the plantation pasts I had so eagerly sought still marked Paramaribo's cityscape in the present. *Combé. Rainville. Tourtonne. Ma Retraite. Morgenstond. Mon Plaisir.* Every city neighborhood was named after plantation lands with every step I took, my feet following in the footsteps not only of the European elite who had turned swamps into profit, but had also of the enslaved and indentured who had toiled for them, and before them, the Indigenous people who had been pushed away from prime coastal lands. I'd searched for my stories in the archives and the rural regions outside the city, but they'd been right there with me the whole time. (248)

After many trips to archives around the world, as well as to plantations where her ancestors were enslaved and indentured, Boon realizes that Paramaribo already encapsulates that history.

Beyond learning more about the author's family, how can Caribbean family life writing help us understand how the past influences the present? One answer comes from Bahadur's deft linking of the legacies of violence from the period of indenture to the present. For Bahadur, her research on Sujaria's life leads her to investigate gender-based violence in contemporary Guyana. The gender imbalance between indentured men and women led to situations of increased power for women, even as women experienced exploitation. An indentured woman's voice reaches us across time, as Bahadur quotes a woman who appears in Canadian missionary Sarah Morton's account proselytizing to Indo-Caribbean people from 1868–1912. Morton recounts her work with women as a missionary: "The loose actions and prevailing practices in respect of women here are quite shocking to the newcomer. I said to an East Indian woman I knew to be the widow of a Brahmin, 'You have no relations in Trinidad, I believe?' 'No, Madame,' she replied, only myself and two children: when the last immigrant ship came I took a 'papa.' I will keep him as long as he treats me well. If he does not treat me well, I shall send him off at once; that's the right way, is it not?' This will be to some a new view of women's rights."[37] This anecdote reflects how the low numbers of Indo-Caribbean women provided some leverage in choosing partners. Polyandry was practiced among indentured communities. Queer sexuality also appears in the archive as colonial administrators wrote of their dismay over same-sex sexuality on the plantations. However, in the majority of cases, the scarcity of women triggered increased surveillance and violence by both sexual partners and plantation overseers eager to claim their rights to a specific woman and/or maintain order among workers. Bahadur uses her skills as a journalist to catalogue newspaper accounts and police records showing that between 1859 to 1917, more than 167 women were killed by intimate partner violence in British Guiana (108). Plantation life was regulated by violence toward workers, and by the state control over their movements. Indentured workers did not have the right to move freely, and needed a pass to travel. Violence against women left its trace in colonial archives rife with anxiety about women's ability to change partners at their whim, and men's anger and violence over their agency.

Bahadur turns from the violence of the past to that of the present, using her skills as a journalist, interviewing officials and analyzing news stories. High rates of intimate partner violence continue within Indo-Caribbean communities, both in the Caribbean and in the diaspora.[38] *Coolie Woman* links the past and present by examining the legacies of the plantation system for contemporary women. The view of domestic violence as an individual issue, an understanding among many cultures until very recently, remains common in public policy and law enforcement in Guyana. Bahadur writes, "Many officers view it as a private affair rather than a method for their intervention, although domestic violence has violated civil law in Guyana since 1996" (201). Ironically, during the colonial period, the state did intervene in violence against women, keeping track of deaths and assaults and prosecuting and hanging violators. The difference is notable between the colonial state's interest in keeping workers under control and protecting its labor force and the interest of an independent state in protecting its citizens. Bahadur writes that one explanation for rising violence is "economic policies pursued to meet conditions attached to loans from the World Bank and International Monetary Fund . . . cuts in social spending, spiraling costs of living and greater unemployment have resulted in the policies, creating a climate of insecurity for the poor" (205). Additionally, more Guyanese now live abroad than in Guyana. Immigration has left women vulnerable to violence since their family members who might provide protection are out of the country.

Just as Bahadur entered the archive to find her great-grandmother and came up with descriptions of Sujaria's body, *Coolie Woman*'s representation of intimate partner violence past and present recirculates representations of women's maimed bodies. From the description of a cutlass attack severing a woman's leg and arm in 1903 to the killing of a woman named Pinky in 2010 who suffered fatal lacerations and dismembered fingers, Bahadur narrativizes archival and contemporary medical and media accounts of the violence done to women's bodies. At times Bahadur's impulse to document and narrate veers into Boon's conception of gawkery, presenting readers repeatedly with images of suffering or dead women for our consumption. Kaneesha Cherelle Parsard trenchantly observes, "It is also here that the limits of archival recovery emerge: Bahadur represents the indentured Indian women . . . only through colonial documents and the *Ramcharitmanas*," concluding, "Bahadur continues to write Indian women as victims of culture."[39] Bahadur's suggestion that cultural influences such as the epic poem Ramayana model violence against unfaithful wives appears to Parsard to pathologize Indo-Caribbean communities and avoid accounting for historical pressures that precipitated violence, such as poverty and the violence the men themselves experienced on the plantation. The sticking point between "history" and "culture" gains traction when we frame it between the pull to document the past and the responsibility of the memoirist to resist recirculating stereotypes. Here archival dust erupts. What should we do with the ash on our hands from "the quiet cataclysm of turning century-old pages?" (47). This tension is a contemporary feminist Caribbean quarrel with history. We either have too much history, with the colonial past given responsibility for the entirety of the present,[40] or have too little, with few historical examples of Indo-Caribbean women outside of their presence as, what Saidiya Hartman called in the context of enslavement, the spectacularized subjects of violence.

Throughout this book I have written about archival impossibility resulting from the limits of evidence in official archives. Archival impossibility also includes the boundaries around what can be known about others from records. Bahadur's postulating about potential causes of intimate partner violence in the last chapter, "Surviving History," certainly is frustrating given the many studies of this phenomenon and its causes. Just one such example is Jacqui Alexander's groundbreaking study on the link between anti-LGBTQ legislation and legal codes about domestic violence as attempts to shore up an anxious and undermined sense of national authority and masculinity, first during nationalist movements and subsequently in the wake of U.S. imperialism.[41] *Coolie Woman* neglects to document the work of many anti-domestic-violence organizations in the Caribbean. Beyond these objections, the categories of history and culture are slippery—what counts as a historical influence on contemporary violence in Guyana, and what comes from Indo-Caribbean culture? How could the two be separated? In attempting to write about both influences, Bahadur does not create these categories but steps into an already fraught debate about history and what it means in the present. Are Caribbean peoples "slaves to history," if the past is only abjection, as Edward Baugh framed it in 1977?[42] Is the postcolonial present best understood through the mode of tragedy, as David Scott argued, for its failure to enact the promise of postcolonial liberation?[43]

Coolie Woman and *What the Oceans Remember* turn to the archive to find evidence of Indo-Caribbean foremothers. What they discover is neither tragic nor deterministic about potential Caribbean futures. Rather, both texts end by quietly marking the resilience of Surinamese and Guyanese people. Boon recalls her grandmother, Sahatoo's daughter, who lived through colonization in Suriname and immigration to the Netherlands in order to marvel at her grandchildren. "Imagine . . . you're all from the same family. And as if none of us had ever thought about this before we all paused and looked around. Oma was right. There we were, my cousins and I, looking for all the world as if we'd tumbled out of box of Crayola multicultural markers" (261–262). This is not a paean to multiculturalism, but a recognition of all that her grandparents survived in order so that Sonja could be born. "There is no logical starting point; I have no single home to return to. Rather the threads of my pasts span the globe" (262). Bahadur is not nearly so optimistic, fittingly for a narrative concerned with violence in the present. Nevertheless, she imagines that culture and history provide ballast against the burdens of history. Recounting the story of a survivor of violence, Bahadur writes, "The past was baggage she had to heft, somehow . . . as generations of coolie women before her had done. To survive her history, she did as they had. She thought of her family, and carried on" (214).

CHAPTER 5

"Put My Mom in There"

MEMORIALIZATION AS CARIBBEAN COUNTER-ARCHIVE

The archive is another way of reconnecting the fragmented ways we're pulled apart in America.

—*Angie Cruz*

In order to write *Dominicana* (2019), a fictionalized version of her mother's coming of age and immigration to the United States, novelist Angie Cruz turned to the archives in the City University of New York's Dominican Studies Institute. Although the majority of immigrants during the 1960s and 1970s from the Dominican Republic to the United States were women and migrated to New York, Cruz found little evidence of the lives of women like her mother.[1] In response to this archival absence, Cruz put out a call for photographs of Dominican women as well as narratives about their lives. She publishes these images and texts on social media through the Instagram account @dominicanasnyc (Dominicanas NYC) to create an alternative archive and allow members of the community to know each other in a new way. Cruz explains, "I started asking people for photos of their mothers, and the experience of submitting and curating that was so joyous. People said, *oh my God, I would love to put my mom in there. I would like to put my grandmother in there. I want to put myself in there.* Someone said, *this is better than a DNA project,* because they'll start finding each other: *is this my cousin? Are you from this town?* The archive is another way of reconnecting the fragmented ways we're pulled apart in America, through images."[2] Dominicanas NYC's placement of the intimate next to the geopolitical, along with a consideration of gender and power, resonates with many other texts considered in this book that write personal narrative in the context of transnational history. Dominicanas NYC politicizes the personal by juxtaposing family photos with an acknowledgment of the transnational forces present in Caribbean people's decision to immigrate. While

Figure 3. @dominicanasnyc "Here is my Grandmother Georgina in the back, Uncle Tony to the left and my mother Nelly to the right. This picture was taken in 1963 on the New York Circle Line." Photo and post credit: Alex Rodriguez @alexis_rod_, November 18, 2019. Image used with permission.

these are usually quietly stated, as in the image here which reads, "My grandfather and grandmother moved to Manhattan due to my grandfather's last name and political reasons during the last few years of the Trujillo era," a reader familiar with the history of the Dominican Republic will know that the caption refers to the U.S. occupation from 1916 to 1924 that led to Rafael Trujillo's dictatorship (1930–1961) (see fig. 3).[3] This picture was taken in 1963, the same year that the Kennedy administration deemed Dominican Juan Bosch's administration to be a potential communist hazard, leading to another occupation by the U.S. military. A seemingly simple family picture of a mother with her children emerges as a legible representation of inter-American politics in this counter-archive, evidence of the transnational migration of people under the threat of state violence.

Cruz documents Dominican women as important for understanding U.S. and Caribbean history, even as these women's stories are not figured that way within official archives. Women's life narratives challenge traditional epistemologies, including whose history counts as evidence and what sources can be drawn upon to write "real" history. Historian Antoinette Burton observes, "For better or worse, it remains the task of historians of women to challenge the residue of objectivist approaches to history-writing and, in the process, to continue to query the gendered presumptions of what counts as evidence, archive, impact . . . we must cite [autobiographies], we must actively use them, as primary sources as well as secondary accounts in order to break the chain of logic between women's work and 'real' history."[4] Building on Burton's and other scholars' emphasis on the importance of life writing, this chapter argues that the genre is not just an important primary source for scholars but also should be seen as intervening in social and historical debates to shape new understandings of the archive.

When Caribbean life writing participates in building new archives, that work comprises an epistemological project of selecting and defining what should be remembered about the past and carried forward into the future.[5] While earlier chapters focused on colonial archives and their absences related to slavery, indenture, and their aftereffects, this final chapter examines life writing that forms an alternative means of memorializing Caribbean lives and history in Caribbean diasporic life writing. It continues the transition begun in chapter 4 of bringing into conversation works by a younger generation of authors who were born in the Caribbean and currently live in North America. I look at the concept of the Caribbean counter-archive presented in a variety of perspectives and forms: Cuban American anthropologist Ruth Behar's ethnographic memoir *An Island Called Home: Returning to Jewish Cuba* (2007), Haitian-American writer Edwidge Danticat's memoir *Brother, I'm Dying* ([2007] 2008) and essay collection *Create Dangerously: The Immigrant Artist at Work* (2010), and Puerto Rican writer Irene Vilar's memoir *The Ladies' Gallery: A Memoir of Family Secrets* ([1996] 2009).[6] All three negotiate the meaning of diasporic identity and the diaspora's relationship to the Caribbean, but from varying perspectives based on social class, race, and religion. Elena Machado Sáez suggests in her study of Caribbean diasporic historical novels that the concept of diaspora itself remains a "contested rhetoric within Caribbean studies."[7] These life writing narratives also challenge a singular understanding of diasporic identity and its relationship to the past. Reading these texts together in an act of interpretive affiliation allows us to see how contemporary Caribbean life narratives stretch our understanding of what archives might look like in the future as they memorialize lives and events not contained within traditional repositories.

Behar's, Danticat's, and Vilar's life writing archives their family histories of immigration from the Caribbean to the United States in order to tell different stories from that of state memory. State memory here includes that of both the Caribbean and the United States, neither of which are responsive to historical claim making of the kind Cruz's interlocutors demand: "put my mom . . . my grandmother . . . myself in there." While popular movements to erect monuments and museums dedicated to remembering slavery and indenture are relatively new in the Caribbean, women's experiences continue to be marginalized within them. What role women's lives should play in projects of memorialization continues as a form of the Caribbean quarrel with history: whose story gets to be represented and why. In his essay "Black Memory versus State Memory," Michael Hanchard notes that projects of memorialization, especially concerning events that might otherwise not be documented in official histories, allow marginalized subjects to make "claims in contemporary life about the relationship between present inequalities and past injustices."[8] This chapter explores what kinds of claims contemporary Caribbean women writers make about history and subjectivity, bringing a feminist decolonial perspective to consider how and why Caribbean diasporic experiences appear in life writing. The slipperiness of personal memory collides in Behar's, Danticat's, and Vilar's work with the gendered expectations of whose story is worth memorializing. In keeping with my analytic focus on gender, this chapter teases apart the politics of memorialization. I find Hanchard's formulation of various forms of memory helpful in distilling these authors' larger engagements with issues of representation and history and with how to memorialize the personal as it is connected to the geopolitical. If, as Hanchard suggests, state memory is vertically constructed as a top-down process, then reading these texts together allows for an understanding of them as co-constructing a horizontal epistemology about the Caribbean in opposition to, but also outside of, neocolonial narratives.[9] This body of writing further troubles typical projects of memorialization, which tend to represent one point of view and one version of history. Instead, Behar works in collaboration with a photographer to present multiple views of Jewish Cuba, Danticat writes from the perspective of "we-moir," or a collective life writing, and Vilar engages in what I call "dememorialization," seeking to undermine simplistic understandings of her grandmother's political activism and Puerto Rican identity.

A major theme within these texts is the impact of U.S. neocolonialism on the lives of Caribbean people.[10] Traumatic historical events, influenced by U.S. international policies, which Behar, Danticat, and Vilar learn about as girls and only "remember" through their family's retelling, take center stage in their writing. Behar writes of her obsession with photographs of herself as a toddler in 1950s Cuba, admitting that she cannot remember Cuban life firsthand. This aporia in Behar's memory precipitates her desire to return repeatedly to Cuba and to advocate for Jews remaining there. Danticat "sees" a television broadcast of a state-sponsored execution of political dissidents in the 1960s first through her relatives' memories and later on in an archive of Haitian television and film.

Her obsession with this event and its filmic representation bears a relationship to her fractured retelling of her uncle's death while in immigration custody. In 1954, Vilar's grandmother Lolita Lebrón opened fire in the U.S. House of Representatives in hopes of furthering the Puerto Rican independence movement. Vilar learns about her grandmother's actions by reading newspaper accounts and court reports of the trial. These archival sources include an image of Lolita Lebrón first published in a newspaper that Vilar returns to throughout her memoir, relating it to her own fragmented sense of self as a Puerto Rican.[11]

Returning to Cruz's Instagram account, it works in this chapter as a useful heuristic since it encapsulates four important characteristics of the feminist decolonial counter-archives also contained in Behar's, Danticat's, and Vilar's writing. Cruz's work demonstrates a deliberate engagement with the existing archive and a wish to describe what exists and what is absent for readers. Second, there is evidence within the text of a curatorial process at work, a consideration my method relies upon. These texts, I maintain, function as archives partly through a narrative recognition that they are selecting and describing certain photographs, memories, and historical events in the service of telling a larger story about gender, Caribbean identities, and immigration.[12] Third, there is a shared recognition that they are creating new archival forms. For Cruz, creating a digital life narrative archive on social media rather than one that is boxed in a physical archive creates conditions for the recognition of shared experiences and affiliation, "*better than a DNA project*," for the New York Dominican community. Finally, Dominicanas NYC foregrounds the relationship between the movement of people and state decisions over borders, identities, and who counts as a citizen.[13] Thus, a recognition that state archives function to regulate citizenship serves in Cruz's work and the other texts considered here as an impetus for creating carefully curated counter-archival texts with innovative formal qualities.

Begged, Borrowed, or Stolen: Memorializing Jewish Cuba

Cuban-born anthropologist Ruth Behar pioneered the practice of combining academic analysis and life writing. Behar has long positioned herself as a proponent of a new methodological intervention in anthropology in which vulnerability and epistemological uncertainty are disclosed upfront, rather than writing from a position of assumed objectivity and authority. Behar's work has been influential in the field of anthropology for its refutation of the idea of the objective viewer and for her insistence on the importance of the anthropologist's identity for ethnographic writing.[14] Behar originated new forms of ethnography and life writing in *Translated Woman: Crossing the Border with Esperanza's Story* (1993) and *The Vulnerable Observer: Anthropology That Breaks Your Heart* (1996). She has been awarded a MacArthur Fellowship as well as other accolades for her innovative formal approaches.

Prefiguring the rise of autotheoretical texts by several decades, Behar's work enabled the development of autobiographical criticism or academic life writing, where a scholar's personal investments and histories become part of the study.[15] Behar's deployment of historiography, ethnography, and personal narrative anticipates the approaches found in Saidiya Hartman's *Lose Your Mother*, Erna Brodber's *Woodside Pear Tree Grove P.O.*, and Sonja Boon's *What the Oceans Remember*. However, when Behar first started publishing, such critical moves were unusual enough that Natalia Rachel Singer coined the term "hybrid memoir" to describe them.[16] "Hybrid" suggests the liminal nature of Behar's work. Neither anthropology nor strictly life writing, it straddles both in its efforts to document Cuban Jewish culture as well as Behar's experience as a child immigrant to the United States.

The life writings discussed in this chapter by Behar, Danticat, and Vilar were published between 2007 and 2010.[17] These dates are significant for a historically informed analysis of Caribbean life writing. A confluence of intellectual currents came together during this time period that created a space where narratives like these could be published. Key among these was the "biographical turn," or the movement within African diaspora studies to understand more about the internal lives or subjectivities of the enslaved.[18] Related to this is the "memoir boom" in publishing. Julie Rak argues that memoir became popular in the 1990s because it allows readers to process global events through narratives of individual lives.[19] Behar's early work marks a boom conterminous with the memoir boom as academics began combining scholarship and life writing. Behar writes of this period, "Can it be an accident that the desire which overtook a wide range of American scholars trained in a variety of academic disciplines to write in newly meaningful ways, which refused anonymity and authority and instead sought connection, intimacy and passion, came as the century was ending?"[20] The work of feminist scholars like Burton and Behar brought down the dividing line between "History," thought of in terms of large-scale political events, and women's experiences, previously relegated to marginal areas of study.

As an anthropologist, poet, and memoirist, Behar writes didactically, teaching her audience how to read her work, and in a sense read her. Behar speaks to multiple audiences, arguing for the inclusion of the personal in violation of older norms of anthropology, while revealing to a lay audience some of the methodological quandaries anthropologists face, such as how to remove the personal when one is writing about conversations and actions one personally witnessed during fieldwork. Behar teaches her academic audience about the potential of life writing to transform academic work, while informing a lay audience how a perspective influenced by critical theory allows for a deeper understanding of experiences that may seem to be singular. Behar's attempt to tie personal narrative and anthropology together is a gendered practice—in an effort to not be interpreted as too emotional or soft (designations coded as feminine) by anthropologists, but also not to be too intellectual—to appear not to have a heart to her family and community, which is also coded as a violation of feminine norms.[21]

Behar's works acknowledge recent popular and scholarly interest in Cuban Jews and Jewish culture in the Caribbean, while arguing for the continuing necessity to explain where she comes from and how Jewish and Cuban identities came to inhabit one body.[22] "Once in America," Behar writes, "they would forever have to explain that they were Cubans who also 'happened' to be Jewish."[23] Behar's family history tells the broader history of Jews in Cuba. Her mother's family was Ashkenazi Jews who emigrated from Poland and Russia to Cuba in the 1920s. Her father's Ladino-speaking family left Turkey in the 1920s, settling into different Cuban neighborhoods and synagogues than the Ashkenazi Jews. Her parents' families were united by religion but separated by much else, including language and class. Behar notes that for her Yiddish-speaking Ashkenazi grandparents, "Spanish . . . was the language of the goyim, but for my paternal grandparents it was precisely the language of their Jewishness, a thread that wound its way back to Ladino, the fifteenth-century Spanish that Sephardim wrote with Hebrew letters."[24] While there have been Jews in Cuba since Europeans first arrived, Behar's family story of immigration represents a swelling of their numbers in the twentieth century, estimated to reach fifteen to twenty thousand before Fidel Castro gained power in 1959. The Behar family's story of emigration is also typical—almost all Cuban Jews left in the years after 1959, fearing that the Cuban government would confiscate religious properties as well as redistribute personal wealth. Most Cuban Jews settled in the United States, but some went to Israel. Behar's family did both—leaving immediately for Israel and then gaining permission to come to the United States, where they lived in Queens, New York.

While Behar's corpus has been justly celebrated, I focus here on *An Island Called Home: Returning to Jewish Cuba* (2007) and how it creates an alternative archive even as it troubles that category. Behar writes from a position of exile and loss, but with a consciousness that the welcome given to Cuban Jews stands in contrast to hostile U.S. immigration policies for other Caribbean and Latinx groups. Referencing Jose Martí's rejection of the new American empire, Behar writes, "I am *cubana* because the border between 'our America' and 'the America which is not ours' is a real border guarded by guns and decorated with ink."[25] Behar repeatedly claims her Cuban identity and her status as an insider, but it is her American passport and occupation as an anthropologist that allow her to travel to Cuba. Behar's profession gives her a freedom of movement unlike that of others in her community in either Cuba or the United States. In order to overcome travel bans to Cuba by the United States and the Cuban government's strict control over the return of Cuban-born exiles, Behar had to organize her trips under the umbrella of anthropological research. Autobiography or creative writing were not state-sanctioned reasons for return, but anthropology as a "scientific" field was (*Island* 18). Anthropology as a profession also allowed Behar to depoliticize her trips, which conflicted with many Cuban exiles' belief that no one should return to Cuba while Fidel Castro was in power.

An Island Called Home begins with Behar's grandmother Esther asking her, "What did you lose in Cuba?" Esther immigrated from Poland and labored to earn passage for her family to Cuba before the Holocaust. The potential for state violence in a place that incarcerates writers and dissidents informs Behar's family's understanding of the dangers of Cuba. For Esther, who left Cuba after Castro came to power, the United States is home. Ruth's repeated returns to a dangerous place do not make sense. For Behar, Cuba represents a longed-for former home. Writing of a longing for Cuba that cannot be fulfilled places Behar in the company of other Cuban American writers. Indeed, Cuban American literature is filled with similar moments, such as in Christina García's novel *Dreaming in Cuban* (1992), where a character muses, "Cuba is a particular exile, I think, an island-colony. We can reach it by a thirty-minute charter flight from Miami, yet never reach it at all."[26] However, Behar's Jewishness creates a sense of urgency for return related to the dwindling numbers of Cuban Jews. The world her parents knew in Havana in the 1950s is nearly gone. She estimates that there are about thirty Cuban people remaining whose parents are both Jewish, and a larger community of between one to two thousand. The family archive comes to represent evidence of Behar's family's life, but also a memorial to the presence of Jews in Cuba generally.

Behar's family photographs of their life in Cuba before immigrating become a way for her to enter into Cuban American history, as something tangible to link her to more public history making. As a child immigrant, Behar's first source of materials about Cuba is her family's photographs as well as their oral histories, rather than her own memories. "Growing up in New York, I was grateful for the little archive of black-and-white photographs my parents and grandparents were able to salvage in the midst of our hurried departure.... Looking at the photographs of my family in Cuba was how I first saw Cuba again, the Cuba I wanted to remember" (13). Labeling her family's collection of photographs an archive, Behar recognizes that they uniquely preserve memories of being Jewish in Cuba in a way official archives of immigration of Cubans to the United States do not. Just as Cruz's Dominicanas NYC represents an alternative archive, *Island Called Home* documents the loss and trauma experienced after the Jewish exodus from Cuba. The photographs testify that her family before leaving Cuba was full of "hope," in contrast to her family post-immigration, when they were "traumatized and scared" (12).

Two formal characteristics help Behar create an absence aesthetic for her counter-archive. First, in *Island Called Home*—and, as we will see later, in Danticat's and Vilar's work as well—time is sped up, slows, or skips as a means of representing how archival absences and epistemological uncertainty influence how knowledge gets transmitted in the present. Second, all three authors mobilize photography or film—either reproduced within the text for Behar and Vilar or vividly described for Danticat. Images serve as evidence of their connection to the Caribbean, of traumatic events, and of the passage of time. The historicity of the Behar family's emigration from Cuba and the transmission of this journey in the present through archival images bear a relationship to Marianne Hirsch's theory of "postmemory." Postmemory describes how trauma is transmitted intergenerationally in life writing, often through photography, so that descendants describe these experiences as their own memories.[27] Not coincidentally, Behar's work bears traces of postmemory, given that some of Hirsch's main examples come from children and grandchildren of those who survived the Holocaust. Behar's family left Europe "just in the nick of time—it was 1934, the eve of the Holocaust when they set foot in the tropics," but they lived with the shadow of how quickly a government could turn against them, a fear reactivated under Castro.[28] Photographs of the Behar family in Cuba provide evidence of their existence there, and for Ruth they become a stand-in for her own memories.[29]

Cuba looms for Behar as a place where some form of recuperation of the losses of history can happen, such as the multiple displacements her family experienced in the twentieth century, which is a form of archival dreams. One of the key differences between Behar's experience of diaspora and those of the Indo- or Afro-Caribbean diasporas explored in this book is that aspects of her family's past are recoverable. Behar's account of visiting her grandparents' hometown during her first visit to Cuba and being offered a list of names of her ancestors contrasts with the absences found by other Caribbean writers. Behar writes, "'Does anybody remember los polacos viejos?' I ask, and as we stand around outside the mint green store entrance, a little circle forms around us, and older men begin to utter the names of my great-grandparents, my grandparents, my great-aunts and great-uncles: Abraham, Hannah, Esther, Maximo, Jaime, Dora, Irene. . . . Just hearing the names coming from the lips of these men, I feel my lifeline extending."[30] Contrast this memory to that of Hartman in Ghana, as discussed in chapter 1, listening to girls in a circle sing about those who were sold into slavery. Only the event of enslavement can be remembered, while learning specific names is impossible.

At the same time as Ruth experiences a sense of belonging in Cuba, it comes to stand in for her *as* the past, a past fraught with anxiety. She must return to Cuba again and again like a dog worrying a bone—because what she searches for cannot be named or perhaps even found. Caribbean writing's relationship to history is one filled with affect—anxiety, repetition, and fear—which can manifest in a lack of narrative confidence. David Scott states, "Indeed, the Caribbean novel almost by definition has been saturated with an obsessive 'quarrel' with the past, one that makes of the past a pervasively recurrent *question*; it has been saturated with an anxious sense that the past, whatever it is, cannot be taken for granted."[31] I read Behar's confession of desire for her own memories, for her own history (both photographic and textual) to be documented in *Island Called Home* through formal choices that reflect a Caribbean relationship to the vexed nature of history—one that informs life writing as much as the novel.

Structurally, the opening and concluding sections rehearse Behar's family history but are accompanied by family photographs, current images of places resonant to her family, such as the Patronato Synagogue in Havana, and images of materials that might be found in a museum or archive of Jewish Cuban life, such as others' passports or tombstones. Periodization, and thus time, becomes blurred as uncaptioned photographs and documents from before 1945 are juxtaposed with images from the 1960s to the present, suggesting the present's continuity with the past. The book creates a memorial as it documents through ethnography and visual evidence what Jewish immigrants brought to the island, such as the uniform one of them wore in a Nazi concentration camp. By attempting to unite anthropology and photography, Behar hoped to avoid exoticizing Cuban Jews through a tourist's gaze. However, the uneven pedantic tone and the presence of explanatory passages for some photographs but not others reveal the multiplicity of the text's intended audience. Depending on their positionality, most readers will move between varying levels of knowledge about Judaism, European and Caribbean history, and U.S. foreign policy.

Behar makes formal choices that also confound an easy understanding of the purpose and audience of *Island Called Home*. First, Behar notes the American "fascination" in the 2000s with Cuban Jews, who are an "over-studied, over-observed, and over-photographed tribe" (31). The archive Behar wishes to create is, by her own admission, not unique. Indeed, many of the people she interviews are also interviewed in *The Chosen Island: Jews in Cuba* (2005) by Mariza Corrales.[32] Behar does not explain how and why she chose the subjects she interviewed. The text's explanation or lack thereof can be vexing—in many instances assuming that the reader knows little to nothing about Caribbean and/or Jewish history, as in its detailed chronology beginning with the expulsion of the Jews from Spain in 1492. Other times, Behar does not define terms, such as "making an aliyah to Israel," or practices that illustrate cultural difference among Jews, such as the Sephardic practice of lighting a bowl of oil rather than Shabbat candles.

From a life writing perspective, the text contains no single narrative point of view because Behar's personal reflections and family history move in and out of focus. Behar's collaboration with photographer Humberto Mayol complicates the interpretation of *Island Called Home* since the text often does not offer the reader information about the photographs. Together they create an image-rich text documenting the lives of Jews still living in Cuba, but the images have no captions and their connection to the text is not always clear. When Mayol declares that his photographs can stand on their own as art, while Behar's contribution is secondary, "documentarian" (259), Behar is injured by his suggestion. She sees her role as offering "epiphanies . . . disturbing flashes of insight that had failed to appear in my fieldnotes, but which haunted me long after the encounters had taken place" (259). In the conclusion to *Island Called Home*, Behar writes that the text emerged in response to the photographs, rather than the more typical example of finding photographs to illustrate an author's text (260–261).

While Behar writes of her ethnographic process of observing and chronicling Jewish Cuban life as a potentially oppositional process to that of including the photographs, I believe this is actually a life narrative problem. The curatorial process for Behar involves a decidedly nondetached or objective anthropological perspective about the Mayol photos, as she memorizes each of them, placing value on them that is the same as those in her family photo album. While documenting the images and daily lives of Jews living in contemporary Cuba, Behar turns their life narratives into hers: "I treated them as I had the old black-and-white family photographs from Cuba, but, unlike the old photographs that were surrogates for the memories I longed to have, Humberto's elicited true memories" (261). Behar's biographical project in *Island Called Home* transforms into the autobiographical as the stories and photographs chosen for publication stand in for the memories she has now made for herself in Cuba. Her "surrogate" memories of Cuba through her family's photographic archive are now supplemented by a text that appears to be about others but instead represents Behar's experiences on the island.

My suggestion that Behar heals through surrogate memories of Cuba until she has her own supports a critique of her privilege and transnational mobility. However, though Behar's approach to curating images and stories in *Island Called Home* reads as somewhat haphazard, it can also be understood as an example of Édouard Glissant's concept of opacity. Glissant calls the state's interest in quantifying identities the "requirement for transparency" for those who are othered.[33] "Transparency" fixes the identity of the other as a known quality, whether real or not, which can subsequently be policed. Instead, Glissant suggests a politics of "opacity," where difference can be recognized without being placed in a hierarchy or even fully understood. "Every Other is a citizen and no longer a barbarian," he suggests.[34] No one voice or portrayal of Cuban Jewish life dominates the narrative, including Behar's. Her family autobiography, woven with her mini-biographies of Cuban Jews, creates a multivocal narrative. Some of the people interviewed support Castro, relieved that communism and religion are now seen as compatible (79). Others subtly critique the suppression of religion and the poverty they experienced after the revolution. Behar calls this "de-assimilation," when an assimilated Cuban chooses to return to the Jewish faith as a sign of their rejection of Castro and communism (85). The multiple origins of Cuban Ashkenazi and Sephardic Jews, archived in the photographs of themselves holding pictures of their parents' Polish or Turkish passports as well as documents related to their own life stories, represent a challenge to the transparency demanded by the state. Sidonie Smith argues that "the autobiographer's specific body is not one culturally charged and categorized body, unified, stable, finite, or final."[35] Behar, like her interlocutors in *Island Called Home*, holds multiple positionalities in her writing that attest to the fluidity of identity in the "I" of life writing: traumatized immigrant, privileged university professor, both Sephardic and Ashkenazi, Jewish, and also Cuban.

Although Behar finds success in working with the Jewish community in Cuba to create an alternative archive of those still living there and a memorial to those who left, her authority as a woman to write and determine a larger narrative does not extend to her family. Family autobiographers depend on family narratives for their writing, with or without approval. Behar describes the aftermath of publishing an essay on encouraging her grandmother, referred to as "Baba" in the essay, to take possession of her father Abraham's handwritten autobiography about Jewish life in Poland before emigrating to Cuba in the 1930s. "The Book," as Behar's family calls it, was long in the possession of Abraham's oldest and wealthiest son. When he asks for the book to be returned, Ruth encourages her grandmother to resist the male prerogative of ownership. "Just as Jacob stole Esau's birthright with the complicity of his mother, my Baba stole 'The Book' from her brother to pass on to me. I am glad we were such good thieves. To want to be a scholar and a writer was not easy in my family."[36] As a child, when Ruth is encouraged to stop reading and focus on a practical career, or just get married, it is Baba who says she takes after Abraham and should be allowed to become a scholar. In Baba's possession, Abraham's words undergo an alchemy of translation; the Yiddish text is read aloud by Baba, who translates it into Spanish so Behar could then put those words back into writing. Behar authorizes herself as a scholar and as the rightful possessor of an important heirloom: "Soon after my grandmother died . . . I rushed it home like looted treasure. I buried it in my fireproof cabinet, where I also keep old family pictures and other memorabilia from Cuba."[37] "The Book" joins the archive of family photographs that served as a catalyst for Behar's life writing in *Island Called Home*, with Behar as chief archivist.

"Such Good Thieves," as the article was titled when it was published in the Jewish women's magazine *Hassadah*, infuriated Behar's extended family since it portrayed Baba as complicit in Behar's desire to own "The Book." No doubt the exposure of this family secret in a magazine read by the Jewish community played a part in her family's reaction. Behar's uncle, in particular, challenges her right to own the original handwritten copy, saying that perhaps the book was meant to be passed down to his father, who was Abraham's son, and not to

Ruth's grandmother. Ruth's uncle calls into question her legitimacy as a scholar, threatening to report Behar to her university: "You're the kind of scholar who'd do anything to get the documents you want, aren't you?" (*Traveling* 43). Her uncle hurls gendered insults, accusing Ruth of being self-serving and careerist, insistent on telling her own story, rather than deferential to older male relatives and bowing to the wishes of her family. Still, even as Ruth cries tears of shame, she refuses to give her uncle the manuscript. She remains the keeper of the family history, the one who will choose how to memorialize their past. Behar claims the right to own her family's archival materials and to control the family history released to the public. While Behar boldly asserts her power, in the next section we will see how Danticat in her own family autobiography writes of her inability to control what happens to her family, and the larger narrative that can be told about them, caught as they are between Haiti and the United States.

"We-moir": Memorializing Haiti

Danticat's work reveals a recurrent theme regarding who has the right to memorialize Haitian history. While Behar claims her right to "looted treasure," Danticat is far more ambivalent about her right to represent her family, or Haiti. Danticat writes in *Create Dangerously*, "Grappling with memory is, I believe, one of the many complicated Haitian obsessions. We have, it seems, a collective agreement to remember our triumphs and gloss over our failures. Thus, we speak of the Haitian revolution as though it happened just yesterday but we rarely speak of the slavery that prompted it" (63–64). Danticat's life writing is thus emplotted by absence, structured by grappling with absence as an epistemological problem that cannot be solved once and for all but must be addressed. Recall from chapter 1 Glissant's formulation of Caribbean history as a "nonhistory" produced through violence, the purposeful colonization of the Caribbean for the purposes of profit in distinction to European nations' "history" as a story of nationalism and culture.[38] Danticat writes into that "nonhistory" by recognizing the silences and absences within what is remembered about Haitian history within Haiti.

What distinguishes Danticat's work in *Create Dangerously* and in her memoir *Brother, I'm Dying* ([2007] 2008) from texts that otherwise have much in common, such as Jamaica Kincaid's nonfiction *A Small Place* (1998), which also addresses issues of the Caribbean postcolonial state, or *My Brother* (1997), a memoir of her brother's death from AIDS, is that Danticat manifests a sustained engagement with the politics of historical absence and recovery. This focus on absence as a motivation for creation distinguishes Danticat's life writing from other Caribbean narratives focused on telling a life story, even those critical of colonization like Kincaid's. Danticat's stylistic choice to have multiple perspectives represents a challenge to the idea of the representativeness of the author of life writing for her community. Instead, she sees documenting a variety of perspectives as important for future readers. Writing "coming from where I come from, with the history I have—having spent the first twelve years of my life under the dictatorships of Papa Doc and his son, Jean-Claude," Danticat reveals that for her, the purpose of "creating dangerously" is the potential that "maybe years in the future, a future we may yet have to dream of, someone may risk his or her life to read us" (*Create* 10). Such an approach of accountability to those reading in the future suggests one method of decolonizing history. Indeed, Glissant resists the idea that there is a sole correct historical account is central to decolonization in the Caribbean: "One of the most disturbing consequences of colonization could well be this notion of a single History, and therefore of power, which has been imposed on others by the West."[39] Holding multiple timelines, narratives, and perspectives in one text is not banal gesturing at a diversity of viewpoints. Instead, such formal choices lay the groundwork for understanding how social, economic, and military power shape the construction of history, and are indeed a central facet of Caribbean poetics.

Though her book is titled *Create Dangerously: The Immigrant Artist at Work*, the opening pages of Danticat's second work of life writing begin with a discussion of neither writing nor immigration. Danticat places the reader in a crowd assembled in Haiti's national cemetery. The crowd is there to witness the execution of two political dissidents, Marcel Numa and Louis Drouin, by firing squad on November 12, 1964. Although Numa and Drouin successfully immigrated to the United States with their families, they later returned to Haiti. Members of the Jeune Haiti movement, they arrived with eleven comrades in August 1964 to incite the overthrow of dictator François Duvalier. Danticat narrates these first pages in a dispassionate tone, describing Numa and Drouin being tied to poles, given last rites, and shot. As with many aspects of Haitian history, the site of their execution is not marked by a memorial. Remarking on this absence, Danticat is told by a Haitian friend that if there were historical plaques everywhere in Haiti where someone was killed, the country would be filled with nothing but these memorials.

No official markers of the execution in the Haitian National cemetery exist, but immediately after the event, film of the execution played in movie theaters and on the state-controlled television stations. François Duvalier, the military dictator of Haiti during this period, used the execution as propaganda, distributing pamphlets praising the execution as evidence of the futility of resisting his regime. Images of Numa and Drouin's corpses were displayed as a reminder of the power of the state. Although their execution happened five years before Danticat's birth in 1969, it looms large in her imaginary. Danticat fills in details by talking to relatives, reading archived newspaper and magazine stories, and finally tracking down the video itself. The first sections are narrated as if Danticat is present, witnessing, and by extension so is the reader. Later in the text, Danticat lets the reader know that she is watching a version of the execution made by the Duvalier regime rather than witnessing the event herself. The film is an archival copy in which "time is slightly compressed . . . in some places the images skip. There is no sound" (*Create* 3).

Danticat's experience of viewing the film, the compression of time, the murkiness of the image, and the lack of sound mirror formal characteristics of the life writing as archives discussed in this chapter. *Brother I'm Dying* also contains these characteristics, as time stretches in the narrative upon learning that her father is dying, and at other times it is compressed, as when her uncle's whereabouts are unknown. Further, writing her family autobiography has similarities to writing recent Haitian history: what she can learn is partial and contains absences that cannot be filled. "What I learned from my father and uncle, I learned out of sequence and in fragments," Danticat writes (*Brother* 26). Although the stories of her father's and uncle's deaths are narrated in roughly chronological order, which I argue below is important to understanding the text as an archive of state violence, the details about their lives and deaths come to the reader in opaque pieces. Unlike Glissant's opacity as a deliberate strategy for recognizing difference without hierarchy, Danticat's relatives' experiences cannot be recovered precisely because they are marked as other and unimportant by the U.S. government.

Referencing archival footage, newspaper articles, and oral histories is a formal means to express affect related to the terror of living under a dictatorship where access to news is often fragmented and biased. "All artists, writers among them," Danticat states, "have several stories—one might call them creation myths—that haunt and obsess them. This is one of mine. I don't even remember when I first heard about it. I feel as though I have always known it, having filled in the curiosity-driven details though photographs, newspapers, books, and films as I have gotten older" (*Create* 5). In Haiti, murderers often remove their victims' eyes, Danticat writes, because of a folk belief that the dead's corneas bear an image of the last thing they saw. This theme of the dead whose history cannot be told relates to the lack of archives or memorials to state violence, making their victims disappear as well. *Create Dangerously* memorializes Numa and Drouin since there is no historical marker in the cemetery concerning their execution and no one knows where they are buried.

The rendering of multiple focal points grounded in historical events in this scene demonstrate Danticat's formal choices in writing what she calls "we-moir" rather than "me-moir."[40] I want to gather up these threads of the scopic, "we-moir," and memory to bring forward the trickiness of gendered self and community representation that Danticat navigates as a means of querying why the execution of Numa and Drouin takes center stage in *Create Dangerously*, and how that centrality offers a key to her other autobiographical writing. Danticat's movement between representativeness for the Haitian diaspora and being seen as an inauthentic figure, a foreigner with no firsthand knowledge, reveals how Caribbean studies shares with autobiography studies concerns over issues of representation and representativeness, authenticity, and testimony.[41]

Create Dangerously helps frame the political import of Danticat's first work of life writing. Danticat's obsession with Numa and Drouin and their return to try to rescue Haiti, and their failure, is a precursor to her own failure to save either her father from a slow death brought on by the stresses of racialized abuse as a cab driver or her uncle while detained by U.S. immigration authorities. *Brother, I'm Dying* is narrated in the present tense and tells the story of her father's and uncle's deaths in chronological order. This structure serves the purpose of relating the story as one would recount a testimony, making sure the beginning, middle, and end are clearly understood. The narrative tells the brothers' life histories, giving their stories complexity and explaining why one brother chose to leave Haiti and one chose to remain. The state demand for transparency, for easy categories of immigrant and visitor, is upended by Danticat's family story, where no one wants to leave Haiti but the political situation makes it impossible to stay.

Lorgia García-Peña suggests that if we want to understand how racialization serves to reinforce the borders of the nation, we must change our focus from geographical borderlands to the bodies that cross these boundaries. Describing "el nié" as a space occupied by those who are between unitary identities, García-Peña writes that it "signifies not the border space that the subject inhabits . . . but rather the body that carries the violent borders that deter them from entering the nation, from access to full citizenship and from public, cultural, historical, and political representation."[42] Danticat writes a hybrid memoir/biography of her father Mira and her uncle Joseph, what happens to their bodies in the course of the narrative, and how they are blocked from full citizenship in both Haiti and the United States. She draws on research on "official documents" as well as the oral histories shared by her father and uncle. However, Danticat carefully states that she is "writing this only because they can't," rather than taking ownership of her family's narrative like Behar (*Brother* 26). In October 2004, UN peacekeepers in conjunction with the Haitian national police carried out incursions against gangs located in Bel Air, where Danticat's uncle Joseph lived in Port-au-Prince. In the wake of neighborhood violence exacerbated by the UN, Joseph flies to Miami, where although he has a valid passport and visa, he is incarcerated. While resisting inflammatory language, Danticat makes it clear that Joseph's neighbors bear some responsibility for his death. Although he served as a minister in Bel Air for decades, local gangs blame him when the roof of his house is used by the military, who kill fifteen people. His church is looted and the altar burned by his neighbors. Joseph subsequently leaves for the United States. The chaos in Haiti and Joseph's sudden departure mean that Edwidge and her family are not sure where he is during this period. *Brother* narrates how an unstable communications infrastructure and political upheaval mean that Edwidge's only source of news about her uncle is online photographs that she has to digitally manipulate to see her uncle's house and the church where he is a pastor (168). Ironically, she must rely on a source of information that she knows is only partial and often inaccurate, provided by a U.S. media that frequently portrays Haiti in the worst possible light.

Joseph arrived in the United States with a valid passport and visa but claimed asylum. Perhaps he became confused by INS questions, or perhaps he truly meant to seek refugee status. The result was that he was taken into detention without access to his medicine and without the device he used to speak after having throat cancer. Joseph experiences a medical emergency in the Krome detention center in Florida, a place Danticat visited previously as a member of the Florida Immigrant Advocacy Center looking into human rights abuses (*Brother* 211). Although some of Danticat's writing about U.S. neocolonialism is stated so politely I wonder if some of her popularity is based on underestimations of her ferocity, the end of *Brother* pulls no punches. "Was my uncle going to jail because he was Haitian? This is a question he probably asked himself. This is a question I still ask myself. Was he going to jail because he was black? If he were white, Cuban, anything other than Haitian, would he be going to Krome?" (223). This moment in *Brother* reminds us that when we read this group of texts, as I suggest we do, as laterally co-constructing epistemologies about Caribbean history, there are hierarchies within them. Behar's family was allowed to migrate to the United States under policies that encouraged those born in Cuba to leave as part of the United States' ideological stance against communism. No such policies exist to assist the Haitian people en masse, although they are also experiencing political and economic turmoil. U.S. policies of anti-Blackness, illustrated in 2018 by U.S. president Donald Trump, who stated that all Haitians have AIDS and that Haiti is a "shithole" country, contributed to Joseph's death.[43]

To communicate this complexity, *Brother, I'm Dying*'s structure leads the reader to believe that this is a story of Danticat's father's illness and death. In reality, *Brother* is as much a way to document her uncle's death while in INS custody in Florida. Beginning from a point of unknowing, with Danticat's father and uncle still alive in the present tense of the narration, demonstrates the constraints on the flow of knowledge across borders. Edwidge as the narrator often does not know what is happening with her family in Haiti as a result of political violence or natural disasters. Such a tension in the narrative is a deliberate result of formal choices. Danticat knows all along, of course, the endings of her father's and uncle's life stories, just as she knows that Numa and Drouin will die through state violence, but she structures the narrative as if the outcome is unknown. Consider that *Brother, I'm Dying* could have had a radically different structure. The narrative could have begun from the perspective of the Edwidge Danticat, whom the public knew as an accomplished author and immigration rights advocate, and proceeded to tell the story of how her uncle's life ended with his entirely avoidable death while being unnecessarily incarcerated.[44]

Danticat holds her father and her uncle in *Brother, I'm Dying* as worthy of memorialization, a gendered distinction between her text and other matrifocal works examined in this book, such as Maryse Condé's tracing of her grandmother's life, Lorna Goodison's celebration of her mother, and Gaiutra Bahadur's writing about her great-grandmother's journey from India to Guyana. More typically, life writing about fathers is written by sons with whom they have a troubled relationship, according to G. Thomas Couser. Couser calls such life writing texts "narratives of filiation," often deliberate attempts to establish a "relationality" between father and son after a lifetime of discord.[45] However, Edwidge is well cared for by both her uncle and father. External forces of economic underdevelopment and neocolonialism in Haiti separate Edwidge from her father, who must go abroad to look for work, and then later from her uncle, after UN peacekeepers make his neighborhood dangerous. Still, I find "filiation" helpful for understanding Danticat's work in *Brother, I'm Dying* from a familial but also transnational perspective. The text insists that both men should have had the right to full citizenship and rights in the United States and Haiti. Edwidge's troubled relationship, then, is with her *patrias*, her homes of Haiti and the United States. In telling the story of her father figures, she also claims her right to be a citizen of Haiti in spite of those who might call her a parasite. Thus, she seeks to filiate herself with Haiti, despite the many contradictions involved in being Haitian American.

Put baldly, even with Danticat's education, connections, and knowledge about the U.S. immigration system, she cannot rescue her uncle when he is taken into detention. Danticat writes in *Create Dangerously*, published three years after *Brother*, "Many of my family members in Haiti [have] always overestimated my ability to do things . . . to get people out of bad situations. . . . I hope I can help. I have sometimes succeeded in helping, but mostly I have failed. Case in point: my elderly uncle died trying to enter the United States. I could not save him" (169). *Brother, I'm Dying* and *Create Dangerously* reveal an archive of Haitian lives impacted by state violence. While *Brother* could have started with the incarceration of her uncle and the death of her father, it instead offers a view of the profound effects of U.S. neocolonialism on their lives. In the context of Haitian-U.S. relationships, these include the invasion of Haiti in the 1930s, Danticat's own painful separation from her parents for nearly a decade as a result of U.S. immigration policies that made it difficult for her to join them, and U.S. policies that supported the Duvalier regime.

Danticat knows she cannot enter into the front door of "History" with the stories of state violence she wants to tell, so she invokes the backstairs as a metaphor, calling to mind the entrance to the Great House for servants and slaves, as well as Haitians trying to reach the United States on barely seaworthy boats. "I want to find those backstairs over and over and keep a map of them for future generations."[46] By naming her process as "mapping," Danticat calls to mind Dionne Brand's story of intergenerational failure to transmit history in *A Map to the Door of No Return*. Brand's grandfather's inability to give her a sense of their ancestors and how they came to be in Trinidad is a gap that cannot be bridged. "It was a rupture in history, a rupture in the quality of being. It was also a physical rupture, a rupture of geography," Brand writes (4–5). Danticat offers her mode of life writing as a map she can give to future generations. This map may not overcome all of the archival absences in these two texts, such as the aporias related to her uncle's death while in state custody. But her work does map those absences in ways that function as an archive of power structures that are important for understanding how the histories of European slavery and American neocolonialism have very real impacts on the valuation of Haitian lives. By emphasizing that her work is a collective reckoning, "we-moir," Danticat's method recalls Maryse Condé's emphasis in chapter 2, that the formal innovation of Caribbean literature consists of its multivalent perspectives. Danticat offers this map to the past, but it is also, in the final analysis, a guide to epistemological questions related to the instability of historical knowledge.

"The Product of Repetitions": A Puerto Rican Quarrel with History

Irene Vilar's *The Ladies' Gallery: A Memoir of Family Secrets* ([1996] 2009) can be understood as a narrative entirely about the instability of historical knowledge.[47] Vilar fuses two seemingly separate stories in her memoir. One narrates the experience of a troubled teenager who leaves Puerto Rico to attend college on the mainland, becomes suicidal, and is committed to a psychiatric hospital in the 1980s. The other is a narrative that creates an archive of the aftermath of an act of political violence toward the U.S. government by Vilar's grandmother, Lolita Lebrón, a woman hailed as a hero by Puerto Rican nationalists. Lebrón famously claimed of her attack on the U.S. Congress, "Yo no vine a matar. Yo vine a morir" (I didn't come here to kill. I came to die), presenting herself as a sacrificial martyr rather than an assassin. *The Ladies' Gallery*, referring to the gender-segregated space in the U.S. Congress, also references the text's preoccupation with understanding what women owe to political movements, and what they owe to their families. Vilar wrestles with Lebrón's gendered framing by the U.S. media as a femme fatale terrorist and with Puerto Rican nationalist interpretations of her as the mother of the nation. Lebrón left her two children with her mother as she became more involved with independence movements and the attack on Congress. Vilar dryly notes, "The Nation is the mother, and

Lolita, who may have had trouble in being a mother before, now would not hesitate to die for that nation" (93). I read Vilar's project as one of "dememorialization," taking apart the mythologies surrounding her grandmother. In contrast to Cruz, Behar, and Danticat, Vilar is not surfacing a little-known story so it can be remembered in the future. By writing about her famous grandmother from an insider's perspective, Vilar destabilizes the idea that a single perspective, whether it is that of the U.S. government, Puerto Rican independence activists, or Lebrón's family, can fully represent the complicated figure of her grandmother. Vilar creates a counter-archive of Puerto Rican women's lives that is different from both state archives *and* that of the Puerto Rican Nationalist Movement in the service of rejecting what she sees as limitations on Puerto Rican women's identity.

In 1954, Lebrón, along with three other activists, entered what was then known as the Ladies' Gallery of the U.S. Congress. Lebrón shouted "Viva Puerto Rico Libre!" and the group fired their weapons, injuring five congressmen. The group claimed that they shot at the seal of the U.S. Congress, and that any injuries were the result of ricocheting bullets.[48] Although the court determined that Lebrón shot in the air and did not bear responsibility for the congressmen's injuries, she nevertheless was sentenced in 1954 to fifty-seven years in prison. Lebrón was given a stay of clemency by President Carter in 1979. The Puerto Rico Nationalist Party's ideas of liberation and sovereignty, predictably, are less well documented by the mainstream press than these dramatic actions. Many Puerto Ricans celebrated Lebrón's actions, meant to draw attention to the cause of Puerto Rican independence, with some calling her "the Joan of Arc of Puerto Rico."[49] Lebrón died in 2010, with *Time* magazine reporting that whether you "call her a hero or a terrorist . . . she will likely be remembered as both."[50] The story was widely covered by the media, and thus Lebrón and her coconspirators' actions entered into the archive of U.S. history, where their actions were labeled as "terrorism" rather than presented with a more complex understanding of their role in the struggle for Puerto Rican sovereignty.

Like the ambiguity of Lebrón's attack on the U.S. Congress, Puerto Rico occupies a liminal space as a U.S. territory. Puerto Ricans are U.S. citizens, but Puerto Rico does not have the same representation within Congress as a state. Most recent polls show that the island remains equally divided over the question of statehood. The *New York Times* reported in 2017 that on the mainland 46 percent of Americans are unaware that Puerto Ricans are U.S. citizens, lumping them into an already-existing category of unwanted Latinx immigrants.[51] As such, the complexity of Puerto Rican identity corresponds to Glissant's idea of opacity, which is "that which cannot be reduced, which is the most perennial guarantee of participation and confluence."[52] These differences in perceptions create differences in resources, such as the austerity measures instituted by the Puerto Rican Oversight, Management and Economic Stability Act

(PROMESA) in 2016, and the documented discrepancies between 2018 recovery efforts in Texas after Hurricane Harvey in comparison to those three weeks later in Puerto Rico after Hurricane Maria.[53] While these are recent examples, the tension between Puerto Ricans' citizenship and the recognition of the unequal distribution of U.S. resources also form the foundation of Lebrón's fight for sovereignty for Puerto Rico. However, the U.S. version of Lebrón's actions does not tell the full story. Lebrón, like Danticat's uncle, exists outside of the filiation required by the state. Outsiders to the state become, as Imani Perry writes, "an obstacle to the ordering of society that therefore, according to the dominant power, must either be made transparent or destroyed. Or, I would add, mapped in ways that mark them, if not for absolute destruction, then for systematic debasement and punishment."[54] Both Lebrón and Joseph are separated from their families and subject to humiliation.

What Lebrón experiences in her long incarceration, including being raped, tortured, and isolated, can be mapped onto Puerto Rico's history first with Spain and then the United States. "Where I come from, rape, metaphorical and literal rape, is considered the spark of our history, and solitude its human consequence" (5), Vilar explains, similar to Danticat's assertion ("Coming from where I come from, with the history I have") of the necessity of writing about dangerous topics as someone who grew up in Haiti with the afterlife of colonialism. This explanation of Puerto Rican origins stemming from rape does not satisfy Vilar because it is told from the male colonizer's point of view. As in previous chapters where the descendants of the enslaved or indentured seek the subjectivity of their ancestors but find it cannot be recovered easily, Vilar demands to know: "But where was *she* all this time?" (5). "She" refers to the stereotype of the inexplicable, or sexualized, or martyred Latin American woman.

Lebrón's actions for the liberation of Puerto Rico allowed her to be understood easily within anticolonial tropes of the mother of the nation. Certainly, Lebrón's story is one of resistance to political and cultural colonization in Puerto Rico, the very definition of an anticolonial romance where folk triumph over their colonial oppressors. In an interview, Lebrón recounts that Pedro Albizu Campos taught her and other members of the party that "*la patria era valor y sacrificio.*"[55] As I have argued elsewhere, mothers of the nation in Caribbean twentieth-century anticolonial discourse are meant to embody the spirit of the people, especially the rural folk, while not typically being active in the work of nation building.[56] Lebrón, with her roots in the Puerto Rican countryside, encapsulates a reverence for the folk and the working class. At the same time, her willingness to sacrifice herself in the name of national freedom is read not in terms of the actions of a leader, but in terms of those of a maternal martyr, also conforming to David Scott's idea that anticolonial romance in the present inevitably turns into tragedy.[57]

Irene describes Lebrón's act and her embodiment of maternal national sacrifice as her "inheritance," and it is this history passed down to her that constitutes the counter-archive created in *The Ladies' Gallery*. This text is not so much a memorialization of Lebrón, unlike some hagiographies passing as interviews of her. Rather, the text accounts for how Lebrón both defied cultural expectations for Puerto Rican women to be nonpolitical but also fulfilled them in her choice to martyr herself for a cause: "In school, a story that became a metaphor for me, a mask magnified by nostalgia. Granddaughter of a Puerto Rican nationalist, a woman who spent twenty-seven years of her life in the women's prison at Alderson, West Virginia" (3). The inheritance of Lebrón's history serves as a screen that for much of the narrative obscures Irene's own identity. Irene's life is not simply one lived in the shadow of a famous relative, but is rather a life altered by Lebrón's absence as well as her actions. This absence, from Irene's perspective, left her mother vulnerable to an early disastrous marriage with no support for her later depression. Intergenerational trauma represents one of the repetitions with a difference Vilar explores, as she repeats aspects of her mother's and grandmother's lives. In Vilar's telling, rather than freeing Lebrón's descendants, her actions precipitated a shattering of her family. Vilar writes that her mother, Gladys Mendez, committed suicide in front of her by jumping out of a car. Lebrón's later religiosity and possible mental illness further strain their relationship in a reenactment of the abandonment Mendez felt in the wake of Lebrón's choice of political work and violent action over staying with her family in Puerto Rico. In turn, Vilar tries repeatedly to end her life while she is in college. The publication of *The Ladies' Gallery* was reported to have led to full estrangement between Vilar and Lebrón. Lebrón described *The Ladies' Gallery* as "full of lies," particularly in reference to Mendez's death being portrayed as a suicide.[58]

In common with representations of time as compressed or sped-up time as in Danticat's and Behar's narratives, *The Ladies' Gallery* lurches back and forth from the psychiatric hospital, where time is described as standing still, to accounts of Puerto Rican history and interactions with Irene's grandmother that are paced very rapidly. This change in narrative tone is part of the liminal status of the archive Vilar builds. One of the purposes of the narrative's turgid passages about Irene's time in the hospital is to link Irene's own experiences to those of her grandmother's related experience of a lengthy incarceration: "Many times, faint at the very sight of a clock's hands turning past the hour, I would sink sideways into my chair, clinging to the second that had just elapsed. . . . In college one has that Borgean sense that it is possible to be many without even trying to be one. . . . And to answer this question demands a sort of expository skill, a shuffling of ideas I was not able to do" (6). Unable to cope with time passing, Irene also cannot respond to the transitions expected of a college student and remains stuck in a suicidal depression.

The rapid changes and challenges to Vilar's identity when she moves to the United States and enrolls in college mirror the multiple modes of the U.S. colonization of Puerto Rico that form the backdrop of *The Ladies' Gallery*. These include the 1917 Jones Act, granting (or forcing, depending on your perspective) U.S. citizenship to Puerto Ricans, Operation Bootstrap, which forcibly rerouted the island's economy from an agrarian basis to industries focused on export and caused widespread unemployment and immigration to the mainland, and the Commonwealth Constitution in 1953, making Puerto Rico a territory but not a state of the United States. Vilar finds herself trapped by imposed identities that subsume her: as an American citizen she is not offered services to accommodate her adjustment to a predominately white and English-speaking university, but neither can she inhabit the figure of the revolutionary dreamed of by her grandmother.

Just as Behar discursively returns to the same events and objects in her past, such as her family's photo archive, and Danticat acknowledges the Haitian pastime of "grappling with memory" that she participates in by rewatching the Numa and Drouin film, Vilar identifies herself as "the product of repetitions" (2). Sandra Ruiz suggests that the many transitions between forms of colonization in Puerto Rico inform contemporary artistic representations that feature "eternal looping [exposing] what is done to the material, national, and discursive body in the name of historical expansionism."[59] Whether we call it "looping" or an obsession with the quarrel with history, *The Ladies' Gallery* contains many examples of recursivity as Irene cycles from one feminine archetype to another. She explores being imprisoned and a mystic or a beautiful martyr to others' wishes. These personal experiences are narrated and renarrated throughout the text, as Irene tries to embody what she perceives to be Puerto Rican female archetypes. In particular, *The Ladies' Gallery* repeatedly references the many press photos of Vilar's grandmother being arrested and during her trial. Like Cruz, Behar, and Danticat, Vilar enters into Caribbean history through images.

Images are central to Lebrón's legacy. Photographs of Lebrón attracted media attention, gaining an "iconic" status. The circulation of Lebrón's image played a key role in establishing her as "the best-known Puerto Rican woman of the twentieth century, national heroine to many Puerto Ricans, and an international symbol of women anti-colonial fighters."[60] Even after her death, Lebrón's obituary in the *Washington Post* referenced photos of her arrest: "In the photograph, a striking Ms. Lebron wears a set jaw and a stylish skirt and jacket" (see fig. 4).[61] In the 1950s, during an era of communist panic, the image of a conventionally attractive woman who was capable of armed resistance challenged gendered American understandings of where the dangers against the state lay.[62]

Vilar reworks this news archive of a terrorist against the state, who is represented as stylish and striking, into an alternative archive. Some of these images are reprinted in the text along with family photos, rendering journalists' impersonal gaze on Lebrón into a broader view of Lebrón's life. Irene describes her grandmother as appearing familiar in these press photos from the 1950s that "show the familiar expression of pain . . . which haunts me since I first saw her,

Figure 4. "Puerto Rican Assault Leader Under Arrest," March 1, 1954. AP Photo. Image courtesy Library of Congress. Used with permission AP.

in 1977, at my mother's funeral" (85). The photos are elevated through the seriousness of Lebrón's actions and the improbable beauty of the clarity of the black-and-white 1950s gelatin silver prints. Vilar creates a new archival record of these images by connecting them together, almost as if she is creating a film from still images of the moments leading up to the shooting in the Capitol building. The photographs allow Irene an imaginative bridge between the present and the past. The narrative takes Lebrón's first-person perspective, something that did not happen in her representations in U.S. media. Laura Halperin observes, "Despite her notoriety/fame, though, immediately following her attack on Congress, none of the public portrayals of Lolita by the politicians or the media grant her a voice with which to explain herself."[63] Replacing the silenced images of Lebrón, Vilar give her a voice as she imagines Lebrón walking up the Capitol steps to what she assumes will be her death. "Hundreds, a thousand, the whole colonial past of America was there, its cruelties echoing at each step, unchanged, unforgotten: Mexico, Panama, Nicaragua, Cuba, Haiti . . . and of course, Puerto Rico, one of Spain's first New World Colonies, one of America's last" (86, ellipsis original). Vilar writes of Lebrón as connecting her action to the oppressions experienced across the Caribbean and in Central America. Yolanda Martínez-San Miguel suggests that another way to imagine these spaces is as "a decolonial archipelago, reimagined from below as a cultural and historical constellation or network of islands and communities and individuals" outside of their current constructions through the legacies of European imperialism and U.S. neoimperialism.[64] *The Ladies' Gallery* imagines from below the history of Puerto Rico as connected to liberation struggles elsewhere.

Indeed, *The Ladies' Gallery* documents a different kind of Caribbean identity. Vilar does not claim Lebrón's revolutionary certainty, nor the tragedy of her mother's suicide for her own life. In turn, she claims neither the political position of the until-now-failed bid for Puerto Rican independence, nor that of assimilation with the United States. She writes about navigating between these two legacies, "getting lost in order to be found, to be born again, thriving like this always on the edge, truly *caribeña*" (320). Vilar's epistemological uncertainty reflects her method of creating her own archive of being Puerto Rican. Writing, like assembling a physical archive, allows for a separation between a lived moment and documentation that it happened: "Distance is a proposition that points to an audience besides yourself. Distance is a book" (7). Gaining distance, for Vilar, involves charting the repetition of history in her grandmother's, mother's and her own life in order to choose for herself her identity.

By returning to her mother's and grandmother's life histories, but retelling their stories with her own, Vilar enacts a narrative intervention. She "untells" a story that comes up against archival limits, since her main sources are government records of her grandmother's crime. *The Ladies' Gallery* ends with a portrait of Lebrón, who is portrayed in her complexity, and with a sense of both the rightness of her cause and the destructive force of violence. Vilar moves into the subject position of "her," the one who was formerly silent but who now has a voice. In doing so, she joins Cruz's efforts to move Dominican women to the center of immigration stories, Behar's work to memorialize the Jewish diaspora in Cuba and the Jewish Cuban diaspora in the United States, and Danticat's portrayal of the human costs of an unyielding U.S. immigration policy. The strategy of writing communal life narratives to create lateral epistemologies allows all four of these writers to create counter-archives of where they are from.

For Cruz, Behar, Danticat, and Vilar to write their stories as immigrants is to write dangerously in the face of neocolonialism. Stretching across islands, their use of the languages of Kreyól, French, Spanish, Yiddish, and Ladino mirrors their differing histories of colonization. Behar articulates the importance of testimonio "as a crucial means of bearing witness and inscribing into history those lived realities that would otherwise succumb to the alchemy of erasure," something all of the texts in this chapter struggle against.[65] These authors address what it means to remember a Caribbean past and to imagine possible futures. Time in these narratives moves unevenly, showing how the project of Caribbean memorialization tells multiple histories in a variety of forms. Writing a collective story, whether it is called "we-moir" by Danticat or *testimonio* by Behar, constitutes a formal feature of these life writings, demonstrating Glissant's idea of the importance of working against the idea of a single historical narrative.[66] The shift in this chapter from a focus on archives created in the colonial period to those of the present day demonstrates that the impact of archival absences related to racialized and gendered determinations of whose lives are worthy of documentation and historicization continues to the present.

Figure 5. Firelei Báez, *Chrono-DREAMer*, 2019. Acrylic and oil on archival printed canvas. Collection of Nish & Pieternel de Gruiter. Courtesy of the artist and James Cohan, New York.

Coda

UNTELLING HISTORY

One hundred seventy years after the publication of the newspaper article, "A Brief Account," a fantasy of a postslavery Caribbean utopia discussed in the introduction to this book, Trinidadian Canadian writer M. NourbeSe Philip used a similar generic strategy, but to reimagine the past rather than the future. Philip writes about the *Gregson v. Gilbert* trial that helped to precipitate the abolition movement. In 1783 British courts litigated over whether throwing overboard one hundred fifty slaves from the slave ship *Zong* constituted murder or an insurance claim. In putting the case before the law of whether Africans were people or property, only representatives from the two sides testified; no one of African descent spoke in court. This unthinkable but archivally documented dystopian debate becomes one of the roots of the Caribbean quarrel with history. Unlike Caribbean writing published in the twentieth century on the *Zong*, but like "A Brief Account," Philip frames her work as life writing.[1] She does so by including on the title page "as told to the author by Setaey Adamu Boateng." This title page follows the format of narratives of the formerly enslaved, who often had to tell their story to another since they were illiterate. Philip dismantles the text of the case to create a prose poem using only words contained within the legal document, encapsulating the limits of colonial archives since the only words in the legal document are those spoken by the colonizers.

Remarkably, Philip's *Zong* achieves what the author of the 1838 newspaper article thought impossible: "Who shall recall from the grave the bodies ye have been employed to agonize, and from eternity the souls into which your iron entered?" by repositioning words and phrases to represent the viewpoint of those who died.[2] Philip explains her process of creation out of such unpromising material: "It's as if we're moving towards an understanding that there's a built-in limit to how much those tools, including the archive, have helped us to this point. And this limit requires new approaches to engage the task at hand, to tell the stories of our time. While I believe that this project—these projects—are particular to this time, I feel that we are coming back to the same story—that is trying to tell itself—by 'untelling'; the same questions, but with different resources, different understandings, building on those who have posed these questions before."[3] Philip's method of "untelling," rather than retelling the story of the murder of one hundred fifty enslaved people, allows her to compose poetry that is also in a sense life writing, as she repurposes language meant to reify African dehumanization to stand in for the voices of the enslaved. Absence for Philip, and as I have argued in relation to contemporary Caribbean writing, becomes a generative source of reimagining the past. "Untelling," as Philip calls it, or Hartman's "critical fabulation," or what I call Condé's "speculative autobiography," or Bahadur and Boon's "archival dust," or framing autobiography as an archive as Behar, Danticat, and Vilar do, foregrounds historical absences as important to the stories they tell rather than papering over them.

Such reimaginings and "untellings" take center stage in Dominican American artist Firelei Báez's work. *Chrono-DREAMer*, (2019) a detail of which is pictured on the cover of this book is printed in its entirety here (see fig. 5). The image's background is a map, intentionally meant to evoke cartography from the colonial period showing shipping lanes from Massachusetts and Halifax to the "Bermudas" with text attesting "Map Showing the Location of the Caribbee Islands," a sixteenth-century term for the region. The text below it obscures who it is engraved for, although the words "History and Guide" are clear. Rather than being displaced or diminished by colonial technologies of mapping and naming, the female figure in *Chrono-DREAMer*, strides across the islands with her body and voluminous coils of hair obscuring much of the United States, claiming the engraving of the map for her own purposes. *Chrono-DREAMer* appears in Báez's installation "A Drexcyen Chronocommons (to win the war you fought it sideways)." This installation evokes a sense of the historical numinous—wonder at the juxtaposition of factual evidence such as colonial maps and historical facts with new ways to imagine decolonial futures. The installation took place under layers of ocean-blue fabric and mesh showing the pattern of the stars on the night of the Haitian revolution in 1791. Viewers have the sense of standing under a night sky as well as being immersed in the ocean. Báez took inspiration from the Detroit electronic music group Drexciya that imagined another site of resistance than the Haitian revolution: an underwater world inhabited by merpeople, descendants of enslaved African women who were thrown off of slave ships during the Atlantic slave trade. Viewers thus entered the installation with the point of view of underwater beings engaging in recuperative acts of dreaming through time in an imagined commons. Bringing together historical fact and Afro-futurist speculative imaginings, Báez's work, like Phillip's, represents another facet of how absence aesthetics work in contemporary feminist Caribbean cultural productions, where women's absence from archival and historical representation becomes a site of artistic creation of new histories and myths.

Rather than a positivist chronicling of the existing archive of eighteenth- and nineteenth-century texts, art, great houses, and slave quarters that remain, the life writing treated here prompts us to ask instead about impossibility, invisibility, haunting, ghosts, dust in the archive, public forgetting, silencing, and disavowing of colonialism's past. Throughout *Dreams of Archives Unfolded* I have argued that contemporary Caribbean life writing speaks to a central predicament of postcoloniality: How and why should the past be remembered? What is necessary to recover from the past to envision decolonized futures? What kinds of fresh Caribbean epistemologies emerge from the innovative formal qualities generated by these first-person narratives? As I navigated between the central concepts of this book used to understand these questions, some were overarching thematic preoccupations of the primary texts such as of archival dreams, absence, and historical ruptures, others were formal qualities, such as absence aesthetics employed to represent gaps in the archive, and some were methodological on my part, such as my emphasis on the importance of reading Caribbean women's life writing together in a communal, if unruly, method of interpretive affiliation, I came to understand their sense of urgency as capturing the precipice of a particular historical moment.

Scholars have yet to account for the power of this generation of life writers, but this book aims for this genre to be seen as necessary to an understanding of twenty-first-century culture. With this genre taken as a collective, we can now see the beginning of a sea change in how history and knowledge are theorized in Caribbean life writing, opening up new possibilities for scholarly engagement with other literary forms than novels, plays, and poetry. Indeed, the majority of the primary texts treated here were published between 2004 and 2014. Each chapter proposes reasons for why these texts at this particular moment—whether the rise in heritage tourism to slave sites in West Africa as in chapter 1, Maryse Condé's participation in the committee on slavery in France as in chapter 2, Erna Brodber's synthesis of existing modes of Caribbean decolonial thought to create her theory of the importance of people to land in Jamaica, which she calls Blackspace, as in chapter 3, the educational attainments of women like Sonja Boon and Gaiutra Bahadur, who are three generations away from indenture, allowing them to name their female ancestors as central to Caribbean history as explored in chapter 4, the success of writers like Ruth Behar and Edwidge Danticat, who found receptive academic and literary markets for their hybrid life writings on diasporic life in the United States as in chapter 5. While all of these statements are true, and are legible as academic assertions of cause and effect, a reader might notice that they do not capture the essence of these writers' contributions.

Instead, as a final word I mark the less formal calling expressed in many of these texts to answer the ancestors, written about as an absent present, but who nevertheless constitute important evidence relevant to the writers' worldview. Ancestors appear in these texts as a spiritual presence as when Goodison calls on "evidence of my generations" (278) for assistance during a time of crisis, when Condé sees her grandmother as a ghost, and when Philip thanks "the Ancestors for bestowing the responsibility of this work on me" in *Zong* (xli) or in a more material and archival sense, as when Hartman finds and then loses an ancestor in the archive, and when Brodber, conscious like Philip of the limitations of the legal archive for descendants of the Middle Passage, worries, "will we find the admissible data on the behavior of people who left no memoirs?"[4] From either a spiritual, community, or political need, all of these narratives are remarkable for finding methodologies to write and theorize the unspeakable acts of colonialism, slavery, and indenture and the disappeared dead. "Untelling" history, a commonality across these writers' work, invokes feelings of a historical numinous. As readers, we find a sense of wonder at what can be imagined as the decolonial future. These imaginaries avoid the tragic vein of much contemporary Caribbean literature, created as they were not in spite of but because of archival absences.

Acknowledgments

For a scholar of autobiography, the acknowledgments section represents a small act of self-presentation and a family tree of the writer's academic kin. Here's mine.

I am indebted to Sue Houchins's model of teaching and scholarship provided to me early on in my academic career. It was Sue who first introduced me to African American and Caribbean literature within a feminist framework, and it was with her that I first read Michelle Cliff and M. NourbeSe Philip. My teaching praxis is directly derived from her. Thank you.

Simon Gikandi, Caroll Smith-Rosenberg, Andrea Henderson, and Arlene Keizer provided encouragement for my obsession with both contemporary Caribbean literature and eighteenth- and nineteenth-century colonial cultures. I want to particularly thank Simon for amplifying my ideas of postcolonial studies and for being a model of scholarly rigor. I wish the luminous and brilliant Patsy Yaeger, who always made me laugh, were here to read my thanks.

At Minnesota State, I was fortunate to find a mentor and friend in Maria Bevacqua. Maria's leadership as department chair sustained this project in its early stages. The President's Teacher Scholar Award provided grant support and made its transnational scope possible. Laura Harrison's friendship is one of the greatest gifts of my time there. The many undergraduate and graduate students in my Global Gender and Autobiography seminars allowed me to think broadly about life writing with them. In particular, the Sophies, Laura, Jeni, Faith, and Blythe made each class memorable.

Thank you to Imogen Giles and Sufang Ng who translated Latin and Dutch for me. Abigail Celis provided translation assistance of French-language materials. I appreciate you all.

My deepest gratitude for friends and colleagues who read early versions of this project. Rosamond King, Ifeona Fulani, and Ylce Irizarry gave me feedback before I fully knew the real subject of this book. Leah Rosenberg, Elena

Machado Sáez, Lisa Ortiz, and Ricia Chansky deserve my thanks for sustaining this project and my sense of why it is vital, even over long distances. Michele Dunnum and Colleen O'Brien sustain me in a thousand ways beyond academic work.

Pallavi Rastogi is my ride or die intellectual companion. Thanks for reading many (many) drafts and quoting my own critical moves back at me. Here's to writing our next books together!

At the University of Michigan Sidonie Smith provided a much-needed impetus to go deeper into autobiography scholarship, and I am grateful beyond measure for her feedback on the argument and structure of the book. Supriya Nair gave me encouragement and generous feedback during a crucial time in writing, and I am thankful for her model of gracious collegiality. Andrea Bolivar lent her expertise in analyzing narratives late in this project. Ruby Tapia is one of my smartest interlocutors. Thank you to Dean Disher and Lilia Cortina for making Ann Arbor a welcoming place.

For Caribbeanist literary scholars, it can be a luxury to have more than one of us at an institution. My friendship with Aliyah Khan has spanned the length of my working on this book, and her kindness and feedback have made it a better project.

Special thanks to Anna Kirkland and everyone at the Institute for Research on Women and Gender for their support of my work. Heidi Bennett was my daily office companion before quarantine and was much missed during the final stages of this book. Zoom meetings are not the same. I want to thank Michigan graduate students Amanda Healy and LaVelle Ridley for being in conversation with me at the beginning and end of the work, respectively. Undergraduate work study students Halie Stuhlmann and Stephanie Campbell provided help with footnotes and the bibliography.

Thank you to the anonymous reviewers and series editors for the Critical Caribbean Studies series at Rutgers University Press. Their comments and feedback have been invaluable in shaping this work. Thanks goes to Jasper Chang for his assistance with the publishing process. Editor Kimberly Guinta's support for this project from our initial meeting at a Caribbean Studies Association conference to publication has allowed me to complete the book I wanted to write. Thank you.

I am grateful to my new colleagues at St. Catherine's University, in particular Dean Tarshia Stanley, for the warm welcome extended to me.

There is no higher tribute I can pay to my parents, Jim and Carolyn Stitt, than to say that they never wavered in their enthusiasm toward my pursuit of a PhD in women's studies and English and an academic career. Neil has loved me through the process of writing this book, which is also high praise. And although my children encouraged me to write in the acknowledgments that I finished this book in spite of them, of course I finished it for them. To Elizabeth and Ramsey.

Portions of chapter 3 were previously published in the *Journal of West Indian Literature* 27, no. 1 (2021). Thanks to editor-in-chief Evelyn O'Callaghan for kind permission to reprint that material here.

Notes

INTRODUCTION

1. "A Brief Account and Familiar Description of Jamaica in Its *Most* Modern Statistics," *Falmouth Post*, June 27, 1838, 2.

2. "A Brief Account" differs from castaway narratives set on tropical islands such as *Robinson Crusoe* (1719) and subsequent Robinsonade narratives such as Thomas Spence's *Crusonia* (1792) that take place in a utopian Caribbean-like island setting. These earlier texts do not portray Caribbean cultural or political institutions, as do the descriptions of Jamaica's General Assembly or towns such as Port Royal in "A Brief Account." For more on utopias and colonial literature, see Bill Ashcroft, "Introduction: Spaces of Utopia: An Electronic Journal," *Spaces of Utopia* 2, no. 1 (2012): 1–17, http://ler.letras.up.pt.

3. "A Brief Account and Familiar Description of Jamaica in Its *Most* Modern Statistics, Con't.," *Falmouth Post*, July 4, 1838, 2, emphasis added.

4. I am grateful for the translation of the line and context of Virgil's writing by Imogen Giles.

5. As an example, all three of the novels praised in a 2016 *Jamaica Gleaner* editorial concern themselves with historical issues. The editorial celebrated Kei Miller's *Augustown* (2016), the Booker Prize winner *A Brief History of Seven Killings* (2015) by Marlon James, and *Here Comes the Sun* (2016) by Nicole Benn-Dennis, as "a renaissance" in Jamaican writing. The first two are historical novels, and Benn-Dennis's work describes the lasting legacy of colonial histories of sexual violence and exploitation. The visions of history in all three can be considered tragic, rather than depictions of anticolonial nationalism. "A Renaissance in Writing," *Jamaica Gleaner*, August 21, 2016, http://jamaica-gleaner.com/article/commentary/20160821/editorial-renaissance-writing. See also Arlene Keizer, *Black Subjects: Identity Formation in the Contemporary Narrative of Slavery* (Ithaca, NY: Cornell University Press, 2004) and Vivian Nun Halloran, *Exhibiting Slavery: The Caribbean Postmodern Novel as Museum* (Charlottesville: University of Virginia Press, 2009).

6. Michel Foucault, *The Archeology of Knowledge* (New York: Vintage, 2010), 7.

7. For an exploration of the urgency of understanding the limits of the archive as an instrument of colonial power, see Simon Gikandi, "Reading at the Limits," *PMLA* 131, no. 3 (2016): 585–593.

8. Julie Rak defines the "memoir boom," much discussed in autobiography studies, as the spike in life narratives written by unknown writers as well as celebrities from 2000 to the present. *Boom! Manufacturing Memoir for the Popular Market* (Waterloo: Wilfrid Laurier University Press, 2013).

9. "In thinking of the methodology of decoloniality, I move to read the social from the cosmologies that inform it, rather than beginning with a gendered reading of cosmologies informing and constituting perception, motility, embodiment, and relation." María Lugones, "Toward a Decolonial Feminism," *Hypatia* 22, no. 4 (2010): 749.

10. Edward Baugh, "The West Indian Writer and His Quarrel with History" (1977), *Small Axe* 16, no. 2 (2012): 60–74. For a succinct account of the tension between recovery and its impossibility in African American studies of enslavement, see Laura Helton, Justine Leroy, Max A. Mishler, Samantha Seely, and Shauna Sweeney, "The Question of Recovery: An Introduction," *Social Text* 33, no. 4 (2015): 1–18.

11. Recently, texts combining life writing and feminist theory have been categorized as "autotheory." Lauren Fournier traces its use by largely white and queer third- and fourth-wave feminist texts in North America, such as Maggie Nelson's *The Argonauts* (Minneapolis: Graywolf, 2015). While this term is useful in describing the increasing publication of personal narrative in conjunction with political critique, one could create a parallel genealogy of earlier feminist texts by women of color such as Sylvia Wynter, Michelle Cliff, Gloria Anzaldúa, Audre Lorde, and Barbara Christian, who trace their political commitments to Mexico and the Caribbean. As I hope this introduction makes clear, I place the texts considered here within a long transnational tradition of Caribbean writing that combines the personal and the historical. "Sick Women, Sad Girls, and Selfie Theory: Autotheory as Contemporary Feminist Practice," *a/b: Auto/Biography Studies* 33, no. 3 (2018): 643–662.

12. See Stephen Best for a critique of the tendency within African diaspora studies since the late 1980s toward "recovery" and "melancholy" as a means of bearing witness to the past through logics that see "the past simply as our present." "On Failing to Make the Past Present," *Modern Language Quarterly* 73, no. 3 (2012): 456, 463; *None Like Us: Blackness, Belonging, Aesthetic Life* (Durham, NC: Duke University Press, 2018).

13. In addition to the works cited in the text, see also Roshini Kempadoo, *Creole in the Archive: Imagery, Presence and the Location of the Caribbean Figure* (London: Rowman & Littlefield, 2016); Marisa J. Fuentes, *Dispossessed Lives: Enslaved Women, Violence, and the Archive* (Philadelphia: University of Pennsylvania Press, 2016); Michel-Rolph Trouillot, *Silencing the Past: Power and the Production of History* (New York: Beacon, 1995); Michael Hanchard, "Black Memory versus State Memory: Notes toward a Method," *Small Axe* 12, no. 2 (2008): 45–62; Simon Gikandi, "Rethinking the Archive of Enslavement," *Early American Literature* 50, no. 1 (2015): 81–102.

14. Jeannette A. Bastian, John A. Aarons, and Stanley H. Griffin, "Introduction," in *Decolonizing the Caribbean Record: An Archives Reader*, ed. Bastian, Aarons, and Griffin (Sacramento, CA: Litwin Books, 2018), 2, 3.

15. Deborah Thomas, "Caribbean Studies, Archive Building, and the Problem of Violence," *Small Axe* 41 (2013): 27.

16. Thomas, "Caribbean Studies," 27.

17. David Scott, "Introduction: On the Archaeologies of Black Memory," *Small Axe* 26, no. 2 (2008): vii.

18. Laurence A. Breiner, "Too Much History, or Not Enough," *Small Axe* 38 (2012): 90.

19. Baugh, "West Indian Writer"; Édouard Glissant, "The Quarrel with History," in *Caribbean Discourse: Selected Essays* (Charlottesville: University of Virginia Press, 1989).

20. The journal *Small Axe* demonstrated the continued relevance of the terms of the debate about history by devoting a 2012 issue to contemporary responses to Baugh's 1977 essay. Alison Donnell's observation that "much of what Baugh argues here remains astute and relevant to the discipline of Caribbean literary criticism today" was shared by other commentators. "All Friends Now? Critical Conversations, West Indian Literature, and the 'Quarrel with History,'" *Small Axe* 38 (2013): 75. See also *Anthurium* 10, no. 2 (2013) on "Intellectual Formations: Locating a Caribbean Critical Tradition," especially essays by Donette Francis, Edward Baugh, and Alison Donnell related to the quarrel with history.

21. Derek Walcott, "The Antilles: Fragments of Epic Memory," in *Caribbean Art at the Crossroads of the World*, ed. Deborah Cullen and Elvis Fuentes (New Haven, CT: Yale University Press, 2012), 22.

22. For a discussion of the paucity of nineteenth-century literature in the Caribbean in contrast to African American literary production and the subsequent necessity for imagination in the contemporary moment to fill those gaps, see Breiner, "Too Much History."

23. See Raphael Dalleo, *Caribbean Literature and the Public Sphere: From the Plantation to the Postcolonial* (Charlottesville: University of Virginia Press, 2011) for an incisive account of the control of the presses by the planter class across the Caribbean during the colonial period and how that impeded the growth of local writers, local histories, and a modern counterpublic.

24. Scott, "Introduction," xii.

25. Best, "On" 464, 466.

26. Aida Levy-Hussen, *How to Read African American Literature: Post–Civil Rights Fiction and the Task of Interpretation* (New York: New York University Press, 2016).

27. Donette Francis, *Fictions of Feminine Citizenship: Sexuality and the Nation in Contemporary Caribbean Literature* (London: Palgrave, 2010).

28. Elena Machado Sáez deploys David Scott's notions of anticolonial romance and tragedy as two poles Caribbean diasporic writers such as Junot Díaz move between in order to articulate their varying relationships to writing history. *Market Aesthetics: The Purchase of the Past in Caribbean Diasporic Fiction* (Charlottesville: University of Virginia Press, 2015), 35–36.

29. David Scott, *Conscripts of Modernity: The Tragedy of Colonial Enlightenment* (Durham, NC: Duke University Press, 2004), 2.

30. David Scott first wrote about anticolonial romance in *Conscripts of Modernity* (2004). Scott declared the impossibility of continuing the anticolonial narratives of early postcoloniality, that triumphant stories of overcoming colonialism should now be replaced with a tragic framework more suitable for understanding contemporary postcoloniality. Questions of the utility of the anticolonial romance, its prevalence in contemporary literature, and the blind spots inherent in this formulation have been taken up by a variety of critics. See Chris Bongie, *Friends and Enemies: Scribal Politics of Post/Colonial Literature* (Liverpool: Liverpool University Press 2008); Francis, *Fictions of Feminine Citizenship*; Sáez, *Market Aesthetics.*

31. Fuentes, *Dispossessed Lives*, 6.

32. Michelle Cliff, *The Land of Look Behind* (Ithaca, NY: Firebrand Books, 1985), 14.

33. Sonja Boon, *What the Oceans Remember: Searching for Belonging and Home* (Waterloo: Wilfrid Laurier University Press, 2019), 262.

34. Donnell, "All Friends Now?," 85.

35. Fuentes, *Dispossessed Lives*, 6.

36. M. Jacqui Alexander, "Not Just (Any) *Body* Can Be a Citizen: The Politics of Law, Sexuality, and Postcoloniality in Trinidad and Tobago and the Bahamas," in *Cultures of Empire: A Reader*, ed. Catherine Hall (New York: Routledge, 2000), 359–376; Francis, *Fictions of Feminine Citizenship*.

37. Jenny Sharpe, *Ghosts of Slavery: A Literary Archeology of Black Women's Lives* (Minneapolis: University of Minnesota Press, 2002), xi.

38. Levy-Hussen describes two modes of reading contemporary African American novels concerned with the aftereffects of slavery as "therapeutic reading," which advocates for recovering the past as a mode of healing, and "prohibitive reading," which advises avoiding texts that bring up the painful past of slavery (*How to Read African American Literature*, 2, 5).

39. Carolyn Steedman, *Dust: The Archive and Cultural History* (New Brunswick, NJ: Rutgers University Press, 2002), 72.

40. Erna Brodber, "Oral History Sources and the Creation of a Social History of the Caribbean," *Jamaica Journal* 16, no. 4 (1983): 2.

41. David Scott, "Introducing Small Axe," *Small Axe* 1 (1997): 24; Rose Réjouis, "Dark Horse Poetics: Lévi-Strauss, Benítez-Rojo, and Caribbean Epistemology," *Small Axe* 43 (2014): 104.

42. Brodber, "Oral History Sources," 4.

43. Brodber, "Oral History Sources," 7.

44. There are few first-person-authored accounts written by those who were indentured in eastern and southern Africa, Fiji, Mauritius, Trinidad, Guyana, and Guadeloupe. Women's testimony exists as given to both Indian and British committees, but that is, of course, mediated by the power differential between the interviewer and interviewee. See Marina Carter and Khal Torabully on the small number of first-person narratives produced by indentured people. *Coolitude: An Anthology of the Indian Labour Diaspora* (London: Anthem Press, 2002), 89. I thank Aliyah Khan for this reference.

45. Bridget Brereton, "Gendered Testimonies: Autobiographies, Diaries and Letters," *Feminist Review* 59 (1998): 144–145.

46. Martha S. Jones, "On Cherokee Rose, Historical Fiction, and Silences in the Archives," *Process*, May 26, 2015, http://www.processhistory.org/on-the-cherokee-rose-historical-fiction-and-silences-in-the-archives/.

47. Breiner, "Too Much History," 90.

48. Siobhan Lambert-Hurley, "Life/History/Archive: Identifying Autobiographical Writing by Muslim Women in South Asia," *Journal of Women's History* 25, no. 2 (2013): 61–62.

49. Steedman, *Dust*, 69; Shari Benstock, "Authorizing the Autobiographical," in *Feminisms: An Anthology of Literary Theory and Criticism*, ed. Robyn R. Warhol and Diane Price Herndl (New Brunswick, NJ: Rutgers University Press, 2007), 1138–1154.

50. In identifying a Caribbean feminist epistemology, I am guided by the work of Patricia Mohammed, who argues for a gendered understanding of "what is accepted and valued as admissible levels of knowledge, and to confront the gatekeepers and conveyors of knowledge" (41). "Unmasking Masculinity and Deconstructing Patriarchy: Problems and Possibilities within Feminist Epistemology," in *Interrogating Caribbean Masculinities: Theoretical and Empirical Analyses*, ed. Rhoda E. Reddock (Kingston: University of the West Indies Press, 2004).

51. Philip Holden argues that genres of life writing have been essential to decolonization, with "speeches, letters and court testimony emerg[ing] as powerful decolonizing gestures. In more recent times, life writing has been a place of continued struggle, drawing on cultural, social and government discourse of both individuation and collectivity." "Postcolonial Auto/Biography," in *The Cambridge History of Postcolonial Literature*, vol. 1, ed. Ato Quayson (Cambridge: Cambridge University Press, 2011), 131.

52. Sidonie Smith and Julia Watson critique autobiography as a masculinist and Eurocentric form in much of their foundational work, including *Reading Autobiography: A Guide for Interpreting Life Narratives*, 2nd ed. (Minneapolis: University of Minnesota Press, 2010), 3. However, rejecting the term "autobiography" in favor of "life writing" is not globally shared. For a reclaiming of the term "autobiographical" as a way of reading rather than a strict generic definition, see Anshu Malhotra and Siobhan Lambert-Hurley, eds., *Speaking of the Self: Gender, Performance, and Autobiography in South Asia* (Durham, NC: Duke University Press, 2015), 7.

53. Gillian Whitlock, *Postcolonial Life Narratives: Testimonial Transactions* (Oxford: Oxford University Press, 2015), 3.

54. Linda Anderson, *Autobiography* (London: Routledge, 2011), 4–5; Whitlock, *Postcolonial Life Narratives*, 3.

55. Sandra Pouchet Paquet, *Caribbean Autobiography: Cultural Identity and Self-Representation* (Madison: University of Wisconsin Press, 2002).

56. Louise Hardwick, *Childhood, Autobiography and the Francophone Caribbean* (Liverpool: Liverpool University Press, 2013). See also Bonnie Thomas, *Connecting Histories: Francophone Caribbean Writers Interrogating Their Past* (Jackson: University of Mississippi Press, 2017). The Francophone Caribbean tradition exhibits several texts that address the autobiographical genre from transnational literary perspectives: Edgard Sankara's *Postcolonial Francophone Autobiographies: From Africa to the Antilles* (Charlottesville: University of Virginia Press, 2011) and Françoise Lionnet's *Autobiographical Voices: Race, Gender, Self-Portraiture* (Ithaca, NY: Cornell University Press, 1989) and *Postcolonial Representations: Women, Literature, Identity* (Ithaca, NY: Cornell University Press, 1995).

57. Lisa R. Brown, "Caribbean Life-Writing and Performative Liberation," in *The Routledge Companion to Anglophone Caribbean Literature*, ed. Michael Bucknor and Alison Donnell (London: Routledge, 2011), 280.

58. Walter Goebel and Saskia Schabio, eds., *Locating Postcolonial Narrative Genres* (London: Routledge, 2013).

59. Holden, "Postcolonial Auto/Biography," 108.

60. Michael W. Twitty's *The Cooking Gene: A Journey through African American History in the Old South* (New York: Amistad, 2017) is an African American cousin to what I have identified as a Caribbean corpus of works that are simultaneously life writing, historical investigation, and cultural critique of racialized archival absence. Twitty investigates the absence of African American foodways in mainstream conceptions of southern food as well as the absence of knowledge about cooking during plantation slavery. With the inclusion of a family tree, ancestry searches, and historical critique and commentary, *Cooking Gene* bears a formal resemblance to the texts considered here.

61. Space considerations prevent me from listing all similar texts to those considered here. Of particular note to this study are texts that combine memoir, travelogue, and historical analysis related to familial ancestry in the Caribbean. See Caryl Phillips's *The Atlantic Sound* (New York: Vintage, 2000), *A New World Order: Essays* (New York: Vintage, 2001),

and *Color Me English: Reflections on Migration and Belonging Before and After 9/11* (New York: New Press, 2011); Carole Boyce Davies's *Caribbean Spaces: Escapes from Twilight Zones* (Urbana: University of Illinois Press, 2013); and Paule Marshall's *Triangular Road: A Memoir* (New York: Perseus, 2009). These texts, however, do not directly engage with the quarrel with history and archival absences and are thus not included in this study.

62. José Esteban Muñoz, "The Sense of Watching Tony Sleep," in *After Sex? On Writing since Queer Theory*, ed. Janet Halley and Andrew Parker (Durham, NC: Duke University Press, 2011), 149.

63. Muñoz, "Sense of Watching," 149.

64. Austin Clarke stands as a central figure in Caribbean life writing, beginning with *Growing Up Stupid under the Union Jack* (1980) through his final work *'Membering* (2015). In Clarke's memoir of childhood in Barbados, he frequently invokes his mother's phrase "dogs amongst doctors," indicating a social inferior trying to gain access to superiors, in describing the prohibition against children asking questions related to their family history. *Growing Up Stupid under the Union Jack* (Toronto: McClelland and Stewart, 1980).

65. For an exploration of the barriers to tracing African diaspora genealogies pre-emancipation and the desire for scientific solutions this historical problem of lack of records, see Alondra Nelson, *The Social Life of DNA: Race, Reparations, and Reconciliation after the Genome* (New York: Beacon, 2017).

66. Yvonne Shorter Brown, *Dead Woman Pickney: A Memoir of Childhood in Jamaica* (Waterloo: Wilfrid Laurier University Press, 2010), 1.

67. Brown, *Dead Woman Pickney*, 2.

68. Maryse Condé, *Victoire: My Mother's Mother* (New York: Atria, 2010); Lorna Goodison, *From Harvey River: A Memoir of My Mother and Her Island* (New York: Amistad/HarperCollins, 2007).

69. Avery Gordon, *Ghostly Matters: Haunting and the Sociological Imagination*, 2nd ed. (Minneapolis: University of Minnesota Press, 2008), 6.

70. For a particularly useful overview of autobiography studies' struggle with defining the genre, see Maria Dibattista and Emily O. Wittman, "Introduction," in *The Cambridge Companion to Autobiography*, ed. Maria Dibattista and Emily O. Wittman (Cambridge: Cambridge University Press, 2014), 1–20.

71. Philip Lejeune, *On Autobiography*, ed. Paul John Eakin, trans. Katherine Leary (Minneapolis: University of Minnesota Press, 1989), 4.

72. Gillian Whitlock, *Soft Weapons: Autobiography in Transit* (Chicago: University of Chicago Press, 2012), 12.

73. Centering the self, C. L. Innes suggests, is a "strategy frequently found in postcolonial writing" because it "sidesteps entering into dialogue on the colonizer's terms by grounding the text in autobiography, starting from the self as a central point of reference." *Cambridge Introduction to Postcolonial Literatures in English* (Cambridge: Cambridge University Press, 2007), 57.

74. Patrick Fuery, *The Theory of Absence: Subjectivity, Signification, and Desire* (Westport, CT: Greenwood, 1995), 2.

75. Gordon argues in *Ghostly Matters* that evidence and history should be considered separate categories of analysis in writing about the past.

76. The reasons for the linguistic and national silos within Caribbean literary history are multifaceted and include differing political statuses between independent nations

and territories with differing histories of colonization. For a critique of the continuing difficulty of enacting an "archipelagic idea of Caribbean identity" (12), see Michelle Stephens, "What Is an Island? Caribbean Studies and the Contemporary Visual Artist," *Small Axe* 41 (2013): 8–57. See also Vanessa Pérez-Rosario, "On the Hispanophone Caribbean Question," *Small Axe* 51 (2016): 21–31, on the continuing difficulty of recognizing the Spanish-speaking Caribbean as a distinct area of study separate from Latin America and as part of Caribbean studies as a whole. Raphael Dalleo's study elucidates the long history within the region of comparative work as well as the political urgency for creating modes of Caribbean analysis that cut across European periodization as well as national boundaries. *Caribbean Literature and the Public Sphere.*

77. Aisha Khan, "Material and Immaterial Bodies: Diaspora Studies and the Problem of Culture, Identity, and Race," *Small Axe* 48 (2015): 31.

78. There are many examples of the integration of work on autobiography into Caribbean literary scholarship, such as an issue of the *Journal of West Indian Literature* on the topic (3, no. 1 [1989]) and the inclusion of chapters related to autobiography within *Teaching Anglophone Caribbean Literature*, ed. Supriya Nair (New York: Modern Language Association, 2012), and *The Routledge Companion to Anglophone Caribbean Literature.* Not as well integrated are life writing texts from the region being analyzed as a genre across linguistic and national boundaries.

79. Lisa Lowe, *The Intimacies of Four Continents* (Durham, NC: Duke University Press, 2015), 2.

80. Alaí Reyes-Santos argues that the language of kinship is central to Caribbean political self-fashioning, determining who can claim solidarity and who is othered. *Our Caribbean Kin: Race and Nation in the Neoliberal Antilles* (New Brunswick, NJ: Rutgers University Press, 2015), 3.

81. In seeking to explore how Caribbean authors make formal choices to signal absence within their self-defined archives, my process does not follow the methodology of symptomatic reading. Stephen Best and Sharon Marcus define symptomatic readings as practices that "often locate outright absences, gaps, and ellipses in texts, and then ask what those absences mean, what forces create them, and how they signify the questions that motivate the text, but that the text itself cannot articulate." "Surface Reading: An Introduction," *Representations* 108, no. 1 (2009): 3.

82. Françoise Lionnet and Shu-mei Shih, "Introduction: Thinking through the Minor, Transnationally," in *Minor Transnationalism*, ed. Lionnet and Shih (Durham, NC: Duke University Press, 2005), 2.

83. Thora Siemsen, "On Working with Archives: An Interview with Writer Saidiya Hartman," *Creative Independent*, April 18, 2018, https://thecreativeindependent.com/people/saidiya-hartman-on-working-with-archives/.

CHAPTER 1 — "AUTOBIOGRAPHY IN A GRAVEYARD"

1. "A Brief Account," 2.

2. Anderson, *Autobiography.*

3. Saidiya Hartman, *Lose Your Mother: A Journey along the Atlantic Slave Route* (New York: Farrar, Straus and Giroux, 2007); Dionne Brand, *A Map to the Door of No Return: Notes to Belonging* (Toronto: Vintage Canada, 2001).

4. Scott, *Conscripts of Modernity*, 4.

5. For an exploration of narratives of return, see Elvira Pulitano, *Transnational Narratives from the Caribbean: Diasporic Literature and the Human Experience* (London: Routledge, 2016).

6. Glissant, "Quarrel with History," 62–63.

7. Citations to primary texts are given parenthetically within the text.

8. Brand's larger body of work contains such references to queer sexuality, especially her collection of poems *No Language Is Neutral* (Toronto: Coach House Press, 1990). Michelle Cliff, for example, praised *No Language Is Neutral* for depicting lesbian sexuality not as foreign import but as originating in Caribbean culture. Judith Raiskin, "The Art of History: An Interview with Michelle Cliff," *Kenyon Review* 15 (1993): 69. For recent examples of scholars placing Brand as part of a queer Caribbean diaspora, see Omise'eke Natasha Tinsley, "Black Atlantic, Queer Atlantic: Queer Imaginings of the Middle Passage," *GLQ* 14 (2008): 191–215; Johanna X. K. Garvey, "Spaces of Violence, Desire, and Queer (Un)belonging: Dionne Brand's Urban Diasporas," *Textual Practice* 25, no. 4 (2011): 757–777; Amar Wahab and Dwaine Plaza, "Queerness in the Transnational Caribbean-Canadian Diaspora," *Caribbean Review of Gender Studies* 3 (2009): 1–34.

9. In keeping with Tinsley's argument that although references to identities such as lesbian or gay are often absent from queer Caribbean texts, writing of Caribbean spiritual practices such as Vodou is a common theme. Brand does refer to Vodou religious practices such as worshiping the goddess Yemaya. Omise'eke Natasha Tinsley, *Ezili's Mirrors: Imagining Black Queer Gender* (Durham, NC: Duke University Press, 2018), 3–4.

10. As another example, Staceyann Chin's *The Other Side of Paradise: A Memoir* (New York: Scribner, 2009), the first lesbian coming out memoir in the Caribbean, does not contain many of the hallmarks of coming-of-age / coming-out narratives from North America. Instead, Chin focuses on her experiences of violence and outsider status as markers of her Asian and queer identities. Jocelyn Fenton Stitt, "Disciplining the Unruly (National) Body in Staceyann Chin's *The Other Side of Paradise*," *Small Axe* 45 (2014): 1–17.

11. Gorée Island is a UNESCO World Heritage Site that memorializes those sold into slavery on the African continent. The island is represented as a place where thousands of slaves were held before they were packed onto slave ships sailing to the Americas. It is one of a number of such places on the west coast of Africa that were marked as important historical sites in the 1940s during decolonization; Léopold Sedar Senghor brought particular attention to Gorée during his presidency while hosting the World Festival of Black Arts in 1966 in Senegal. Ana Lucia Araujo, "Welcome the Diaspora: Slave Trade Heritage Tourism and the Public Memory of Slavery," *Ethnologies* 32, no. 2 (2010), 149–150. Subsequently, the island and its Slave House became well known globally, with visits by Nelson Mandela and other luminaries.

12. Maryse Condé, *What Is Africa to Me? Fragments of a True-to-Life Autobiography* (London: Seagull Books, 2017), 71.

13. Araujo, "Welcome the Diaspora," 146. Araujo makes an important point that although ten times the number of enslaved people were taken to Brazil than to the United States, few Afro-Brazilians make African heritage trips due to the expense.

14. Yaa Gyasi's *Homegoing* (New York: Vintage, 2017) subverts both the *Roots* narrative of triumphant return and the idea that reconnection cannot take place at the Door of No Return. *Homegoing* fits with other contemporary narratives of return espousing a

cautious optimism as explored in Michelle D. Commander's *Afro-Atlantic Flight: Speculative Returns and the Black Fantastic* (Durham, NC: Duke University Press, 2017).

15. Orlando Patterson, *Slavery and Social Death: A Comparative Study* (Cambridge, MA: Harvard University Press, 1982).

16. In the contemporary moment, genetic testing now allows, for those who can afford it, the possibility of going beyond records that often end at emancipation to discover and travel to ancestral origins. Alondra Nelson writes of the particular importance of such tests to the African diaspora in the Americas, whose knowledge of their family's past is often fractured due to the deliberate separation of families under slavery as well as the absence of records that identify slaves by name that would allow for confirmation of a person's tie to an enslaved person's origins. *Social Life of DNA*, 73.

17. Hartman's text served as one of the centerpieces of the 2008 Rites of Return conference at CUNY and Columbia University; Marianne Hirsch and Nancy K. Miller, eds., *Rites of Return: Diaspora Politics and the Politics of Memory* (New York: Columbia University Press, 2011) was published as an edited collection. See also Harvey Neptune, "Loving through Loss: Reading Saidiya Hartman's History of Black Hurt," *Anthurium* 6, no. 1 (2008): 1–9; Yogita Goyal, "Introduction: Africa and the Black Atlantic," *Research in African Literatures* 45, no. 3 (2014): v–xxv; Jocelyn Fenton Stitt, "The Aftereffects of Slavery: A Black Feminist Genealogy," *Meridians* 17, no. 1 (2018): 150–162.

18. Saidiya Hartman, "Venus in Two Acts," *Small Axe* 28 (2008): 1–14.

19. Christina Sharpe, *In the Wake: On Blackness and Being* (Durham, NC: Duke University Press, 2016), 33.

20. Commander, *Afro-Atlantic Flight*, 3.

21. Commander, *Afro-Atlantic Flight*, 79.

22. Aida Levy-Hussen provides an analysis of the competing claims of the past on the present, including her idea of "therapeutic reading," in *How to Read African American Literature*.

23. Best, "On Failing to Make the Past Present," 453. As a prime example, Best points to the character of Sethe in Toni Morrison's *Beloved*. Sethe asserts that the slave past will never die—"it will always be waiting if you go there—you who never was there—if you go there and stand in the place where it was, it will happen again." Toni Morrison, *Beloved* (New York: Knopf, 1987), 34.

24. Since the publication of Mary Louise Pratt's foundational *Imperial Eyes: Travel Writing and Transculturation* (London: Routledge, 1992) and David Spurr's *The Rhetoric of Empire: Colonial Discourse in Journalism, Travel Writing, and Imperial Administration* (Durham, NC: Duke University Press, 1993), the connection between travel narratives and the colonial project has become a subfield in and of itself.

25. Frederick Cooper, Thomas C. Holt, and Rebecca J. Scott note that until recently historians of Africa did not see themselves as studying post-emancipation societies in the same way as Americanists. Further, the "archives were filled with silences" regarding African participation in the slave trade (2). *Beyond Slavery: Explorations of race, Labor and Citizenship in Postemancipation Societies* (Chapel Hill: University of North Carolina Press, 2000). Hartman addresses these silences among contemporary scholars in *Lose Your Mother*, especially in chapters 8, 10, and 12.

26. For a discussion of Hartman's innovation of thinking about slavery as starting in Africa, see Gikandi, "Rethinking the Archive of Enslavement," 85–86, 100.

27. Doig Simmonds, "A Note on the Excavations in Cape Coast Castle," *Transactions of the Historical Society of Ghana* 14, no. 2 (1973): 268.

28. Yogita Goyal, *Romance, Diaspora, and Black Atlantic Literature* (Cambridge: Cambridge University Press, 2010), 1.

29. Kelly Baker Josephs, "Articulating Caribbean Epistemologies," *Small Axe* 43 (2014): 99.

30. Rebecca Wolff, "Maryse Condé," *Bomb* 68 (1999), https://bombmagazine.org/articles/maryse-cond%C3%A9/.

31. "'Lose Your Mother' Author Finds Heritage in Africa," National Public Radio, January 23, 2007, https://www.npr.org/templates/story/story.php?storyId=6955366.

32. I would like to thank Sufang Ng for her kind help with translating this document.

33. There are first-person narratives representing the experience of colonization and enslavement from the perspective of Europeans. Eighteenth- and nineteenth-century narratives written by Lady Nugent, Matthew Lewis, Bryan Edwards, and Thomas Thistlewood are prime examples. Autobiographical texts such as these helped constitute the Caribbean in the European imagination, Helen Tiffin reasons, and so offer a particularly resonant genre with which to write postcolonial counternarratives. "Rites of Resistance: Counter-Discourse and West Indian Biography," *Journal of West Indian Literature* 3, no. 1 (1989): 30.

34. Nicole N. Aljoe, *Creole Testimonies: Slave Narratives from the British West Indies, 1709–1838* (New York: Palgrave Macmillan, 2012), 29.

35. Aljoe, *Creole Testimonies*, 28.

36. Marisa Fuentes suggests that when presented with the lack of first-person accounts of slavery, trying to uncover additional records related to enslavement created by the powerful only reproduces the very archival absences scholars are trying to fill. *Dispossessed Lives*, 6.

37. In the text, Hartman records her source as "a musty trial transcript" (138), but she actually consults four texts published in 1792 concerning the trial of John Kimber (250n).

38. Steedman, *Dust*.

39. Brodber, "Oral History Sources," 4.

40. Sáez, *Market Aesthetics*, 82–83.

41. Gayatri Gopinath sees queer affiliation in *Lose Your Mother*'s ending. I am less persuaded by this argument, which Gopinath acknowledges is "transitory and fleeting," given that the majority of the text is about being unable to find connections through kinship, racial identity, and even experiences. However, Gopinath's larger argument about the possibilities of non-kinship affiliations to question and create alternative archives is most useful. "Archive, Affect, and the Everyday: Queer Diasporic Re-visions," in *Political Emotions: New Agendas in Communication*, ed. Janet Staiger, Ann Cvetkovich, and Ann Reynolds (London: Routledge, 2010), 167.

42. Writing caustically of his own experience of a Through the Door of No Return ritual in Ghana, Caryl Phillips points to the trope of diaspora as a sickness and Africa as a cure as a fallacy. "Africa cannot cure. Africa cannot make anybody feel whole. Africa is not a psychiatrist." *Atlantic Sound*, 216. Phillips's formulation of fantasies of return as healing anticipates Aida Levy-Hussen's notion of reading the slave past as a "therapeutic reading" in *How to Read African American Literature*.

43. *Lose Your Mother* echoes Brand in centering absence genealogical and spatial absence when Hartman writes, "For me, the rupture was the story" (42).

44. See Heather Andrea Williams, *Help Me to Find My People: The African American Search for Family Lost in Slavery* (Chapel Hill: University of North Carolina Press, 2012) for an extended study of the barriers to genealogical searches for the descendants of the enslaved.

45. Alison Donnell, "Quarrels with the Quarrels with History," *Anthurium* 10, no. 2 (2013): 3.

46. Lauren J. Gantz, "Archiving the Door of No Return in Dionne Brand's *At the Full and Change of the Moon*," *Meridians* 13, no. 2 (2016): 126–127.

47. Steedman, *Dust*; John Frow, *Time and Commodity Culture: Essays on Cultural Theory and Postmodernity* (Oxford: Oxford University Press, 1997), 225.

48. The text's subtitle, *Notes to Belonging*, invokes Joan Riley's novel *The Unbelonging* (London: Women's Press, 1985), one of the first works of fiction written by a diasporic Caribbean woman in the United Kingdom. *The Unbelonging* is notable for the despair that the protagonist experiences when she returns to the Caribbean after living in the United Kingdom for many years. Place is not a solution to unbelonging in this novel as it is not in Brand's life writing.

49. Best, "On Failing," 455.

50. Nira Yuval-Davis, "Belonging and the Politics of Belonging," *Patterns of Prejudice* 40, no. 3 (2006): 197–214.

51. Ann Cvetkovich, *An Archive of Feelings: Trauma, Sexuality, and Lesbian Public Cultures* (Durham, NC: Duke University Press, 2003), 7.

52. Sharpe, *In the Wake*, 107.

53. I am using "queer" here to describe a reading of Brand's *Map* from a queer studies perspective. Brand identifies as a lesbian. The term "queer" is contested in the Caribbean, where it is used as a slur. Other regional expressions are often more culturally appropriate. Thomas Glave, *Our Caribbean: A Gathering of Lesbian and Gay Writing from the Antilles* (Durham, NC: Duke University Press, 2008), 8–9.

54. Ronald Cummings writes of the use of "marronage as a way of narrating the experiences of gays and lesbians" in Caribbean writing. "(Trans)Nationalisms, Marronage, and Queer Caribbean Subjectivities," *Transforming Anthropology* 18, no. 2 (2010): 177.

55. Nadia Ellis, *Territories of the Soul: Queered Belonging in the Diaspora* (Durham, NC: Duke University Press, 2015), 3.

56. Nicole Phillip-Dowe, "Women in the Grenada Revolution, 1979–1983," *Social and Economic Studies* 62, nos. 3–4 (2013): 45–82. For a discussion of the importance of women who participated in the Grenada Revolution in current feminist activism in the Caribbean, see Horace G. Campbell, "Challenges for Revolutionary Change in the Caribbean," in *The Grenada Revolution: Reflections and Lessons*, ed. Wendy C. Grenade (Jackson: University Press of Mississippi, 2015), 179–209.

57. David Scott, *Omens of Adversity: Tragedy, Time, Memory, Justice* (Durham, NC: Duke University Press, 2014), 103.

58. Phillip-Dowe, "Women in the Grenada Revolution," 55.

59. On the occasion of the release of the imprisoned members of the New Jewel Movement (NJM) in 2009, Grenadian scholar Patsy Lewis wrote of her experience at a Caribbean Studies Association panel that same year, where the trauma of the overthrow of the NJP seemed to be fresh for the non-Grenadians in attendance, while Grenadians, in her view, had worked to heal those wounds. Patsy Lewis, "Grenadian Reflections," *Stabroek News*, September 14, 2009, http://www.stabroeknews.com/2009/features/09/14

/grenadian-reflections/. Brian Meeks agrees with Lewis, characterizing the reactions of other Caribbean people as "suspended in the moment of crisis in 1983." "Grenada Once Again: Revisiting the 1983 Crisis and Collapse of the Grenada Revolution," in *The Grenada Revolution: Reflections and Lessons*, ed. Wendy C. Grenade (Jackson: University of Missouri Press, 2015), 88.

60. Merle Collins, "Foreword," *The Grenada Revolution*, ed. Wendy C. Grenade (Jackson: University of Mississippi Press, 2015), vii.

61. Shalini Puri, "Fielding the Field: Notes on Caribbean Cultural Criticism, Area Studies, and the Forms of Engagement," *Small Axe* 17, nos. 2 and 4 (2013): 60, 68.

62. Shalini Puri, *The Grenadian Revolution in the Caribbean Present: Operation Urgent Memory* (New York: Palgrave Macmillan, 2014), 14.

63. Dionne Brand, "Marlene Green," *Now Toronto*, November 2, 2002, https://nowtoronto.com/news/marlene-green-1940-2002/.

64. Sharpe, *Ghosts of Slavery*, xi.

65. Recently Bernard Coard used a similar question as part of the title of his own account of his role in the coup and his seventeen-year-long imprisonment. *The Grenada Revolution: What Really Happened* (CreateSpace, 2017).

66. Merle Collins, "What Happened? Grenada: A Retrospective Journey," *Social and Economic Studies* 62, nos. 3–4 (2013): 19.

67. Collins, "What Happened?"

68. Brand, *No Language Is Neutral*.

69. See David Scott's discussion of *Angel* by Merle Collins as representative of the "temporal standstill" that the failure of the Grenada Revolution caused in both literary and political discourse. *Omens of Adversity*, 71–87.

70. Raphael Dalleo identifies the revolution as a repeated theme in Brand's work across her poetry, life writing, and fiction. See *Caribbean Literature and the Public Sphere*, 231. As Collins suggests in "What Happened?," it is perhaps more accurate to say that Grenada's past is not completely silenced but unresolved and to some extent unresolvable.

71. Collins, "What Happened?," 20.

72. Steedman, *Dust*, 62.

73. Cummings, "(Trans)Nationalisms," 169.

74. Patricia Saunders, "Fugitive Dreams of Diaspora: Conversations with Saidiya Hartman," *Anthurium* 6, no. 1 (2008): 13.

CHAPTER 2 — SPECULATIVE AUTOBIOGRAPHY

1. Foundational texts related to the line between fiction and autobiography include Paul John Eakin, *Fictions of Autobiography: Studies in the Art of Self-Invention* (Princeton: Princeton University Press, 1985), Timothy Dow Adams, *Telling Lies in Modern American Autobiography* (Chapel Hill: University of North Carolina Press, 2000), and Leigh Gilmore, *The Limits of Autobiography* (Ithaca, NY: Cornell University Press, 1990). My framework for the Caribbean "quarrel with history" includes Edward Baugh, "West Indian Writer," and Glissant, "Quarrel with History."

2. For an overview of the West's figuring of the Global South as outside of history and modernity as well as how power works to create or elide historical "truth," see Trouillot, *Silencing the Past*. Mimi Sheller's *Consuming the Caribbean: From Arawaks to Zombies* (London: Routledge, 2003) takes up these themes in detail as they related to European exploitation of the Caribbean.

3. Some of the major feminist efforts in Caribbean literature and criticism, in a rough chronological order from the 1970s to the present, include highlighting women's presence in historical and political movements, as well as bringing forward underrecognized writers; offering positive representations of rural and working-class Caribbean women; representing women as agential subjects; spotlighting women's role in nationalist movements; and theorizing sexuality and domesticity. As I discuss in this chapter, some Francophone Caribbean feminist projects differ from Anglophone ones in that places like Martinique and Guadeloupe are not independent nations, and so issues of women's agency and erasure from history tend to be more prominent than women's embrace of nationalism in works from here. For an encapsulated discussion of some of the main thrusts of Caribbean feminist literary productions and feminist literary criticism, see Donette Francis, "Strategies of Caribbean Feminism," in Bucknor and Donnell, *Routledge Companion*, 332–343.

4. Condé is a prolific author, publishing over fifteen novels since her first work *Heremakhonon* (1976) as well as essays, stories, plays, and children's fiction. She is one of most well-known and successful writers of the African diaspora, with her novels in particular generating critical attention from scholars of Caribbean, African diaspora, Francophone literature, and women's literature. There are over twenty-nine monographs devoted in part or in full to Condé's novels. Major works include Dawn Fulton, *Signs of Dissent: Maryse Condé and Postcolonial Criticism* (Charlottesville: University of Virginia Press, 2006); Vera Broichhagen, *Feasting on Words: Maryse Condé, Cannibalism, and the Caribbean Text* (Princeton: Program in Latin American Studies, Princeton University, 2006); Simone A. James Alexander, *Mother Imagery in the Novels of Afro-Caribbean Women* (Columbia: University of Missouri Press, 2001); Eva Sansavior, *Maryse Condé and the Space of Literature* (London: Legenda, 2012); and Deborah M. Hess, *Maryse Condé: Mythe, Parabole Et Complexité* (Paris: L'Harmattan, 2011). Significant critical treatments of Condé's life writing include Edgard Sankara, *Postcolonial Autobiographies: From Africa to the Antilles* (Charlottesville: University of Virginia Press, 2011); Laurie Corbin, "The Return to and Beyond the Mother: Maryse Condé and Representations of Maternity," *Life Writing* 4, no. 2 (2007): 231–245; and Thomas, *Connecting Histories*.

5. Paquet, *Caribbean Autobiography*, 5.

6. Maryse Condé, "Order, Disorder, Freedom, and the West Indian Writer," *Yale French Studies* 97, no. 2 (2000): 163.

7. Francis, *Fictions of Feminine Citizenship*, 143.

8. The autobiographical pact was theorized by Philip Lejeune in *On Autobiography*. More recently, James Phelan calls instances in life writing where the author alerts the reader that a pure invention will follow "fictionality." I distinguish fictionality as a method of representing the truth that has some connection to real events (such as Phelan's example of a writer depicting his actual psychiatrist as the White Rabbit from *Alice in Wonderland*) from speculative autobiography that responds to absences in the historical record that cannot be bridged through metaphor or through additional archives or other forms of research. "Fictionality," *a/b: Auto/Biography Studies* 32, no. 2 (2017): 235–238.

9. Joe Fassler, "How Surrealism Enriches Storytelling about Women: Interview with Carmen Maria Machado," *Atlantic*, October 12, 2017, https://www.theatlantic.com/entertainment/archive/2017/10/how-surrealism-enriches-storytelling-about-women/542496/#article-comments.

10. "The French republican and integrationist model is built upon the prerequisite that foreigners and minorities should assimilate, erasing the possibility for an individual to have a dual identity. The model dictates that a black citizen from the Antilles or from Africa should become 'French,' all ties to his native culture must be severed and any feeling of belonging to his former group erased. Equally, this immigrant can make no claims on behalf of his slave ancestors and has no right whatsoever of having his particular history recognized by the State." Jean-Yves Camus, "The Commemoration of Slavery in France and the Emergence of a Black Political Consciousness," *European Legacy* 11, no. 6 (2006): 650.

11. Camus, "Commemoration of Slavery," 649; Crystal M. Fleming, "White Cruelty or Republican Sins? Competing Frames of Stigma Reversal in French Commemorations of Slavery," *Ethnic and Racial Studies* 35, no. 3 (2012): 493.

12. Christopher L. Miller, *The French Atlantic Triangle: Literature and Culture of the Slave Trade* (Durham, NC: Duke University Press, 2008), 38.

13. François Vergés, "Cartographies of Memory, Politics of Emancipation," in *At the Limits of Memory: Legacies of Slavery in the Francophone World*, ed. Nicola Frith and Kate Hodgson (Liverpool: Liverpool University Press, 2015), 229.

14. Of course, the second time slavery was abolished in France was 1848. Camus, "Commemoration of Slavery," 649; Fleming, "White Cruelty," 493. The hundredth anniversary of emancipation was celebrated in both France and its Caribbean departments. Charles Forsdick, "Contrapuntal Memories of Slavery and Abolition in the French-Speaking World," in *Slavery, Memory, and Identity: National Representations and Global Legacies*, ed. Douglas Hamilton, Kate Hodgson, and Joel Quirk (London: Pickering & Chatto, 2012), 105. Guadeloupe recently opened a museum devoted to slavery, Memorial ACTe, built on the site of a former factory that used slave labor. It has received criticism for what some believe to be its Eurocentric narrative about the origins of slavery and its paternalistic view of the current relationship between France and its overseas departments. Maddy Crowell, "The Island Where France's Colonial Legacy Lives On," *Atlantic*, April 21, 2018, https://www.theatlantic.com/international/archive/2018/04/france-macron-guadeloupe-slavery-colonialism/557996/.

15. Notable is Haiti's exclusion from official committees and acts of remembrance. See Forsdick, "Contrapuntal Memories."

16. "La recherche sur la traite négrière, l'esclavage et leurs abolitions est une preoccupation centrale pour le CPME. Son développement contribuera utilement à l'apaisement des controverses actuelles, qui reposent trop souvent sur une méconnaissance des faits établis par les chercheurs des différents pays. Cela concerne notamment la connaissance des chiffres de la traite au cours des siècles de son existence, légale puis illégale. En outre, la recherché universitaire française sur ces sujets longtemps délaissés ou occultés a pris un immense retard par rapport aux travaux des chercheurs britanniques, nord-américains, jamaïcains, cubains ou brésiliens. Fournir à la recherche française en ces domaines les moyens, matériels et institutionnels, doit être considéré comme une priorité absolue. Dans l'immédiat, l'objectif visé doit être de mettre cette recherche au niveau de ses devancières de langue anglaise, qui ont été longtemps les seules à prospecter ce terrain vierge des sciences historiques et sociales." Comité pour la mémoire de l'esclave, "Mémoires de la traite négriére, del l'esclave et leurs abolitions," Rapport á Monsieur le Premier Ministre, April 12, 2005, 49.

17. Stiina Löytömäki, "French Memory Laws and the Ambivalence about the Meaning of Colonialism," in *The Palgrave Handbook of State Sponsored History after 1945*, ed. Berber Bevernage and Nico Wouters (Basingstoke, UK: Palgrave Macmillan, 2018), 87–92.

18. Condé is a divisive figure within Caribbean literature, notable for rejecting notions of cultural essentialism such as that to write in Creole is a more authentic expression of Antillean culture than to write in standard French. A further example of Condé's rejection of essentialism is her characterization of Negritude and Pan-Africanism as early forms of globalization that effaced cultural differences among the African diaspora and embraced a faulty belief in commonalities based on race. See Anne W. Gulick, "Africa, Pan-Africanism, and the Global Caribbean in Maryse Condé's *The Story of the Cannibal Women*," *Global South* 4, no. 2 (2010): 49–75.

19. Helen Buss, *Repossessing the World: Reading Memoirs by Contemporary Women* (Waterloo: Wilfrid Laurier University Press, 2002), 86; James Alexander, *Mother Imagery.*

20. To contextualize the distance in time and class status between Victoire's illiteracy and her granddaughter's international acclaim as a writer, it is important to note that Condé was born in 1938 into an upwardly mobile family who were part of the elite Grands Négres, the emerging Black bourgeois of 1920s and 1930s Guadeloupe. The Grands Négres, in Condé's historical vision, are portrayed as little better than their white creole predecessors. They scorn the mixed race of Guadeloupe and revere the French language and culture. Contrary to their revolutionary rhetoric, they wish to remake the power structure to their own advantage. Ironically, as I explore in this chapter, as an illegitimate child born to an illiterate mother, Condé's mother Jeanne is able to join the Grands Négres only through the sacrifices of Victoire, who embarrassed her through her servitude and inability to speak French. The distance between Maryse and Victoire is not only one of class and race, but also one of time and language.

21. Megan Doll, "Interview with Maryse Condé," *Bookslut*, February 2010, http://www.bookslut.com/features/2010_02_015665.php.

22. Yarimar Bonilla, *Non-sovereign Futures: Caribbean Politics in the Wake of Disenchantment* (Chicago: University of Chicago Press, 2015), 136.

23. The term "archival impossibility" is inspired by Lisa Lowe's powerful framing of the limits of archives in *Intimacies of Four Continents.*

24. Forsdick, "Contrapuntal Memories," 107.

25. Cheryl Wall, *Worrying the Line: Black Women Writers, Lineage, and Literary Tradition* (Chapel Hill: University of North Carolina Press, 2005), 9.

26. Trouillot, *Silencing the Past*, 52.

27. Avery Gordon, "Introduction to the New Edition," in *Ghostly Matters*, xvi.

28. Baugh, "West Indian Writer," 64.

29. Patricia Yaeger, "Ghosts and Shattered Bodies, or What Does it Mean to Still be Haunted by Southern Literature," *South Central Review* 22, no. 1 (2005): 97.

30. Here, as throughout this study, I refer to the authors of life writing texts by their last name and to their self-representation within the text by their first name.

31. Condé does not provide a date for this photograph, but we may assume it was taken when Victoire was an adult and probably paid for by her daughter. According to Michael Ayre, the period encompassing Victoire's life (1874–1915) was also years of rapid change in photography in the Caribbean. The invention of dry plate photography allowed photographers to travel throughout the Caribbean, even to smaller towns such as Pointe-á-Pitre.

Around 1905 photographs became more accessible to Caribbean people. *The Caribbean in Sepia: A History in Photographs 1840–1900* (Kingston: Ian Randle, 2012).

32. For an instructive reading of photographs of Guadeloupean women from this time period, see Claire Tancons, "Women in the Whirlwind: Withholding Guadeloupe's Archipelagic History," *Small Axe* 16, no. 3 (2012): 143–165.

33. Gordon, "Introduction to the New Edition," xvi.

34. Wolff, "Maryse Condé."

35. Arif Dirlik cautions, "As literature has been placed at the service of exploring ethnic and transnational (or diasporic) identities, the construction of identities in literary work has been confounded with the ethnography of culture, subjecting the writer to pressures that subvert the autonomy of creative work." "Literature/Identity: Transnationalism, Narrative and Representation," *Review of Education, Pedagogy, and Cultural Studies* 24, no. 3 (2002): 210.

36. See Doll, "Interview," for Condé's assertion that her publisher labeled *Victoire* as "autofiction"; she wanted it to be categorized as a "tale," like *Tales from the Heart: True Stories from My Childhood* (New York: Soho Press, 2004).

37. Smith and Watson, *Reading Autobiography*, 256. Condé's life writing also might be categorized as serial autobiography—autobiographical works published in multiple volumes. These texts could be termed "memoirs" since they are less of a birth to an old-age story but rather seek to position Condé and her family within the context of the continued colonization of Guadeloupe (Smith and Watson, *Reading Autobiography*, 280).

38. Leigh Gilmore, *Autobiographics: A Feminist Theory of Women's Self-Representation* (Ithaca, NY: Cornell University Press 1994), 2.

39. Hartman, "Venus in Two Acts," 11.

40. Documentation of the newspapers or periodicals Condé mentions that were published during the time period can be found in Archives Départementales de la Guadeloupe, *Journaz et revues: Catalogue des collections de presse conservées aux Archives départementales* (Gourbeyre: Archives Départementales de la Guadeloupe, 2000), 332.

41. Fuentes, *Dispossessed Lives*, 7.

42. Doll, "Interview."

43. Andrea Stuart, *Sugar in the Blood: One Family's Story of History and Empire* (London: Portobello Books, 2012), xviii.

44. Stuart, *Sugar in the Blood*, xvii.

45. Stuart, *Sugar in the Blood*, xvii.

46. Lucia Llano Puertas, "Touching the Past: The Inscription of Trauma and Affect in Francophone Neo-Slave Narratives," *Callaloo* 40, no. 4 (2017): 78–79.

47. Catherine Reinhardt, *Claims to Memory: Beyond Slavery and Emancipation in the French Caribbean* (New York: Berghahn Books, 2006), 15. See also Diana Paton, "Telling Stories about Slavery," *History Workshop Journal* 59 (2005): 252.

48. Françoise Lionnet, "Narrating the Americas: Transcolonial Métissage and Maryse Condé's La Migration des coeurs," in *Mixing Race, Mixing Culture*, ed. Monika Kaup and Debra J. Rosenthal (Austin: University of Texas Press, 2002), 69.

49. Rice-Maximin terms this period in Guadeloupean history "le siècle oublié." Micheline Rice-Maximin, *Karukéra: Presence littéraire de la Guadeloupe* (New York: Peter Lang, 1988), 84. Mary Jean Green's essay "Maryse Condé's Victoire: Thinking

Back through Her Mothers," *Nottingham French Studies* 53, no. 3 (2014): 297–313, very helpfully pointed me toward this text. Abigail Celis provided translation assistance of French portions of Green's essay as well as other French-language materials.

50. Laurent Dubois notes that slavery and emancipation are the primary focuses within Guadeloupean history as well as in historical fiction. "Solitude's Statue: Confronting the Past in the French Caribbean," *Outre-Mers* 94, nos. 350–351 (2006): 34–36.

51. Anne Eller, "Rumors of Slavery: Defending Emancipation in a Hostile Caribbean," *American Historical Review* 122, no. 3 (2017): 675.

52. Rice-Maximin, *Karukéra*, 84.

53. Rice-Maximin, *Karukéra*, 84–85; Green, "Maryse Condé's Victoire," 301.

54. Hortense J. Spillers, "Mama's Baby, Papa's Maybe: An American Grammar Book," *Diacritics* 17, no. 2 (1987): 67.

55. *Victoire* contradicts the story Condé tells in *Tales from the Heart* about Jeanne's father. (Victoire is called Elodie in *Tales*.) "A stranger had raped Elodie and fifteen years earlier a factory worker had sexually assaulted her own mother" (72).

56. The image is from a family trip in 1946. "A picture taken at the end of that particular visit to France shows us in the Luxembourg Gardens. My brothers and sisters all in a row. My father, sporting a mustache, dressed in an overcoat with a fur collar. My mother smiling with all her pearly white teeth, her almond shaped eyes squinting under her shiny rabbit-skin fedora" (*Tales from the Heart*, 8).

57. Timothy Dow Adams, *Light Writing and Life Writing: Photography in Autobiography* (Chapel Hill: University of North Carolina Press, 2000), 5.

58. Dawn Fulton, in her study of Condé's work, argues that "one unwelcome consequence of the drive towards inclusivity is thus the glamorization of the oppressed subject that accompanies his or her transparent apparition in theoretical discourse: on the stage of cultural relativism, the marginal condition attains a state of moral immunity and unnuanced goodness" (*Signs of Dissent*, 7).

59. "The goodness of the father. He takes care of his children; it is up to them to be well-behaved, to deserve his attention. The intrusion of sentiment in socio-political relations." Glissant, "Quarrel with History," 28.

60. Lauren Derby, "Beyond Fugitive Speech: Rumor and Affect in Caribbean History," *Small Axe* 18, no. 2 (2014): 132, 124.

61. Francis, *Fictions of Feminine Citizenship*, 3.

62. Lisa A. Lindsay and John Wood Sweet, "Introduction: Biography and the Black Atlantic," in *Biography and the Black Atlantic*, ed. Lindsay and Sweet (Philadelphia: University of Pennsylvania Press, 2014), 8.

63. Reinhardt, *Claims to Memory*, 1–21.

64. As Lowe notes, social stratification "charts the historically differentiated access to the domains of liberal personhood, from interiority and individual will, to the possession of property and domesticity" (*Intimacies of Four Continents*, 18).

65. Adolphe Catan, *La Guadeloupe à travers l'oeil d'Adolphe Catan: 50 ans de photos depuis 1920* (Guadeloupe: Association Photo Cat, 1999).

66. Gayatri Chakravorty Spivak, "Three Women's Texts and Circumfession," in *Postcolonialism & Autobiography: Michelle Cliff, David Dabydeen, Opal Palmer Adisa*, ed. Alfred Horung and Ernstpeter Ruhe (Amsterdam: Rodopi, 1998), 21.

67. Spivak, "Three Women's Texts," 9.

68. Chris Bongie argues that Condé intentionally invokes postcolonial critical frameworks in her fiction (such as the revision of canonical novels as in *Windward Heights*), only to frustrate expectations, such as that the postcolonial future will be better than the colonial past. Bongie, *Friends and Enemies*, 331.

69. Adams, *Telling Lies*, 8–9.

70. Eakin, *Fictions of Autobiography*, 287.

71. Joan Wallach Scott foundationally defines a feminist historian's standpoint as beginning with "a refusal of the fixed and permanent quality of the binary opposition, a genuine historicization and deconstruction of the terms of sexual difference. . . . The history of feminist thought is a history of the refusal of the hierarchical construction of the relationship between male and female in its specific contexts and an attempt to reverse or displace its operations." "Gender: A Useful Category of Historical Analysis," *American Historical Review* 91, no. 5 (1989): 1065–1066.

72. See Green, "Maryse Condé's Victoire," esp. 311 and n. 32, for a discussion of stories about Légitimus's private life in Guadeloupean popular culture.

73. "The grammar of black feminist futurity is a performance of a future that hasn't yet happened but must. It is an attachment to a belief in what should be true. . . . It is the power to imagine beyond current fact and to envision that which is not, but must be." Tina M. Campt, *Listening to Images: An Exercise in Counterintuition* (Durham, NC: Duke University Press, 2017), 17.

74. Victoire's skill in inventing dishes is often linked in the text to Condé's own feelings of pleasure and mastery in writing as most scholarship on *Victoire* acknowledges. See Bonnie Thomas, "The Cook and the Writer: Maryse Condé's Journey of Self-Discovery," *PORTAL* 10, no. 2 (2013): 1–12. For an overview of representations of food in French Caribbean writing, see Valérie Loichot, *The Tropics Bite Back: Culinary Coups in Caribbean Literature* (Minneapolis: University of Minnesota Press, 2013).

75. Victor Schoelcher was a French abolitionist who was an elected deputy from Guadeloupe to the French legislature.

76. Nick Nesbitt, "Caribbean Literature in French: Origins and Development," in *The Cambridge History of African and Caribbean Literature*, ed. F. Abiola Irele and Simon Gikandi. (Cambridge: Cambridge University Press, 2008), 653.

77. For an overview of the role of marronage in Caribbean resistance practices, see Neil Roberts, *Freedom as Marronage* (Chicago: University of Chicago Press, 2015).

78. Fred Moten, "Preface for a Solo by Miles Davis," *Women and Performance: A Journal of Feminist Theory* 17, no. 2 (2007): 223.

79. Jean Rhys, "Heat," *New Yorker*, May 17, 1976, 36–37.

80. Alexander, "Not Just (Any) *Body*."

CHAPTER 3 — REPICTURING THE PICTURESQUE

1. The new emphasis within Caribbean studies on environmental humanities and its difference from North American versions informs this reading. The editors of *Caribbean Literature and the Environment* note that while North American ecocriticism often harkens to a landscape unmarked by history or human labor, this is an impossible project in the Caribbean. In the Caribbean what we think of now as "natural" was constructed through the wholesale importation of crops and fauna. For example, the palm tree, coconut drinks, and sugar cane—synonymous with the region—are the products of plants imported from India. Elizabeth M. DeLoughrey, Renée K. Gosson, and George B.

Handley, "Introduction," in *Caribbean Literature and the Environment*, ed. DeLoughrey, Gosson, and Handley (Charlottesville: University of Virginia Press, 2005), 1–30.

2. Krista Thompson, "Evidence of Things Not Photographed: Slavery and Historical Memory in the British West Indies," *Representations* 113, no. 1 (2011): 40.

3. Helton, et. al, 1.

4. Sandra Pouchet Paquet, "Autobiography and Autobiographical Fiction in the Caribbean," in *The Novel in Africa and the Caribbean since 1950*, ed. Simon Gikandi (Oxford: Oxford University Press, 2016), 332.

5. My approach to thinking about categories of identity and the meaning made of them in feminist historiography is influenced by Evelyn Brooks Higginbotham's groundbreaking 1992 essay on the co-constituting categories of race and gender. Her recent revisiting of that essay focuses on the still understudied connections between race, sexuality, and African American women's history, noting the necessity of bringing multiple identities into an analysis. "African-American Women's History and the Metalanguage of Race," *Signs* 17, no. 2 (1992): 251–274; "'The Metalanguage of Race,' Then and Now," *Signs* 42, no. 3 (2017): 628–642.

6. Steedman, *Dust*, 67.

7. For a definition of descendant communities and overview of the relationship between descendant communities and social science and historical interpretation, see Chip Colwell, "Collaborative Archaeologies and Descendant Communities," *Annual Review of Anthropology* 45 (2016): 113–127.

8. Megan Gannon, "Kitchen of Thomas Jefferson's Enslaved Chef Is Uncovered," *Live Science*, January 10, 2018, https://www.livescience.com/61388-thomas-jefferson-james-hemings-kitchen.html.

9. In the United States, slaves were counted by age and sex rather than by name through the 1860 federal census. U.S. census data can vary by state.

10. For example, even in a resource-rich country such as the United States, President James Monroe's plantation Highland (currently owned and managed by the College of William & Mary) did not acknowledge the role of slaves in their tours and educational materials until recently. Tours of former slave plantations often focus on the prosperous trappings of the Big House, with little focus on the identities of the enslaved or their living conditions. What became of the enslaved and their families post-emancipation was also little remarked upon. At Highland, historians accepted the oral history that Monroe's slaves were sold and sent to Florida, ignoring the fact that African Americans living in a nearby area called Monroetown knew themselves to be descendants of Monroe's slaves. The descendant community of Monroetown advocated for their history to change the way Highland told the story of the plantation to visitors. Jordy Yager, "A Former Plantation Begins to Tell as Fuller Story of Slavery in America," National Public Radio, December 9, 2018, https://www.npr.org/2018/12/09/672349672/a-former-plantation-begins-to-tell-a-fuller-story-of-slavery-in-america.

11. National Trust for Historic Preservation and African American Cultural Heritage Action Fund, "Engaging Descendant Communities in the Interpretation of Slavery: A Rubric of Best Practices Established by the National Summit of Teaching Slavery" (September 26, 2018), https://assets.documentcloud.org/documents/5348132/Interpreting-Slavery-9-26-18.pdf.

12. William Gilpin, *Observations of the River Wye, and Several Parts of Wales, &c: Relative Chiefly to Picturesque Beauty Made in the Summer of 1770*, 2nd ed. (London: Blamire, 1789). https://archive.org/stream/observationsonr00gilpgoog#page/n42/mode/2up.

13. Gilpin, *Observations of the River Wye*, 44. I was directed to this passage in Gilpin's writing by Krista Thompson's *Eye for the Tropics* (35).

14. James Hakewill, *A Picturesque Tour of the Island of Jamaica from Drawing Made in the Years 1820 and 1821* (London: Hurst and Robinson, 1825).

15. Elizabeth A. Bohls, *Slavery and the Politics of Place: the Colonial Caribbean, 1772—1833* (Cambridge: Cambridge University Press, 2015), 22–23.

16. John E. Crowley, "Picturing the Caribbean in the Global British Landscape," *Studies in Eighteenth-Century Culture* 32 (2003): 323.

17. Édouard Glissant, *Poetics of Relation*, trans. Betsy Wing (Ann Arbor: University of Michigan Press, 1997), 70.

18. Charmaine A. Nelson, *Slavery, Geography and Empire in Nineteenth-Century Marine Landscapes of Montreal and Jamaica* (New York: Routledge, 2016), 303.

19. Thompson, *Eye for the Tropics*, 27–29.

20. Erna Brodber, "Afro-Jamaican Women at the Turn of the Century," *Social and Economic Studies* 35, no. 3 (1980): 23–50. For an illuminating gloss of Brodber's first novels and early historical writings, see Veronica Gregg, "'This Past That Waits for Me': Erna Brodber's Critical Remembrance and the Challenge to History," in *Engendering Caribbean History: Cross-Cultural Perspectives*, ed. Verene Shepherd (Kingston: Ian Randle, 2011), 789–799. See also Alison Donnell's invaluable essay on the importance of Brodber's work focused on the local in the midst of critical emphasis on diaspora "What It Means to Stay: Reterritorializing the Black Atlantic in Erna Brodber's Writing of the Local," *Third World Quarterly* 26, no. 3 (2005): 479–486.

21. There are several videos documenting the work of Blackspace as a site of oral transmission of knowledge on YouTube including "Erna Brodber on Blackspace," August 12, 2013. https://www.youtube.com/watch?v=3z_vMfGyQX8.

22. Erna Brodber, *The People of My Jamaican Village 1817–1948* (St. Mary/St. Catherine: Blackspace, 1999) and *Woodside Pear Tree Grove P.O.* (Kingston: University of the West Indies Press, 2004).

23. Erna Brodber, "Re-engineering Blackspace," *Caribbean Quarterly* 43, nos. 1–2 (1997): 70, 72.

24. Brodber, "Re-engineering Blackspace," 72.

25. A tension exists within autobiography studies between views of genealogy as an inherently conservative impulse in contrast to life writing's potential to generate narratives of affiliation that are not about legitimacy and blood kinship. These arguments are not necessarily relevant to the communities attempting to recover histories obscured by slavery, indenture, and colonial rule. See Julia Watson, "Ordering the Family: Genealogy as Autobiographical Pedigree" (1996), in *Life Writing in the Long Run: A Smith and Watson Autobiography Studies Reader*, ed. Sidonie Smith and Julia Watson (Ann Arbor: Michigan Publishing, 2017), and Julie Rak, "Radical Connections: Genealogy, Small Lives, Big Data," *a/b: Auto/Biography Studies* 32, no. 3 (2017): 479–497.

26. Kamau Brathwaite, *The Development of Creole Society in Jamaica, 1770–1820* (Oxford: Clarendon, 1972); Rex Nettleford, *Caribbean Cultural Identity: The Case of Jamaica* (Los Angeles: Center for Afro-American Studies and UCLA Latin American Center, 1979); Barbara Bush, *Slave Women in Caribbean Society* (Bloomington: Indiana University Press, 1990).

27. Catherine John states that Brodber's embedded research and publications coupled with her localized community work is a "new kind of model for a Caribbean organic

intellectual" in distinction to current modes of theorization emphasizing hybrid and globalized subjects (73). "Caribbean Organic Intellectual: The Legacy and Challenge of Erna Brodber's Life's Work," *Small Axe* 39 (2012): 72–88.

28. Antonia MacDonald, "Erna Brodber: A Poetics of Redemption," in *The Routledge Companion to Caribbean Literature*, ed. Michael A. Bucknor and Alison Donnell (London: Routledge, 2011), 20.

29. Hartman, *Lose Your Mother*, 130.

30. Sheri-Marie Harrison, *Jamaica's Difficult Subjects: Negotiating Sovereignty in Anglophone Caribbean Literature and Criticism* (Columbus: Ohio State University, 2014), 2, 15–16.

31. John A. Aarons and Sharon Alexander-Gooding, "Historical Developments in Caribbean Archives and Record Keeping," in Bastian, Aarons, and Griffin, *Decolonizing the Caribbean Record*, 14.

32. Sylvia Wynter, "Novel and History, Plot and Plantation," *Savacou* 5, (1971): 95.

33. Brodber, "Oral History Sources," 7.

34. Mary Prince, *History of Mary Prince, a West Indian Slave. Related by Herself. With a Supplement by the Editor. To Which Is Added, the Narrative of Asa-Asa, a Captured African* (London: F. Westley and A. H. Davis, 1831); James Williams, *A Narrative of Events since the First of August, 1834, by James Williams an Apprenticed Labourer in Jamaica* (Durham, NC: Duke University Press, 2001).

35. See Barbara Bush, "'Sable Venus,' 'She Devil' or 'Drudge'? British Slavery and the 'Fabulous Fiction' of Black Women's Identities, c. 1650–1838," *Women's History Review* 9, no. 4 (2000): 761–789.

36. Hakewill, *Picturesque Tour*, 8.

37. Trevor Burnard, *Mastery, Tyranny, and Desire: Thomas Thistlewood and His Slaves in the Anglo-Jamaican World* (Chapel Hill: University of North Carolina Press, 2004), 154–156.

38. See, for example, the entry on John Neilson in Legacies of British Slave-Ownership, https://www.ucl.ac.uk/lbs/person/view/2146646129.

39. Jessica Marie Johnson, "Markup Bodies: Black [Life] Studies and Slavery [Death] Studies at the Digital Crossroads," *Social Text* 36, no. 4 (2018): 58.

40. Johnson, "Markup Bodies," 59.

41. National Trust for Historic Preservation and African American Cultural Heritage Action Fund, "Engaging Descendant Communities."

42. Erna Brodber "Where Are All the Others?," in *Caribbean Creolization: Reflections on the Cultural Dynamics of Language, Literature, and Identity*, ed. Kathleen M. Blutansky and Mare-Agnes Sourieau (Kingston: University Press of the West Indies, 1998), 69.

43. Sidonie Smith and Julia Watson characterize *From Harvey River* as autoethnography, a term distinguishing life writing that centers a polity rather than an individual, which accurately describes Goodison's work. I distinguish descendant community life writing from autoethnography as Brodber's and Goodison's narratives focus on place as much as people. *Reading Autobiography*, 259. Goodison, *From Harvey River.*

44. For scholarship on themes in Goodison's poetry related to ancestry and land, see Hugh Hodges, "Possession Rites and Healing Rituals in the Poetry of Lorna Goodison," *Research in African Literatures* 36, no. 2 (2005): 19–32; Mac Fenwick, "Simply There: Lorna Goodison's Gardens," *Journal of Commonwealth Literature* 46 (2011): 433–453; and Jahan Ramazi, "Lorna Goodison," *Caribbean Quarterly* 64, nos. 3–4 (2018): 560–580.

45. Christopher Winks suggests that *From Harvey River* might be read as "microhistory" (140). "From Harvey River: A Memoir of My Mother and Her Island," *Review: Literature and Arts of the Americas* 42, no. 1 (2009):138–140.

46. Lorna Goodison, "Reporting Back to Queen Isabella, Donette Francis, and Sandra Pouchet Paquet," *Small Axe* 14, no. 2 (2010): 183.

47. Omise'eke Natasha Tinsley, *Thiefing Sugar: Eroticism between Women in Caribbean Literature* (Durham, NC: Duke University Press, 2010), 164.

48. When Doris fears her son has been killed in a train crash, she is described as returning to Harvey River to cope: "Calm, for some reason my mother became completely calm, her mind goes underwater, for the next few hours she will do everything as if she was swimming under the waters of the Harvey River" (239).

49. Here, as throughout this study, I refer to the authors of life writing texts by their last name and to their self-representation within the text by their first name.

50. Sarah Phillips Casteel categorizes much of recent diasporic criticism as having an "exaggerated stress on displacement, dislocation, and movement at the expense of place," especially the rural (3). *Second Arrivals: Landscape and Belonging in Contemporary Writing of the Americas* (Charlottesville: University of Virginia Press, 2007).

51. Francis, *Fictions of Feminine Citizenship*.

52. Supriya Nair, *Pathologies of Paradise: Caribbean Detours* (Charlottesville: University of Virginia Press, 2013), 75.

53. Alison Donnell, *Twentieth-Century Caribbean Literature: Critical Moments in Anglophone Literary History* (London: Routledge, 2005), 71. These critiques persist, despite poems by Goodison such as "Jamaica 1980," which questions the Caribbean as a paradise in the wake of Jamaican violence.

54. *From Harvey River* does not speak directly to many of the central themes of late twentieth- and early twenty-first-century literature such as migration, diaspora, and cultural dislocation that also align with key critical theoretical models. These include Paul Gilroy's *The Black Atlantic: Modernity and Double-Consciousness* (Cambridge, MA: Harvard University Press, 1994) and Antonio Benítez-Rojo's postmodern take in *The Repeating Island: The Caribbean and the Postmodern Perspective* (Durham, NC: Duke University Press, 1997). Gilroy's emphasis on multiple sites of Black cultural production in the Atlantic world, like Benítez-Rojo's reliance on chaos theory and cultures without borders, does not map easily onto Goodison's text, which is about local spaces and is an attempt to order and recover family history. While Benítez-Rojo theorized the linguistic and cultural virtuosity of the Caribbean as hybrid cultures constantly in motion, speaking back to imperial ideologies of Caribbean cultures as being either poor imitations of the mother country or as barbaric holdovers from Africa and Asia, *From Harvey River* depicts a local Jamaican culture that is largely unconcerned with these debates.

55. Donnell, *Twentieth-Century Caribbean Literature*, 94, 93.

56. *From Harvey River* was reviewed widely, but in the decade since its publication it has received few critical treatments. With the exception of the articles published in *Small Axe*, there has been no sustained critical treatment of the work.

57. In *Fictions of Feminine Citizenship*, Francis notes the presence of the Caribbean picturesque in romances from the nationalist period, which then "give way to the antiromance of the late postcolonial period" (5). In this chapter I argue that Goodison's

recuperation of the picturesque is neither an antiromance nor an idealized vision of the Caribbean allying her with earlier representations by Caribbean nationalists.

58. Donette Francis, "The Last Stitch: A Praise Song for My Mother Who Mothered Me," *Small Axe* 14, no. 2 (2010): 161.

59. Sandra Pouchet Paquet, "Sewing Up Questions of Cultural Identity: Lorna Goodison's *From Harvey River*," *Small Axe* 14, no. 2 (2010): 168.

60. "The pleasure here lies in the recognition of the elements that gave pleasure before and the desire to revisit that experience. The excess creates the need for more repetition, more recognition, and the generation of more meanings that are not identical to what has gone before, but can be *identified*. They are almost, but not quite, the same." Rak, *Boom!*, Kindle 637.

61. Maternal memoirs are usually focused on the subjectivity of the mother/autobiographer or more directly on the mother/child relationship. Elizabeth Podnieks and Andrea O'Reilly, "Maternal Literatures in Text and Tradition: Daughter-Centric, Matrilineal and Matrifocal Perspectives," in *Textual Mothers, Maternal Texts: Motherhood in Contemporary Women's Literatures*, ed. Podnieks and O'Reilly (Waterloo: Wilfrid Laurier University Press, 2010), 1–27.

62. Goodison, "Reporting Back," 183, emphasis added.

63. In discussing the CUNY Graduate Center's Caribbean Epistemologies Seminar (2010–2012), Josephs argues that definitions of the Caribbean are central to the region's epistemologies because intellectual framings create what can be known about a place and its culture. "Articulating Caribbean Epistemologies."

64. Crowley, "Picturing the Caribbean," 324–325. In the years that have passed since Crowley's essay, it has been necessary to temper his argument that Caribbeanists have been inattentive to colonial modes of visual production. Leon Wainwright noted in his review of Thompson's *An Eye for the Tropics* that Caribbean studies was experiencing a visual turn. The subsequent publication of Mary Lou Emery's *Modernism, the Visual, and Caribbean Literature* (Cambridge: Cambridge University Press, 2007) and Simon Gikandi's *Slavery and the Culture of Taste* (Princeton: Princeton University Press, 2011) would seem to confirm interdisciplinary interest in Caribbean and British colonial visual productions. Nevertheless, Crowley's larger point about the absence of the picturesque from critical accounts of colonial rule is still relevant.

65. Peasant women washing clothes is a well-known image in nineteenth-century painting. *Washerwomen in a Grotto* by Wolfgang-Adam Töpffer (1825–1830) and *Washerwomen of Fouesnant* by William-Adolphe Bouguereau (1869) are two examples. The male gaze on women working is expected, but what is notable about Hakewill's depiction is the decontextualization and depersonalization of the washerwomen. Despite his ability to etch detailed leaves, the humans depicted in *Bridge, over the White River* are faceless in distinction to the detailed faces and distinguishable identities of the women portrayed by Töpffer and Bouguereau.

66. Nancy Lee Peluso is recognized as developing the term "counter mapping," which has subsequently been used in many different contexts by geographers and others interested in land and the equitable distribution of resources. "Whose Woods are These? Counter-Mapping Forest Territories in Kalimantan, Indonesia," *Antipode* 27, no. 4 (1995): 383–406.

67. "The existence of family land throughout the region . . . provides evidence of ancestor-focused, landholding, cognatic descent corporations" that recognize the claims

of all descendants. The symbolic valuing of land that even in the contemporary Caribbean is mostly owned by large corporations) is seen as "providing freehold rights for generations in perpetuity in these plantation dominated societies." Jean Besson, "A Paradox in Caribbean Attitudes to Land," in *Land and Development in the Caribbean*, ed. Jean Besson and Janet Momsen (London: Macmillan Caribbean, 1987), 19, 21.

68. The Jamaican Harvey family claim William Harvey, born 1578, physician to James I and Charles I and discoverer of blood circulation as an ancestor, while Susan Harvey locates her ancestry in Northern Ireland. The http://harveyfamilyhistory.com website has been taken down.

69. Zora Neale Hurston, *Their Eyes Were Watching God* (1937; repr., New York: Harper, 2010), 20.

70. Jana Evans Braziel, *Caribbean Genesis Jamaica Kincaid and the Writing of New Worlds* (Albany: State University of New York Press, 2009), 3.

CHAPTER 4 — ASHES TO ASHES, DUST TO DUST

1. José Esteban Muñoz, "Ephemera as Evidence: Introductory Notes to Queer Acts," *Women & Performance* 8, no. 2 (January 1996): 5–16, https://doi.org/10.1080/07407709608571228; Cvetkovich, *Archive of Feelings*.

2. Racquel Stratchan-Innerarity, "Preserving Archival Collections in the 21st Century: The Caribbean Experience," in Bastian, Aarons, and Griffin, *Decolonizing the Caribbean Record*, 364–365.

3. Gaiutra Bahadur, *Coolie Woman: The Odyssey of Indenture* (Chicago: University of Chicago Press, 2014); Boon, *What the Oceans Remember*.

4. Lowe, *Intimacies of Four Continents*, 2.

5. Sharpe, *Ghosts of Slavery*, xi.

6. Cynthia Enloe, *Bananas, Beaches and Bases: Making Feminist Sense of International Politics* (Berkeley: University of California Press, 2014).

7. Indian indenture took place in over twelve locations globally, not just the Caribbean. Bahadur and Boon's narratives represent just two locations indentured workers were sent: British Guiana and Suriname. British Guiana "pioneered" indentured labor in the Caribbean and received 55.6 percent of Indian immigrants. Verene A. Shepherd, "Indian Women and Labor Migration to the Caribbean: An Overview," in Shepherd, *Engendering Caribbean History*, 554.

8. Suriname received the third largest number of indentured workers. Even within the Caribbean, immigrant experiences differed because the sites of plantation work were governed by varying colonial rules set down by the British, Dutch, and French. The traditional explanation for importation of indentured workers to the Caribbean by European powers involves the post-emancipation refusal of the formerly enslaved to work for meager wages on plantations. Immigration patterns support this theory to a degree, with British colonies first sending ships from India in 1838, the year the apprenticeship program ended. The need for labor from outside the Caribbean may also have been a method to suppress wages and keep control over the existing populations. During this period France began importing workers for its plantations. Ten years after emancipation in the Dutch colonies in 1863, Suriname began to import Indian workers. This program continued until 1918, with a total of 34,000 indentured people arriving in Suriname. Shepherd, "Indian Women," 553.

9. D. Alissa Trotz, "The Caribbean Family?," in *A Companion to Gender Studies*, ed. Philomena Essed, David Theo Goldberg, and Audrey Kobayashi (Malden, MA: Blackwell, 2005), 370.

10. Intriguingly, ash carries religious significance for Hindus. Bahadur describes the Hindu religious rituals practiced in her family but does not mention ash in particular. Anna S. King describes how cremated remains are referred to as flowers in Hindi. King notes their connection, with flowers as "symbols of luxuriance and fertility, [which] itself suggests the language of death is also the language of birth and creation." The association between archival remains and the creation of new knowledge resonates with Bahadur and Boon's projects. "Ashes and Flowers: Some Hindu Approaches to Death and Dying," *Journal of Beliefs and Values* 19, no. 1 (1998): 21.

11. As Aliyah Khan puts it, mutual suffering during colonial transoceanic ship journeys has proved to be a relatively crude basis for ethnic affiliation and alliance in postcolonial Trinidad and Guyana, where many Indo-Caribbean people still embrace the Bhojpuri Hindi-Caribbean nationalist slogan *apan jaat*, "voting with one's race or cast." "Voyages across Indenture: From Ship Sister to Mannish Woman," *GLQ* 22, no. 2 (2016): 251. See also Verene A. Shepherd, *Maharani's Misery: Narratives of a Passage from India to the Caribbean* (Mona: University of the West Indies Press, 2002), xvii.

12. Kamau Brathwaite, "Caribbean Man in Space and Time," *Savacou*, nos. 11–12 (1975): 1.

13. "[Dust] is about the circularity, the impossibility of things disappearing, or going away, or being gone. Nothing *can be* destroyed." Steedman, *Dust*, 164.

14. Steedman, *Dust*, 70.

15. Trouillot, *Silencing the Past*; Thomas Richards, *The Imperial Archive: Knowledge and the Fantasy of Empire* (London: Verso, 1993).

16. U.S. National Archives and Records Administration, "Dusting" (August 15, 2016), https://www.archives.gov/preservation/holdings-maintenance/dusting.html.

17. Aarons and Alexander-Gooding, "Historical Developments," 23.

18. Rita Tjien Fooh, "Return of the Historical Archives (1661–1975) from the Netherlands to Suriname," in Bastian, Aarons, and Griffin, *Decolonizing the Caribbean Record*, 79–92.

19. Brodber, "Oral History Sources," 2.

20. *Coolie Woman* is one of ten sources cited by Gabrielle Jamela Hosein and Lisa Outar as being foundational among recent studies of Indo-Caribbean feminism. Gabrielle Jamela Hosein and Lisa Outar, "Introduction: Interrogating an Indo-Caribbean Feminist Epistemology," in *Indo-Caribbean Feminist Thought: Genealogies, Theories, Enactments*, ed. Hosein and Outar (New York: Palgrave Macmillan, 2016), 1–19.

21. For an overview of political, economic, cultural, and environmental factors endangering Caribbean archives, see Aarons and Alexander-Gooding, "Historical Developments." For an account of attempts to modernize national archives in Guyana from the 1960s to the present, see Hugh Payne, "Working at the National Archives of Guyana: Experiences, Challenges & Lessons," in Bastian, Aarons, and Griffin, *Decolonizing the Caribbean Record*, 115–135.

22. Joy Mahabir and Mariam Pirbhai, "Introduction: Tracing an Emerging Tradition," in *Critical Perspectives on Indo-Caribbean Women's Literature*, vol. 4, ed. Mahabir and Pirbhai (New York: Routledge, 2013). See also Gabrielle Jamela Hosein and Lisa

Outar, "Indo-Caribbean Feminisms: Charting Crossings in Geography, Discourse, and Politics," *Caribbean Review of Gender Studies* 6 (2012): 1.

23. Here, as throughout this study, I refer to the authors of life writing texts by their last name and to their self-representation within the text by their first name.

24. Jacques Derrida, *Archive Fever: A Freudian Impression* (Chicago: University of Chicago Press, 1998).

25. Gaiutra Bahadur, "How Could I Write about Women Whose Existence Is Barely Acknowledged?," *Guardian*, June 14, 2016, https://www.theguardian.com/books/2016/jun/14/gaiutra-bahadurindentured-female-labourers-coolie-woman.

26. The text appears on Bahadur's great-grandmother's emigration pass reproduced in *Coolie Woman*, n.p.

27. Shepherd, *Maharani's Misery*, xxii.

28. Fuentes, *Dispossessed Lives*.

29. "In autobiography the desire for origin and rooting has to be relocated from the verifiable past to a sense of emergent and incomplete history existing in a productive tension between individual and public notions of experience." Watson, "Ordering the Family."

30. Lorgia García-Peña, *The Borders of Dominicanidad: Race, Nation, and Archives of Contradiction* (Durham, NC: Duke University Press, 2016), 2.

31. Elsewhere in the Caribbean, Boon's Indo-Caribbean and African heritage might identify her as Dougla, someone of mixed race, which is an identity that can carry stigma. Boon does not use this terminology, however, to refer to herself or others. See Gabrielle Jamela Hosein, "Dougla Poetics and Politics in Indo-Caribbean Feminist Thought: Reflection and Reconceptualization," in Hosein and Outar, *Indo-Caribbean Feminist Thought*.

32. Hosein and Outar, "Introduction," 9.

33. Eve Tuck and K. Wayne Yang, "R-Words: Refusing Research," in *Humanizing Research: Decolonizing Qualitative Inquiry with Youth and Communities*, ed. Django Paris and Maisha T. Winn (Thousand Oaks, CA: Sage, 2014), 224.

34. For a discussion of literary stereotypes of Indo-Caribbean women and contemporary novels writing back to that literary tradition, see Mariam Pirbhai, "Recasting *Jahaji-Bhain*: Plantation History and the Indo-Caribbean Women's Novel in Trinidad, Guyana and Martinique," in Mahabir and Pirbhai, *Critical Perspectives on Indo-Caribbean Women's Literature*, 25–47.

35. Johnson, "Markup Bodies."

36. V. S. Naipaul, *The Middle Passage: The Caribbean Revisited* (London: Macmillan, 1962), 197.

37. Sarah E. Morton, *John Morton of Trinidad* (Toronto: Westminster, 1916), 342.

38. Odessa D. Despot, "Indo-Caribbean Women from Trinidad and Guyana: Hardships, Conflict, and Resiliency," *Meridians* 13, no. 2 (2016): 1–27.

39. Kaneesha Cherelle Parsard, "Cutlass: Objects toward a Theory of Representation," in Hosein and Outar, *Indo-Caribbean Feminist Thought*, 247, 250.

40. Breiner, "Too Much History."

41. M. Jacqui Alexander, "Erotic Autonomy as a Politics of Decolonization: An Anatomy of Feminist and State Practice in the Bahamas Tourist Economy," in *Feminist Genealogies, Colonial Legacies, Democratic Futures*, ed. M. Jacqui Alexander and Chandra Talpade Mohanty (New York: Routledge, 1997), 63–100.

42. Baugh, "West Indian Writer," 64.

43. Scott, *Conscripts of Modernity*.

CHAPTER 5 — "PUT MY MOM IN THERE"

1. Chiamaka Nwosu and Jeanne Batalova, "Immigrants from the Dominican Republic in the United States," Migration Policy Institute, July 18, 2014, http://migrationpolicy.org/article/immigrants-dominican-republic-united-states#:~:targetText=Large-scale%20migration%20from%20the,and%20other%20government%20agencies%20intervened.

2. Bindu Bansinath, "She Couldn't Find Dominican Women in the Official Archives. So She Started Her Own," *The Cut*, October 31, 2019, https://www.thecut.com/2019/10/angie-cruz-on-her-instagram-archive-dominicanas-nyc.html.

3. Dominicanas NYC, "Here Is My Grandmother Georgina in the Back, Uncle Tony to the Left and My Mother Nelly to the Right. This Picture Was Taken in 1963 on the New York Circle Line," *Instagram*, November 18, 2019, https://www.instagram.com/p/B5A8HmSj-OV/.

4. Antoinette Burton, "'An Assemblage/Before Me': Autobiography as Archive," *Journal of Women's History* 25, no. 2 (2013): 186.

5. See Josephs, "Articulating Caribbean Epistemologies," for a discussion of how and why the Caribbean becomes known in contemporary scholarship.

6. Ruth Behar, *An Island Called Home: Returning to Jewish Cuba* (New Brunswick, NJ: Rutgers University Press, 2007); Irene Vilar, *The Ladies' Gallery: A Memoir of Family Secrets*, trans. Gregory Rabassa (1996; repr., New York: Other Press, 2009); Edwidge Danticat, *Brother, I'm Dying* (New York: Vintage, 2008); Edwidge Danticat, *Create Dangerously: The Immigrant Artist at Work* (New York: Vintage, 2010).

7. Sáez, *Market Aesthetics*, 13.

8. Hanchard, "Black Memory," 48.

9. Hanchard, "Black Memory," 46.

10. During the Spanish-American War, when the United States first invaded Cuba, it also invaded Puerto Rico, eventually gaining possession of it in 1899. U.S. intervention in and occupation of Cuba (1898–1902, 1906–1909, 1912, 1917–1922), the Dominican Republic (1916–1924), and Haiti (1915–1934) exacerbated the destabilization of their political systems and paved the way for dictators such as Castro in Cuba, Trujillo in the Dominican Republic, and the Duvaliers in Haiti. Suzy Caster and Lynn Garafola, "The American Occupation of Haiti (1915–1934) and the Dominican Republic (1916–1924)," *Massachusetts Review* 15, nos. 1–2 (1974): 253–275; Alejandra Bronfman, *On the Move: The Caribbean since 1989* (London: Zed Books, 2007).

11. Although Puerto Rico is not independent, I refer to it as Vilar's country since that is how she characterizes it. Like Guadeloupe, which is a territory of France, Puerto Rico is a territory of the United States. Both are places with contested sovereignty.

12. While the focus of this chapter is on U.S.-Caribbean immigrant identities and neocolonialism, it is worth noting the complex relationship among these Caribbean cultures. Dominicans experience racialization and discrimination in Puerto Rico, while the Dominican Republic engages in anti-Haitian polices. See Reyes-Santos, *Our Caribbean Kin*.

13. García-Peña, *Borders of Dominicanidad*, 192–193.

14. Behar's many publications are outside the scope of this chapter. For an excellent overview of Behar's work as an anthropologist and a life writer within the context of Jewish studies, see Rocío G. Davis, "Vulnerable Observation in *An Island Called Home*: Ruth Behar's Story of the Jews of Cuba," *Prooftexts* 31, no. 3 (2011): 263–268.

15. For context on Behar's influence on autobiography studies, see Diane P. Freedman and Olivia Frey, "Self/Discipline: An Introduction," in *Autobiographical Writing across the Disciplines: A Reader*, ed. Freedman and Frey (Durham, NC: Duke University Press, 2003), 2, and Smith and Watson, *Reading Autobiography*, 253. For more on autotheory, see Lauren Fournier, "Sick Women, Sad Girls, and Selfie Theory," 643–662.

16. Natalia Rachel Singer, "Life Experiences through Hybrid Memoirs," *Chronicle of Higher Education*, October 22, 2004, https://www.chronicle.com/article/The-Most-Influential-Books/6356.

17. Vilar's *The Ladies' Gallery* has a complicated translation and publishing history. Vilar wrote the text in Spanish although the text was never published in that language. It was translated into English by Gregory Rabassa and published in 1996 under the title *A Message from God in the Atomic Age.* Vilar's text was then republished by Vintage Random House in 1996 as *The Ladies Gallery.* Subsequently, following on the success and notoriety of her *Impossible Motherhood: Testimony of an Abortion Addict* published by Other Press in 2009, *The Ladies Gallery* was republished by Other Press also in 2009. I read the 2009 text as part of a turn within publishing in the first decade of the twenty-first century that made life writing by Caribbean women authors marketable. Following on this train of thought, I do not believe it is a coincidence that most of the scholarship published on *The Ladies Gallery* occurred during this decade and the next and not during the 1990s.

18. Lindsay and Sweet, "Introduction."

19. Rak, *Boom!*.

20. Ruth Behar, "Foreword," in Freedman and Frey, *Autobiographical Writing*, xv.

21. For an overview of the criticism Behar received after publishing her first book combining anthropology and life writing, *Translated Woman* (1993), see Gelya Frank, "Ruth Behar's Biography in the Shadow: A Review of Reviews," *American Anthropologist* 97, no. 2 (1995): 357–359.

22. Sarah Phillips Casteel, *Calypso Jews: Jewishness in the Caribbean Literary Imagination* (New York: Columbia University Press, 2016); and Robert M. Levine, *Tropical Diaspora: The Jewish Experience in Cuba* (Gainesville: University Press of Florida, 1993).

23. Ruth Behar, "Juban," in Freedman and Frey, *Autobiographical Writing*, 335.

24. Ruth Behar, *Traveling Heavy: A Memoir between Journeys* (Durham, NC: Duke University Press, 2013), 22.

25. Behar, "Juban," 335.

26. Christina García, *Dreaming in Cuban* (New York: Knopf, 1992), 219.

27. Marianne Hirsch, "The Generation of Postmemory," *Poetics Today* 29, no. 1 (2008): 111.

28. Behar, *Traveling Heavy*, 29.

29. Here, as throughout this study, I refer to the authors of life writing texts by their last name and to their self-representation within the text by their first name.

30. Behar, "Juban," 345.

31. Scott, *Omens of Adversity*, 75.

32. Mariza Corrales, *The Chosen Island: Jews in Cuba* (Chicago: Salsedo Press, 2005).

33. Glissant, *Poetics of Relation*, 190.

34. Glissant, *Poetics of Relation*, 190.

35. Sidonie Smith, *Subjectivity, Identity, and the Body: Women's Autobiographical Practices in the Twentieth Century* (Bloomington: Indiana University Press, 1993), 130.

36. Ruth Behar, "Such Good Thieves," *Hassadah Magazine*, February 26, 2008, https://www.hadassahmagazine.org/2008/02/26/family-matters-good-thieves/.

37. Behar, "Such Good Thieves."

38. Glissant, "Quarrel with History," 62–63.

39. Édouard Glissant, "History, Time, Identity," in *Caribbean Discourse*, 93.

40. Edwidge Danticat, "Edwidge Danticat," in *Why We Write about Ourselves: Twenty Memoirists on Why They Expose Themselves (and Others) in the Name of Literature*, ed. Meredith Maran (New York: Plume, 2016), 64.

41. Danticat writes of "being called a parasitic *dyaspora*, a foreign being but still not a *blan*," (*Create* 51).

42. García-Peña, *Borders of Dominicanidad*, 4.

43. Michael D. Shear and Julie Hirschfeld Davis, "Stoking Fears, Trump Defied Bureaucracy to Advance Immigration Agenda," *New York Times*, December 23, 2017, https://www.nytimes.com/2017/12/23/us/politics/trump-immigration.html; Leighton Akio Woodhouse, "Trump's 'Shithole Countries' Remark Is at the Center of a Lawsuit to Reinstate Protections for Immigrants," *The Intercept*, June 28, 2018, https://theintercept.com/2018/06/28/trump-tps-shithole-countries-lawsuit/.

44. At the time of *Brother, I'm Dying*'s publication, Danticat had received an elite education at Barnard and Brown, was a *New York Times* best-selling author of an Oprah's Book Club pick, and had been awarded prestigious literary prizes such as the American Book Award in 1999 and the Anisfield-Wolf Book Award in 2005.

45. G. Thomas Couser, "Genre Matters: Form, Force, and Filiation," *Life Writing* 2, no. 2 (2005): 151.

46. Danticat, "Edwidge Danticat," 64.

47. Laura Halperin's *Intersections of Harm* is one of a handful of works to analyze Vilar's writing in depth. It also covers *Impossible Motherhood: Testimony of an Abortion Addict* (2009), which is outside of the scope of my project. *Intersections of Harm: Narratives of Latina Deviance and Defiance* (Newark, NJ: Rutgers University Press, 2015).

48. Sandra Ruiz, *Ricanness: Enduring Time in Anticolonial Performance* (New York: New York University Press, 2019), 56.

49. Manuel Roig-Franzia, "A Terrorist in the House," *Washington Post Magazine*, February 22, 2004, https://www.washingtonpost.com/archive/lifestyle/magazine/2004/02/22/a-terrorist-in-the-house/293c52cd-8794-47bd-9960-9c7a871e009c/.

50. Frances Romero, "Fond Farewells: Lolita Lebron," *Time*, August 16, 2010, http://content.time.com/time/specials/packages/article/0,28804,2036683_2036477_2036974,00.html.

51. Kyle Dropp and Brendan Nyhan, "Nearly Half of Americans Don't Know Puerto Ricans Are Fellow Citizens," *New York Times*, September 26, 2017, https://www.nytimes.com/2017/09/26/upshot/nearly-half-of-americans-dont-know-people-in-puerto-ricoans-are-fellow-citizens.html.

52. Glissant, *Poetics of Relation*, 191.

53. Danny Vinik, "How Trump Favored Texas over Puerto Rico," *Politico*, March 27, 2018, https://www.politico.com/story/2018/03/27/donald-trump-fema-hurricane-maria-response-480557; Ed Morales, "Hurricane Maria Swept Away the Illusion of Puerto Ricans' Citizenship," *Washington Post*, June 7, 2018, https://www.washingtonpost.com/news/post-nation/wp/2018/06/07/for-many-puerto-ricans-hurricane-maria-swept-away-the-illusion-of-u-s-citizenship/.

54. Imani Perry, *Vexy Thing: On Gender and Liberation* (Durham, NC: Duke University Press, 2018), 191.

55. Margaret Power, "Interview with Lolita Lebrón," *Radical History Review* 128 (2017): 38.

56. Jocelyn Fenton Stitt, "Gendered Legacies of Romantic Nationalism in the Works of Michelle Cliff," *Small Axe* 24 (2007): 52–72.

57. Scott, *Conscripts of Modernity*, 2.

58. Manuel Roig-Franzia and Nina Rauch, "Women: Sins of the Mothers," *Guardian*, December 1, 1998.

59. Ruiz, *Ricanness*, 3.

60. Power, "Interview," 37.

61. Emma Brown, "Lolita Lebron, Jailed for Gun Attack at U.S. Capital in 1954, Dies at 90," *Washington Post*, August 2, 2010, https://www.washingtonpost.com/wp-dyn/content/article/2010/08/01/AR2010080103400.html.

62. For more on the performative aspects of Lebrón's femininity, see Ruiz, *Ricanness*.

63. Halperin, *Intersections of Harm*, 31.

64. Yolanda Martínez-San Miguel, "Colonial and Mexican Archipelagoes: Reimagining Colonial Caribbean Studies," in *Archipelagic American Studies*, ed. Brian Russell Roberts and Michelle Ann Stephens (Durham, NC: Duke University Press, 2017), 169.

65. Latina Feminist Group, *Telling to Live: Latina Feminist Testimonios* (Durham, NC: Duke University Press, 2001), 2.

66. Glissant, "History, Time, Identity," 93.

CODA

1. Contemporary texts referencing the *Zong* incident include Michelle Cliff's *Free Enterprise* (1993), Fred D'Aguiar's *Feeding the Ghosts* (1999), and David Dabydeen's *Turner: New and Selected Poems* (1994).

2. "A Brief Account and Familiar Description of Jamaica in Its *Most* Modern Statistics, Con't.," *Falmouth Post*, July 4, 1838, 2; M. NourbeSe Philip, *Zong, as Told to the Author by Setaey Adamu Boateng* (Middletown, CT: Wesleyan University Press, 2008).

3. Patricia Saunders, "Defending the Dead, Confronting the Archive: A Conversation with M. NourbeSe Philip," *Small Axe* 26 (2008): 71.

4. Brodber, "Oral History Sources," 7.

Bibliography

Aarons, John A., and Sharon Alexander-Gooding. "Historical Development in Caribbean Archives and Record Keeping." In *Decolonizing the Caribbean Record: An Archives Reader*, edited by Jeannette A. Bastian, John A. Aarons, and Stanley H. Griffin, 11–53. Sacramento, CA: Litwin Books, 2018.

Adams, Timothy Dow. *Light Writing and Life Writing: Photography in Autobiography.* Chapel Hill: University of North Carolina Press, 2000.

———. *Telling Lies in Modern American Autobiography.* Chapel Hill: University of North Carolina Press, 2000.

Adesocan, Akin. "New African Writing and the Question of Audience." *Research in African Literatures* 43, no. 3 (2012): 1–20.

Adichie, Chimamanda. "The Danger of a Single Story." TEDGlobal, July 2009. https://www.ted.com/talks/chimamanda_adichie_the_danger_of_a_single_story.

Alexander, M. Jacqui. "Erotic Autonomy as a Politics of Decolonization: An Anatomy of Feminist and State Practice in the Bahamas Tourist Economy." In *Feminist Genealogies, Colonial Legacies, Democratic Futures*, edited by M. Jacqui Alexander and Chandra Talpade Mohanty, 63–100. New York: Routledge, 1997.

———. "Not Just (Any) *Body* Can Be a Citizen: The Politics of Law, Sexuality, and Postcoloniality in Trinidad and Tobago and the Bahamas." In *Cultures of Empire: A Reader*, edited by Catherine Hall, 359–376. New York: Routledge, 2000.

Aljoe, Nicole N. *Creole Testimonies: Slave Narratives from the British West Indies, 1709–1838.* New York: Palgrave Macmillan, 2012.

Anderson, Linda. *Autobiography.* London: Routledge, 2011.

Araujo, Ana Lucia. "Welcome the Diaspora: Slave Trade Heritage Tourism and the Public Memory of Slavery." *Ethnologies* 32, no. 2 (2010): 145–175.

Archives Départementales de la Guadeloupe. *Journaz et revues: Catalogue des collections de presse conservées aux Archives départementales.* Gourbeyre: Archives Départementales de la Guadeloupe, 2000.

Ashcroft, Bill. "Introduction: Spaces of Utopia: An Electronic Journal." *Spaces of Utopia* 2, no. 1 (2012): 1–17. http://ler.letras.up.pt.

Ayre, Michael. *The Caribbean in Sepia: A History in Photographs 1840–1900*. Kingston: Ian Randle, 2012.

Bahadur, Gaiutra. *Coolie Woman: The Odyssey of Indenture*. Chicago: University of Chicago Press, 2014.

Bansinath, Bindu. "She Couldn't Find Dominican Women in the Official Archives. So She Started Her Own." *The Cut*, October 31, 2019. https://www.thecut.com/2019/10/angie-cruz-on-her-instagram-archive-dominicanas-nyc.html.

Bastian, Jeannette A., John A. Aarons, and Stanley H. Griffin. "Introduction." In *Decolonizing the Caribbean Record: An Archives Reader*, edited by Jeannette A. Bastian, John A. Aarons, and Stanley H. Griffin, 1–7. Sacramento: Litwin Books, 2018.

Baugh, Edward. "The West Indian Writer and His Quarrel with History" (1977). *Small Axe* 16, no. 2 (2012): 60–74.

Behar, Ruth. "Foreword." In *Autobiographical Writing across the Disciplines: A Reader*, edited by Diane P. Freedman and Olivia Frey, xiii–xviii. Durham, NC: Duke University Press, 2003.

———. *An Island Called Home: Returning to Jewish Cuba*. New Brunswick, NJ: Rutgers University Press, 2007.

———. "Juban América." In *Autobiographical Writing across the Disciplines: A Reader*, edited by Diane P. Freedman and Olivia Frey, 331–348. Durham, NC: Duke University Press, 2003.

———. "Such Good Thieves." *Hassadah Magazine*, February 26, 2008. https://www.hadassahmagazine.org/2008/02/26/family-matters-good-thieves/.

———. *Traveling Heavy: A Memoir between Journeys*. Durham, NC: Duke University Press, 2013.

———. "While Waiting for the Ferry to Cuba: Afterthoughts about Adio Kerida." *Michigan Quarterly Review* 41, no. 4 (2002): 651–667.

Benítez-Rojo, Antonio. *The Repeating Island: The Caribbean and the Postmodern Perspective*. Durham, NC: Duke University Press, 1997.

Benstock, Shari. "Authorizing the Autobiographical." In *Feminisms: An Anthology of Literary Theory and Criticism*, edited by Robyn R. Warhol and Diane Price Herndl, 1138–1154. New Brunswick, NJ: Rutgers University Press, 2007.

Besson, Jean. "A Paradox in Caribbean Attitudes to Land." In *Land and Development in the Caribbean*, edited by Jean Besson and Janet Momsen, 13–45. London: Macmillan Caribbean, 1987.

Best, Stephen. *None Like Us: Blackness, Belonging, Aesthetic Life*. Durham, NC: Duke University Press, 2018.

———. "On Failing to Make the Past Present." *Modern Language Quarterly* 73, no. 3 (2012): 453–474.

Best, Stephen, and Sharon Marcus. "Surface Reading: An Introduction." *Representations* 108, no. 1 (2009): 1–21.

Bohls, Elizabeth A. *Slavery and the Politics of Place: the Colonial Caribbean, 1772–1833*. Cambridge: Cambridge University Press, 2015.

Bongie, Chris. *Friends and Enemies: Scribal Politics of Post/Colonial Literature*. Liverpool: Liverpool University Press, 2008.

Bonilla, Yarimar. *Non-sovereign Futures: Caribbean Politics in the Wake of Disenchantment*. Chicago: University of Chicago Press, 2015.

Boon, Sonja. *What the Oceans Remember: Searching for Belonging and Home*. Waterloo: Wilfrid Laurier University Press, 2019.

Brand, Dionne. *Bread Out of Stone: Recollections, Sex, Recognitions, Race, Dreaming, Politics*. Toronto: Coach House Press, 1994.

———. *A Map to the Door of No Return: Notes to Belonging*. Toronto: Vintage Canada, 2001.

———. "Marlene Green." *Now Toronto*, November 2, 2002. https://nowtoronto.com/news/marlene-green-1940-2002/.

———. *No Language Is Neutral*. Toronto: Coach House Press, 1990.

Brathwaite, Kamau. "Caribbean Man in Space and Time." *Savacou*, nos. 11–12 (1975): 1–11.

———. *The Development of Creole Society in Jamaica, 1770–1820*. Oxford: Clarendon, 1972.

Braziel, Jana Evans. *Caribbean Genesis Jamaica Kincaid and the Writing of New Worlds*. Albany: State University of New York Press, 2009.

Breiner, Laurence A. "Too Much History, or Not Enough." *Small Axe* 38, no. 2 (2012): 86–98.

Brennan, Timothy. "The National Longing for Form." In *Nation and Narration*, edited by Homi Bhabha, 44–70. London: Routledge, 1990.

Brereton, Bridget. "Gendered Testimonies: Autobiographies, Diaries and Letters." *Feminist Review* 59 (1998): 144–145.

"A Brief Account and Familiar Description of Jamaica in Its *Most* Modern Statistics." *Falmouth Post*, June 27, 1838, 2.

"A Brief Account and Familiar Description of Jamaica in Its *Most* Modern Statistics, Con't." *Falmouth Post*, July 4, 1838, 2.

Brodber, Erna. "Afro-Jamaican Women at the Turn of the Century." *Social and Economic Studies* 35, no. 3 (1980): 23–50.

———. "Oral History Sources and the Creation of a Social History of the Caribbean." *Jamaica Journal* 16, no. 4 (1983): 2–11.

———. *The People of My Jamaican Village 1817–1948*. St. Mary/St. Catherine: Blackspace, 1999.

———. "Re-engineering Blackspace." *Caribbean Quarterly* 43, nos. 1–2 (1997): 70–81.

———. "Where Are All the Others?" In *Caribbean Creolization: Reflections on the Cultural Dynamics of Language, Literature, and Identity*, edited by Kathleen M. Blutansky and Mare-Agnes Sourieau, 68–75. Kingston: University Press of the West Indies, 1998.

———. *Woodside Pear Tree Grove P.O.* Kingston: University of the West Indies Press, 2004.

Broichhagen, Vera. *Feasting on Words: Maryse Condé, Cannibalism, and the Caribbean Text*. Princeton: Program in Latin American Studies, Princeton University, 2006.

Bronfman, Alejandra. *On the Move: The Caribbean since 1989*. London: Zed Books, 2007.

Brown, Emma. "Lolita Lebron, Jailed for Gun Attack at U.S. Capital in 1954, Dies at 90." *Washington Post*, August 2, 2010. https://www.washingtonpost.com/wp-dyn/content/article/2010/08/01/AR2010080103400.html.

Brown, Lisa R. "Caribbean Life-Writing and Performative Liberation." In *The Routledge Companion to Anglophone Caribbean Literature*, edited by Michael Bucknor and Alison Donnell, 255–264. London: Routledge, 2011.

Brown, Yvonne Shorter. *Dead Woman Pickney: A Memoir of Childhood in Jamaica*. Waterloo: Wilfrid Laurier University Press, 2010.

Burnard, Trevor. *Mastery, Tyranny, and Desire: Thomas Thistlewood and His Slaves in the Anglo-Jamaican World*. Chapel Hill: University of North Carolina Press, 2004.

Burton, Antoinette. "'An Assemblage/Before Me': Autobiography as Archive." *Journal of Women's History* 25, no. 2 (2013): 185–188.

Bush, Barbara. "'Sable Venus,' 'She Devil' or 'Drudge'? British Slavery and the 'Fabulous Fiction' of Black Women's Identities, c. 1650–1838." *Women's History Review* 9, no. 4 (2000): 761–789.

———. *Slave Women in Caribbean Society, 1650–1838*. Bloomington: Indiana University Press, 1990.

Buss, Helen. *Repossessing the World: Reading Memoirs by Contemporary Women*. Waterloo: Wilfrid Laurier University Press, 2002.

Campbell, Horace G. "Challenges for Revolutionary Change in the Caribbean." In *The Grenada Revolution: Reflections and Lessons*, edited by Wendy C. Grenade, 179–210. Jackson: University Press of Mississippi, 2015.

Campt, Tina M. *Listening to Images: An Exercise in Counterintuition*. Durham, NC: Duke University Press, 2017.

Camus, Jean-Yves. "The Commemoration of Slavery in France and the Emergence of a Black Political Consciousness." *European Legacy* 11, no. 6 (2006): 649–650.

Carter, Marina, and Khal Torabully. *Coolitude: An Anthology of the Indian Labour Diaspora*. London: Anthem Press, 2002.

Casteel, Sarah Phillips. *Calypso Jews: Jewishness in the Caribbean Literary Imagination*. New York: Columbia University Press, 2016.

———. *Second Arrivals: Landscape and Belonging in Contemporary Writing of the Americas*. Charlottesville: University of Virginia Press, 2007.

Caster, Suzy, and Lynn Garafola. "The American Occupation of Haiti (1915–1934) and the Dominican Republic (1916–1924)." *Massachusetts Review* 15, nos. 1–2 (1974): 253–275.

Catan, Adolphe. *La Guadeloupe à travers l'oeil d'Adolphe Catan: 50 ans de photos depuis 1920*. Guadeloupe: Association Photo Cat, 1999.

Chancy, Myriam J. A. "Recovering History 'Bone by Bone': Conversation with Edwidge Danticat." *Calabash: A Journal of Caribbean Arts and Letters* 1, no. 2 (2001): 15–38.

Chin, Staceyann. *The Other Side of Paradise: A Memoir*. New York: Scribner, 2009.

Clarke, Austin. *Growing Up Stupid under the Union Jack*. Toronto: McClelland and Stewart, 1980.

Cliff, Michelle. *The Land of Look Behind*. Ithaca, NY: Firebrand Books, 1985.

Coard, Bernard. *The Grenada Revolution: What Really Happened*. CreateSpace, 2017.

Collins, Merle. "Foreword." In *The Grenada Revolution*, edited by Wendy C. Grenade, vii–ix. Jackson: University of Mississippi Press, 2015.

———. "What Happened? Grenada: A Retrospective Journey." *Social and Economic Studies* 62, nos. 3–4 (2013): 15–19.

Colwell, Chip. "Collaborative Archaeologies and Descendant Communities." *Annual Review of Anthropology* 45 (2016): 113–127.

Combe, Dominique. "Preface." In *Postcolonial Poetics*, edited by Patrick Crowley and Jane Hiddleston, vii–xii. Liverpool: Liverpool University Press, 2011.

Comité pour la mémoire de l'esclave. "Mémoires de la traite négriére, del l'esclave et leurs abolitions." Rapport á Monsieur le Premier Ministre, April 12, 2005.

Commander, Michelle D. *Afro-Atlantic Flight: Speculative Returns and the Black Fantastic*. Durham, NC: Duke University Press, 2017.

Condé, Maryse. *Heremakhonon*. 1976. Translated by Richard Philcox. Washington, DC: Three Continents Press, 1982.

———. *Of Morsels and Marvels*. 2015. Translated by Richard Philcox. London: Seagull Books, 2020.

———. "Order, Disorder, Freedom, and the West Indian Writer." *Yale French Studies* 97, no. 2 (2000): 151–165.

———. *Tales from the Heart: True Stories from My Childhood*. 1999. Translated by Richard Philcox. New York: Soho Press, 2004.

———. *Victoire: My Mother's Mother*. 2006. Translated by Richard Philcox. New York: Atria, 2010.

———. *What Is Africa to Me? Fragments of a True-to-Life Autobiography*. 2012. Translated by Richard Philcox. London: Seagull Books, 2017.

"A Conversation with Stuart Hall." *Journal of the International Institute* 7, no. 1 (1990). http://quod.lib.umich.edu/j/jii/4750978.0007.107/—conversation-with-stuart-hall?rgn=main;view=fulltext.

Cooper, Frederick, Thomas C. Holt, and Rebecca J. Scott. *Beyond Slavery: Explorations of Race, Labor, and Citizenship in Postemancipation Societies*. Chapel Hill: University of North Carolina Press, 2000.

Corbin, Laurie. "The Return to and Beyond the Mother: Maryse Condé and Representations of Maternity." *Life Writing* 4, no. 2 (2007): 231–245.

Corrales, Mariza. *The Chosen Island: Jews in Cuba*. Chicago: Salsedo Press, 2005.

Couser, G. Thomas. "Genre Matters: Form, Force, and Filiation." *Life Writing* 2, no. 2 (2005): 139–156.

Crowell, Maddy. "The Island Where France's Colonial Legacy Lives on." *Atlantic*, April 21, 2018. https://www.theatlantic.com/international/archive/2018/04/france-macron-guadeloupe-slavery-colonialism/557996/.

Crowley, John E. "Picturing the Caribbean in the Global British Landscape." *Studies in Eighteenth-Century Culture* 32 (2003): 323–346.

Cummings, Ronald. "(Trans)Nationalisms, Marronage, and Queer Caribbean Subjectivities." *Transforming Anthropology* 18, no. 2 (2010): 169–180.

Cvetkovich, Ann. *An Archive of Feelings: Trauma, Sexuality, and Lesbian Public Cultures*. Durham, NC: Duke University Press, 2003.

Dalleo, Raphael. *Caribbean Literature and the Public Sphere: From the Plantation to the Postcolonial*. Charlottesville: University of Virginia Press, 2011.

Danticat, Edwidge. *After the Dance: A Walk through Carnival in Jacmel, Haiti*. New York: Vintage, 2002.

———. *The Art of Death: Writing the Final Story*. Minneapolis: Graywolf Press, 2017.

———. *Brother, I'm Dying*. New York: Vintage, 2008. First published 2007 by Knopf.

———. *Create Dangerously: The Immigrant Artist at Work*. New York: Vintage, 2010.

———. "Edwidge Danticat." In *Why We Write about Ourselves: Twenty Memoirists on Why They Expose Themselves (and Others) in the Name of Literature*, edited by Meredith Maran, 59–72. New York: Plume, 2016.

———. "Trump Reopens an Old Wound for Haitians." *New Yorker*, December 29, 2017. https://www.newyorker.com/news/news-desk/trump-reopens-an-old-wound-for-haitians.

Davies, Carole Boyce. *Caribbean Spaces: Escapes from Twilight Zones*. Urbana: University of Illinois Press, 2013.

Davis, Rocío G. "Vulnerable Observation in *An Island Called Home*: Ruth Behar's Story of the Jews of Cuba." *Prooftexts* 31, no. 3 (2011): 263–268.

DeLoughrey, Elizabeth M., Renée K. Gosson, and George B. Handley. "Introduction." In *Caribbean Literature and the Environment*, edited by Elizabeth M. DeLoughrey, Renée K. Gosson, and George B. Handley, 1–30. Charlottesville: University of Virginia Press, 2005.

Derby, Lauren. "Beyond Fugitive Speech: Rumor and Affect in Caribbean History." *Small Axe* 18, no. 2 (2014): 123–140.

Derrida, Jacques. *Archive Fever: A Freudian Impression*. Chicago: University of Chicago Press, 1998.

Despot, Odessa D. "Indo-Caribbean Women from Trinidad and Guyana: Hardships, Conflict, and Resiliency." *Meridians* 13, no. 2 (2016): 1–27.

Dibattista, Maria, and Emily O. Wittman. "Introduction." In *The Cambridge Companion to Autobiography*, edited by Maria Dibattista and Emily O. Wittman, 1–20. Cambridge: Cambridge University Press, 2014.

Dirlik, Arif. "Literature/Identity: Transnationalism, Narrative and Representation." *Review of Education, Pedagogy, and Cultural Studies* 24, no. 3 (2002): 209–234.

Doll, Megan. "Interview with Maryse Condé." *Bookslut*, February 2010. http://www.bookslut.com/features/2010_02_015665.php.

Donnell, Alison. "All Friends Now? Critical Conversations, West Indian Literature, and the 'Quarrel with History.'" *Small Axe* 38 (2013): 75–85.

———. "Happenings, Histories, and Literary Healing." In *The Routledge Companion to Anglophone Caribbean Literature*, edited by Michael A. Bucknor and Alison Donnell, 422–431. New York: Routledge, 2011.

———. "Quarrels with the Quarrel with History." *Anthurium* 10, no. 2 (2013): 1–4.

———. *The Routledge Companion to Anglophone Caribbean Literature*. Edited by Michael A. Bucknor and Alison Donnell. New York: Routledge, 2011.

———. *Twentieth-Century Caribbean Literature: Critical Moments in Anglophone Literary History*. London: Routledge, 2005.

———. "What It Means to Stay: Reterritorializing the Black Atlantic in Erna Brodber's Writing of the Local." *Third World Quarterly* 26, no. 3 (2005): 479–486.

Dubois, Laurent. "Solitude's Statue: Confronting the Past in the French Caribbean." *Outre-Mers* 94, nos. 350–351 (2006): 34–36.

Eakin, Paul John. *Fictions of Autobiography: Studies in the Art of Self-Invention*. Princeton: Princeton University Press, 1985.

Edmondson, Belinda. *Making Men: Gender, Literary Authority, and Women's Writing in Caribbean Narrative*. Durham, NC: Duke University Press, 1998.

Eller, Anne. "Rumors of Slavery: Defending Emancipation in a Hostile Caribbean." *American Historical Review* 122, no. 3 (2017): 653–679.

Ellis, Nadia. *Territories of the Soul: Queered Belonging in the Diaspora*. Durham, NC: Duke University Press, 2015.

Emery, Mary Lou. *Modernism, the Visual, and Caribbean Literature*. Cambridge: Cambridge University Press, 2007.

Enloe, Cynthia. *Bananas, Beaches and Bases: Making Feminist Sense of International Politics*. Berkeley: University of California Press, 2014.

Fassler, Joe. "How Surrealism Enriches Storytelling about Women: Interview with Carmen Maria Machado." *Atlantic*, October 12, 2017. https://www.theatlantic.com

/entertainment /archive/2017/10/how-surrealism-enriches-storytelling-about-women /542496/#article-comments.

Fenwick, Mac. "Simply There: Lorna Goodison's Gardens." *Journal of Commonwealth Literature* 46 (2011): 433–453.

Fleming, Crystal M. "White Cruelty or Republican Sins? Competing Frames of Stigma Reversal in French Commemorations of Slavery." *Ethnic and Racial Studies* 35, no. 3 (2012): 488–505.

Fooh, Rita Tjien. "Return of the Historical Archives (1661–1975) from the Netherlands to Suriname." In *Decolonizing the Caribbean Record: An Archives Reader*, edited by Jeannette A. Bastian, John A. Aarons, and Stanley H. Griffin, 79–92. Sacramento, CA: Litwin Books, 2018.

Forsdick, Charles. "Contrapuntal Memories of Slavery and Abolition in the French-Speaking World." In *Slavery, Memory, and Identity: National Representations and Global Legacies*, edited by Douglas Hamilton, Kate Hodgson, and Joel Quirk, 105–114. London: Pickering & Chatto, 2012.

Foucault, Michel. *The Archeology of Knowledge*. New York: Vintage, 2010.

Fournier, Lauren. "Sick Women, Sad Girls, and Selfie Theory: Autotheory as Contemporary Feminist Practice." *a/b: Auto/Biography Studies* 33, no. 3 (2018): 643–662.

Francis, Donette. *Fictions of Feminine Citizenship: Sexuality and the Nation in Contemporary Caribbean Literature*. London: Palgrave, 2010.

———. "The Last Stitch: A Praise Song for My Mother Who Mothered Me." *Small Axe* 14, no. 2 (2010): 160–167.

———. "Strategies of Caribbean Feminism." In *The Routledge Companion to Anglophone Caribbean Literature*, edited by Michael Bucknor and Alison Donnell, 332–343. London: Routledge, 2010.

Frank, Gelya. "Ruth Behar's Biography in the Shadow: A Review of Reviews." *American Anthropologist* 97, no. 2 (1995): 357–359.

Freedman, Diane P., and Olivia Frey, eds. *Autobiographical Writing across the Disciplines: A Reader.* Durham, NC: Duke University Press, 2004.

———. "Self/Discipline: An Introduction." In *Autobiographical Writing across the Disciplines: A Reader*, edited by Diane P. Freedman and Olivia Frey, 1–37. Durham, NC: Duke University Press, 2003.

Froude, James Anthony. *The English in the West Indies or The Bow of Ulysses*. London: Longman, Green, and Co, 1888.

Frow, John. *Time and Commodity Culture: Essays on Cultural Theory and Postmodernity.* Oxford: Oxford University Press, 1997.

Fuentes, Marisa J. *Dispossessed Lives: Enslaved Women, Violence, and the Archive*. Philadelphia: University of Pennsylvania Press, 2016.

Fuery, Patrick. *The Theory of Absence: Subjectivity, Signification, and Desire*. Westport, CT: Greenwood, 1995.

Fulton, Dawn. *Signs of Dissent: Maryse Condé and Postcolonial Criticism*. Charlottesville: University of Virginia Press, 2006.

Gannon, Megan. "Kitchen of Thomas Jefferson's Enslaved Chef Is Uncovered." *Live Science*, January 10, 2018. https://www.livescience.com/61388-thomas-jefferson-james -hemings-kitchen.html.

Gantz, Lauren J. "Archiving the Door of No Return in Dionne Brand's *At the Full and Change of the Moon*." *Meridians* 13, no. 2 (2016): 126–127.

García, Christina. *Dreaming in Cuban*. New York: Knopf, 1992.
García-Peña, Lorgia. *The Borders of Dominicanidad: Race, Nation, and Archives of Contradiction*. Durham, NC: Duke University Press, 2016.
Garvey, Johanna X. K. "Spaces of Violence, Desire, and Queer (Un)belonging: Dionne Brand's Urban Diasporas." *Textual Practice* 25, no. 4 (2011): 757–777.
Gikandi, Simon. "Reading at the Limits." *PMLA* 131, no. 3 (2016): 585–593.
———. "Rethinking the Archive of Enslavement." *Early American Literature* 50, no. 1 (2015): 81–102.
———. *Slavery and the Culture of Taste*. Princeton: Princeton University Press, 2011.
Gilmore, Leigh. *Autobiographics: A Feminist Theory of Women's Self-Representation*. Ithaca, NY: Cornell University Press, 1994.
———. *The Limits of Autobiography*. Ithaca, NY: Cornell University Press, 1990.
Gilpin, William. *Observations of the River Wye, and Several Parts of Wales, &c: Relative Chiefly to Picturesque Beauty Made in the Summer of 1770*. 2nd ed. London: Blamire, 1789. https://archive.org/stream/observationsonroogilpgoog#page/n42/mode/2up.
Gilroy, Paul. *The Black Atlantic: Modernity and Double-Consciousness*. Cambridge, MA: Harvard University Press, 1994.
Glave, Thomas. *Our Caribbean: A Gathering of Lesbian and Gay Writing from the Antilles*. Durham, NC: Duke University Press, 2008.
Glissant, Édouard. "History, Time, Identity." In *Caribbean Discourse: Selected Essays*, 92–96. Charlottesville: University of Virginia Press, 1989.
———. *Poetics of Relation*. Translated by Betsy Wing. Ann Arbor: University of Michigan Press, 1997.
———. "The Quarrel with History." In *Caribbean Discourse: Selected Essays*, 61–66. Charlottesville: University of Virginia Press, 1989.
Goebel, Walter, and Saskia Schabio, eds. *Locating Postcolonial Narrative Genres*. London: Routledge, 2013.
Goodison, Lorna. *From Harvey River: A Memoir of My Mother and Her Island*. New York: Amistad/HarperCollins, 2007.
———. "Reporting Back to Queen Isabella, Donette Francis, and Sandra Pouchet Paquet." *Small Axe* 14, no. 2 (2010): 179–183.
Gopinath, Gayatri. "Archive, Affect, and the Everyday: Queer Diasporic Re-visions." In *Political Emotions: New Agendas in Communication*, edited by Janet Staiger, Ann Cvetkovich, and Ann Reynolds, 165–192. London: Routledge, 2010.
Gordon, Avery. *Ghostly Matters: Haunting and the Sociological Imagination*. 2nd ed. Minneapolis: University of Minnesota Press, 2008.
———. "Introduction to the New Edition." In *Ghostly Matters: Haunting and the Sociological Imagination*, xv–xx. Minneapolis: University of Minnesota Press, 2008.
Goyal, Yogita. "Introduction: Africa and the Black Atlantic." *Research in African Literatures* 45, no. 3 (2014): v–xxv.
———. *Romance, Diaspora, and Black Atlantic Literature*. Cambridge: Cambridge University Press, 2010.
Green, Mary Jean. "Maryse Condé's Victoire: Thinking Back through Her Mothers." *Nottingham French Studies* 53, no. 3 (2014): 297–313.
Gregg, Veronica. "'This Past That Waits for Me': Erna Brodber's Critical Remembrance and the Challenge to History." In *Engendering Caribbean History: Cross-Cultural Perspectives*, edited by Verene Shepherd, 789–799. Kingston: Ian Randle, 2011.

Gulick, Anne W. "Africa, Pan-Africanism, and the Global Caribbean in Maryse Condé's *The Story of the Cannibal Women.*" *Global South* 4, no. 2 (2010): 49–75.

Gyasi, Yaa. *Homegoing.* New York: Vintage, 2017.

Hakewill, James. *A Picturesque Tour of the Island of Jamaica from Drawing Made in the Years 1820 and 1821.* London: Hurst and Robinson, 1825.

Hall, Stuart. *Familiar Strangers: A Life between Two Words.* Durham, NC: Duke University Press, 2017.

Halloran, Vivian Nun. *Exhibiting Slavery: The Caribbean Postmodern Novel as Museum.* Charlottesville: University of Virginia Press, 2009.

Halperin, Laura. *Intersections of Harm: Narratives of Latina Deviance and Defiance.* New Brunswick, NJ: Rutgers University Press, 2015.

Hanchard, Michael. "Black Memory versus State Memory: Notes toward a Method." *Small Axe* 12, no. 2 (2008): 45–62.

Hardwick, Louise. *Childhood, Autobiography and the Francophone Caribbean.* Liverpool: Liverpool University Press, 2013.

Harrison, Sheri-Marie. *Jamaica's Difficult Subjects: Negotiating Sovereignty in Anglophone Caribbean Literature and Criticism.* Columbus: Ohio State University Press, 2014.

Hartman, Saidiya. *Lose Your Mother: A Journey along the Atlantic Slave Route.* New York: Farrar, Straus and Giroux, 2007.

———. "Venus in Two Acts." *Small Axe* 28 (2008): 1–14.

Hartman, Saidiya, Eva Hoffman, and Daniel Mendelson. "Memoirs of Return." In *Rites of Return: Diaspora Poetics and the Politics of Memory,* edited by Marianne Hirsch and Nancy K. Miller, 107–123. New York: Columbia University Press, 2011.

Helton, Laura, Justine Leroy, Max A. Mishler, Samantha Seely, and Shauna Sweeney. "The Question of Recovery: An Introduction." *Social Text* 33, no. 4 (2015): 1–18.

Hess, Deborah M. *Maryse Condé: Mythe, Parabole Et Complexité.* Paris: L'Harmattan, 2011.

Higginbotham, Evelyn Brooks. "African-American Women's History and the Metalanguage of Race." *Signs* 17, no. 2 (1992): 251–274.

———. "'The Metalanguage of Race,' Then and Now." *Signs* 42, no. 3 (2017): 628–642.

Hirsch, Marianne. "The Generation of Postmemory." *Poetics Today* 29, no. 1 (2008): 103–128.

Hirsch, Marianne, and Nancy K. Miller, eds. *Rites of Return: Diaspora Politics and the Politics of Memory.* New York: Columbia University Press, 2011.

Hodges, Hugh. "Possession Rites and Healing Rituals in the Poetry of Lorna Goodison." *Research in African Literatures* 36, no. 2 (2005): 19–32.

Holden, Philip. *Autobiography and Decolonization: Modernity, Masculinity, and the Nation-State.* Madison: University of Wisconsin Press, 2008.

———. "Postcolonial Auto/Biography." In *The Cambridge History of Postcolonial Literature,* vol. 1, edited by Ato Quayson, 107–136. Cambridge: Cambridge University Press, 2011.

Hosein, Gabrielle Jamela. "Dougla Poetics and Politics in Indo-Caribbean Feminist Thought: Reflection and Reconceptualization." In *Indo-Caribbean Feminist Thought: Genealogies, Theories, Enactments,* edited by Gabrielle Jamela Hosein and Lisa Outar, 205–222. New York: Palgrave Macmillan, 2016.

Hosein, Gabrielle Jamela, and Lisa Outar. "Indo-Caribbean Feminisms: Charting Crossings in Geography, Discourse, and Politics." *Caribbean Review of Gender Studies* 6 (2012): 1–10.

———. "Introduction: Interrogating an Indo-Caribbean Feminist Epistemology." In *Indo-Caribbean Feminist Thought: Genealogies, Theories, Enactments*, edited by Gabrielle Jamela Hosein and Lisa Outar, 1–19. New York: Palgrave Macmillan, 2016.

Huddart, David. "Postcolonialism." In *Encyclopedia of Life Writing: Autobiographical and Biographical Forms*, edited by M. Jolly, 253–254. London: Routledge, 2001.

Hurston, Zora Neale. *Their Eyes Were Watching God*. 1937. Reprint, New York: Harper, 2010.

Innes, C. L. *Cambridge Introduction to Postcolonial Literatures in English*. Cambridge: Cambridge University Press, 2007.

James Alexander, Simone A. *Mother Imagery in the Novels of Afro-Caribbean Women*. Columbia: University of Missouri Press, 2001.

John, Catherine. "Caribbean Organic Intellectual: The Legacy and Challenge of Erna Brodber's Life's Work." *Small Axe* 39 (2012): 72–88.

Johnson, Jessica Marie. "Markup Bodies: Black [Life] Studies and Slavery [Death] Studies at the Digital Crossroads." *Social Text* 36, no. 4 (2018): 57–79.

Jones, Martha S. "On Cherokee Rose, Historical Fiction, and Silences in the Archives." *Process*, May 26, 2015. http://www.processhistory.org/on-the-cherokee-rose-historical-fiction-and-silences-in-the-archives/.

Josephs, Kelly Baker. "Articulating Caribbean Epistemologies." *Small Axe* 43 (2014): 99–102.

Keizer, Arlene. *Black Subjects: Identity Formation in the Contemporary Narrative of Slavery*. Ithaca, NY: Cornell University Press, 2004.

Kempadoo, Roshini. *Creole in the Archive: Imagery, Presence and the Location of the Caribbean Figure*. London: Rowman & Littlefield, 2016.

Khan, Aisha. "Material and Immaterial Bodies: Diaspora Studies and the Problem of Culture, Identity, and Race." *Small Axe* 48 (2015): 21–49.

Khan, Aliyah. "Voyages across Indenture: From Ship Sister to Mannish Woman." *GLQ* 22, no. 2 (2016): 249–280.

Kincaid, Jamaica. *Autobiography of My Mother*. New York: Farrar, Straus & Giroux, 1996.

King, Anna S. "Ashes and Flowers: Some Hindu Approaches to Death and Dying." *Journal of Beliefs and Values* 19, no. 1 (1998): 19–31.

Lambert-Hurley, Siobhan. "Life/History/Archive: Identifying Autobiographical Writing by Muslim Women in South Asia." *Journal of Women's History* 25, no. 2 (2013): 61–84.

Latina Feminist Group. *Telling to Live: Latina Feminist Testimonios*. Durham, NC: Duke University Press, 2001.

Lejeune, Philip. *On Autobiography*. Edited by Paul John Eakin, translated by Katherine Leary. Minneapolis: University of Minnesota Press, 1989.

Levine, Robert M. *Tropical Diaspora: The Jewish Experience in Cuba*. Gainesville: University Press of Florida, 1993.

Levy-Hussen, Aida. *How to Read African American Literature: Post–Civil Rights Fiction and the Task of Interpretation*. New York: New York University Press, 2016.

Lewis, Patsy. "Grenadian Reflections." *Stabroek News*, September 14, 2009. http://www.stabroeknews.com/2009/features/09/14/grenadian-reflections/.

Lindsay, Lisa A., and John Wood Sweet. "Introduction: Biography and the Black Atlantic." In *Biography and the Black Atlantic*, edited by Lisa A. Lindsay and John Wood Sweet, 1–16. Philadelphia: University of Pennsylvania Press, 2014.

Lionnet, Françoise. *Autobiographical Voices: Race, Gender, Self-Portraiture*. Ithaca, NY: Cornell University Press, 1995.

———. "Narrating the Americas: Transcolonial Métissage and Maryse Condé's La Migration des coeurs." In *Mixing Race, Mixing Culture*, edited by Monika Kaup and Debra J. Rosenthal, 65–87. Austin: University of Texas Press, 2002.

———. *Postcolonial Representations: Women, Literature, Identity*. Ithaca, NY: Cornell University Press, 1995.

Lionnet, Françoise, and Shu-mei Shih. "Introduction: Thinking through the Minor, Transnationally." In *Minor Transnationalism*, edited by Françoise Lionnet and Shu-mei Shih, 1–23. Durham, NC: Duke University Press, 2005.

Loichot, Valérie. *The Tropics Bite Back: Culinary Coups in Caribbean Literature*. Minneapolis: University of Minnesota Press, 2013.

"'Lose Your Mother' Author Finds Heritage in Africa." National Public Radio, January 23, 2007. https://www.npr.org/templates/story/story.php?storyId=6955366.

Lowe, Lisa. *The Intimacies of Four Continents*. Durham, NC: Duke University Press, 2015.

Löytömäki, Stiina. "French Memory Laws and the Ambivalence about the Meaning of Colonialism." In *The Palgrave Handbook of State Sponsored History after 1945*, edited by Berber Bevernage and Nico Wouters, 87–92. Basingstoke, UK: Palgrave Macmillan, 2018.

Lugones, María. "Toward a Decolonial Feminism." *Hypatia* 22, no. 4 (2010): 742–759.

MacDonald, Antonia. "Erna Brodber: A Poetics of Redemption." In *The Routledge Companion to Caribbean Literature*, edited by Michael A. Bucknor and Alison Donnell, 20–26. London: Routledge, 2011.

Mahabir, Joy, and Mariam Pirbhai. "Introduction: Tracing an Emerging Tradition." In *Critical Perspectives on Indo-Caribbean Women's Literature*, vol. 4, edited by Joy Mahabir and Mariam Pirbhai, 1–21. New York: Routledge, 2013.

Malhotra, Anshu, and Siobhan Lambert-Hurley, eds. *Speaking of the Self: Gender, Performance, and Autobiography in South Asia*. Durham, NC: Duke University Press, 2015.

Marshall, Paule. *Triangular Road: A Memoir*. New York: Perseus, 2009.

Martínez-San Miguel, Yolanda. "Colonial and Mexican Archipelagoes: Reimagining Colonial Caribbean Studies." In *Archipelagic American Studies*, edited by Brian Russell Roberts and Michelle Ann Stephens, 155–173. Durham, NC: Duke University Press, 2017.

Meeks, Brian. "Grenada Once Again: Revisiting the 1983 Crisis and Collapse of the Grenada Revolution." In *The Grenada Revolution: Reflections and Lessons*, edited by Wendy C. Grenade, 87–113. Jackson: University of Mississippi Press, 2015.

Miller, Christopher L. *The French Atlantic Triangle: Literature and Culture of the Slave Trade*. Durham, NC: Duke University Press, 2008.

Mohammed, Patricia. "Unmasking Masculinity and Deconstructing Patriarchy: Problems and Possibilities within Feminist Epistemology." In *Interrogating Caribbean Masculinities: Theoretical and Empirical Analyses*, edited by Rhoda E. Reddock, 38–67. Kingston: University of the West Indies Press, 2004.

Morrison, Toni. *Beloved*. New York: Knopf, 1987.

Morton, Sarah E. *John Morton of Trinidad*. Toronto: Westminster, 1916.

Moten, Fred. "Preface for a Solo by Miles Davis." *Women and Performance: A Journal of Feminist Theory* 17, no. 2 (2007): 217–246.

Muñoz, José Esteban. "Ephemera as Evidence: Introductory Notes to Queer Acts." *Women & Performance* 8, no. 2 (January 1996): 5–16. https://doi.org/10.1080/07407709608571228.

———. "The Sense of Watching Tony Sleep." In *After Sex? On Writing since Queer Theory*, edited by Janet Halley and Andrew Parker, 142–150. Durham, NC: Duke University Press, 2011.

Naipaul, V. S. *The Middle Passage: The Caribbean Revisited*. London: Macmillan, 1962.

Nair, Supriya. "Caribbean Groundings and Limbo Gateways." In *Teaching Anglophone Caribbean Literature*, edited by Supriya Nair, 1–28. New York: Modern Language Association, 2012.

———. *Pathologies of Paradise: Caribbean Detours*. Charlottesville: University of Virginia Press, 2013.

———. *Teaching Anglophone Caribbean Literature*. Edited by Supriya Nair. New York: Modern Language Association, 2012.

Nelson, Alondra. *The Social Life of DNA: Race, Reparations, and Reconciliation after the Genome*. New York: Beacon, 2017.

Nelson, Charmaine A. *Slavery, Geography and Empire in Nineteenth-Century Marine Landscapes of Montreal and Jamaica*. New York: Routledge, 2016.

Nelson, Maggie. *The Argonauts*. Minneapolis: Graywolf, 2015.

Neptune, Harvey. "Loving through Loss: Reading Saidiya Hartman's History of Black Hurt." *Anthurium* 6, no. 1 (2008): 1–9.

Nesbitt, Nick. "Caribbean Literature in French: Origins and Development." In *The Cambridge History of African and Caribbean Literature*, edited by F. Abiola Irele and Simon Gikandi, 643–669. Cambridge: Cambridge University Press, 2008.

———. *Voicing Memory: History and Subjectivity in French Caribbean Literature*. Charlottesville: University of Virginia Press, 2003.

Nettleford, Rex. *Caribbean Cultural Identity: The Case of Jamaica*. Los Angeles: Center for Afro-American Studies and UCLA Latin American Center, 1979.

Nwosu, Chiamaka, and Jeanne Batalova. "Immigrants from the Dominican Republic in the United States." Migration Policy Institute, July 18, 2014. http://migrationpolicy.org/article/immigrants-dominican-republic-united-states#:~:targetText=Large-scale%20migration%20from%20the,and%20other%20government%20agencies%20intervened.

Paquet, Sandra Pouchet. "Autobiography and Autobiographical Fiction in the Caribbean." In *The Novel in Africa and the Caribbean since 1950*, edited by Simon Gikandi, 332–343. Oxford: Oxford University Press, 2016.

———. *Caribbean Autobiography: Cultural Identity and Self-Representation*. Madison: University of Wisconsin Press, 2002.

———. "The Mediated Self in the Contested Domain of Caribbean Autobiography." In *Auto/Biography across the Americas*, edited by Ricia A. Chansky, 111–126. New York: Routledge, 2016.

———. "Sewing Up Questions of Cultural Identity: Lorna Goodison's *From Harvey River*." *Small Axe* 14, no. 2 (2010): 168–178.

Parsard, Kaneesha Cherelle. "Cutlass: Objects toward a Theory of Representation." In *Indo-Caribbean Feminist Thought: Genealogies, Theories, Enactments*, edited by Gabrielle Jamela Hosein and Lisa Outar, 241–260. New York: Palgrave Macmillan, 2016.

Paton, Diana. "Telling Stories about Slavery." *History Workshop Journal* 59 (2005): 251–262.

Patterson, Orlando. *Slavery and Social Death: A Comparative Study*. Cambridge, MA: Harvard University Press, 1982.

Payne, Hugh. "Working at the National Archives of Guyana: Experiences, Challenges & Lessons." In *Decolonizing the Caribbean: An Archives Reader*, edited by Jeanette A. Bastian, 115–135. Sacramento, CA: Litwin Books, 2018.

Peluso, Nancy Lee. "Whose Woods Are These? Counter-Mapping Forest Territories in Kalimantan, Indonesia." *Antipode* 27, no. 4 (1995): 383–406.

Pérez-Rosario, Vanessa. "On the Hispanophone Caribbean Question." *Small Axe* 51 (2016): 21–31.

Perry, Imani. *Vexy Thing: On Gender and Liberation*. Durham, NC: Duke University Press, 2018.

Phelan, James. "Fictionality." *a/b: Auto/Biography Studies* 32, no. 2 (2017): 235–238.

Philip, M. NourbeSe. *Zong! as Told to the Author by Setaey Adamu Boateng*. Middletown, CT: Wesleyan University Press, 2008.

Phillip-Dowe, Nicole. "Women in the Grenada Revolution, 1979–1983." *Social and Economic Studies* 62, nos. 3–4 (2013): 45–82.

Phillips, Caryl. *The Atlantic Sound*. New York: Vintage, 2000.

———. *Color Me English: Reflections on Migration and Belonging Before and After 9/11*. New York: New Press, 2011.

———. *A New World Order: Essays*. New York: Vintage, 2001.

Pirbhai, Mariam. "Recasting *Jahaji-Bhain*: Plantation History and the Indo-Caribbean Women's Novel in Trinidad, Guyana and Martinique." In *Critical Perspectives on Indo-Caribbean Women's Literature*, vol. 4, edited by Joy Mahabir and Mariam Pirbhai, 25–47. New York: Routledge, 2013.

Podnieks, Elizabeth, and Andrea O'Reilly. "Introduction: Maternal Literatures in Text and Tradition: Daughter-Centric, Matrilineal and Matrifocal Perspectives." In *Textual Mothers, Maternal Texts: Motherhood in Contemporary Women's Literatures*, edited by Elizabeth Podnieks and Andrea O'Reilly, 1–27. Waterloo: Wilfrid Laurier University Press, 2010.

Power, Margaret. "Interview with Lolita Lebrón." *Radical History Review* 128 (2017): 37–45.

Pratt, Mary Louise. *Imperial Eyes: Travel Writing and Transculturation*. London: Routledge, 1992.

Prince, Mary. *History of Mary Prince, a West Indian Slave. Related by Herself. With a Supplement by the Editor. To Which Is Added, the Narrative of Asa-Asa, a Captured African*. London: F. Westley and A. H. Davis, 1831.

Puertas, Lucia Llano. "Touching the Past: The Inscription of Trauma and Affect in Francophone Neo-Slave Narratives." *Callaloo* 40, no. 4 (2017): 78–93.

Pulitano, Elvira. *Transnational Narratives from the Caribbean: Diasporic Literature and the Human Experience*. London: Routledge, 2016.

Puri, Shalini. "Fielding the Field: Notes on Caribbean Cultural Criticism, Area Studies, and the Forms of Engagement." *Small Axe* 17, nos. 2 and 4 (2013): 60, 68.

———. *The Grenadian Revolution in the Caribbean Present: Operation Urgent Memory*. New York: Palgrave Macmillan, 2014.

Raiskin, Judith. "The Art of History: An Interview with Michelle Cliff." *Kenyon Review* 15 (1993): 57–71.

Rak, Julie. *Boom! Manufacturing Memoir for the Popular Market*. Waterloo: Wilfrid Laurier University Press, 2013.

———. "Radical Connections: Genealogy, Small Lives, Big Data." *a/b: Auto/Biography Studies* 32, no. 3 (2017): 479–497.

Ramazi, Jahan. "Lorna Goodison." *Caribbean Quarterly* 64, nos. 3–4 (2018): 560–580.

Rauch, Nina. "Women: Sins of the Mothers Her Grandmother Risked Death in an Act of Terrorism That Involved Shooting Five Men." *Guardian*, December 1, 1998: A6.

Reinhardt, Catherine. *Claims to Memory: Beyond Slavery and Emancipation in the French Caribbean*. New York: Berghahn Books, 2006.

Réjouis, Rose. "Dark Horse Poetics: Lévi-Strauss, Benítez-Rojo, and Caribbean Epistemology." *Small Axe* 43 (2014): 103–113.

"A Renaissance in Writing." *Jamaica Gleaner*, August 21, 2016. http://jamaica-gleaner.com/article/commentary/20160821/editorial-renaissance-writing.

Reyes-Santos, Alaí. *Our Caribbean Kin: Race and Nation in the Neoliberal Antilles*. New Brunswick, NJ: Rutgers University Press, 2015.

Rhys, Jean. "Heat." *New Yorker*, May 17, 1976, 36–37.

Rice-Maximin, Micheline. *Karukéra: Presence littéraire de la Guadeloupe*. New York: Peter Lang, 1988.

Richards, Thomas. *The Imperial Archive: Knowledge and the Fantasy of Empire*. London: Verso, 1993.

Riley, Joan. *The Unbelonging*. London: Women's Press, 1985.

Roberts, Elizabeth F. S. "Bioethnography and the Birth Cohort: A Method for Making New Kinds of Anthropological Knowledge about Transmission (Which Is What Anthropology Has Been about All Along)." *Science, Medicine, and Anthropology*, November 19, 2019. http://somatosphere.net/2019/bioethnography-anthropological-knowledge-transmission.html/.

Roberts, Neil. *Freedom as Marronage*. Chicago: University of Chicago Press, 2015.

Rodríquez, Ileana. *Transatlantic Topographies: Islands, Highlands, Jungles*. Minneapolis: University of Minnesota Press, 2004.

Roig-Franzia, Manuel. "A Terrorist in the House." *Washington Post Magazine*, February 22, 2004. https://www.washingtonpost.com/archive/lifestyle/magazine/2004/02/22/a-terrorist-in-the-house/293c52cd-8794-47bd-9960-9c7a871e009c/.

Roig-Franzia, Manuel, and Nina Rauch. "Women: Sins of the Mothers." *Guardian*, December 1, 1998.

Rosenberg, Leah Reade. "Anglophone Caribbean Literature and the Canon." In *The Routledge Companion to Anglophone Caribbean Literature*, edited by Michael A. Bucknor and Alison Donnell, 347–364. London: Routledge, 2011.

Rubin, Gayle. "The Traffic in Women: Notes on the 'Political Economy' of Sex." In *Toward an Anthropology of Women*, edited by Rayna R. Reiter, 157–210. New York: Monthly Review Press, 1975.

Ruiz, Sandra. *Ricanness: Enduring Time in Anticolonial Performance*. New York: New York University Press, 2019.

Sáez, Elena Machado. *Market Aesthetics: The Purchase of the Past in Caribbean Diasporic Fiction*. Charlottesville: University of Virginia Press, 2015.

Sankara, Edgard. *Postcolonial Autobiographies: From Africa to the Antilles*. Charlottesville: University of Virginia Press, 2011.

———. *Postcolonial Francophone Autobiographies: From Africa to the Antilles*. Charlottesville: University of Virginia Press, 2011.

Sansavior, Eva. *Maryse Condé and the Space of Literature*. London: Legenda, 2012.

Saunders, Patricia. "Defending the Dead, Confronting the Archive: A Conversation with M. NourbeSe Philip." *Small Axe* 26 (2008): 63–79.

———. "Fugitive Dreams of Diaspora: Conversations with Saidiya Hartman." *Anthurium* 6, no. 1 (2008): 1–16.

Schwarz-Bart, Simone. *Between Two Worlds*. New York: Harper & Row, 1981.

Scott, David. *Conscripts of Modernity: The Tragedy of Colonial Enlightenment*. Durham, NC: Duke University Press, 2004.

———. "Introducing Small Axe." *Small Axe* 1 (1997): 1–3.

———. "Introduction: On the Archaeologies of Black Memory." *Small Axe* 26, no. 2 (2008): v–xvi.

———. *Omens of Adversity: Tragedy, Time, Memory, Justice*. Durham, NC: Duke University Press, 2014.

Scott, Joan Wallach. "Gender: A Useful Category of Historical Analysis." *American Historical Review* 91, no. 5 (1989): 1053–1075.

Sharpe, Christina. *In the Wake: On Blackness and Being*. Durham, NC: Duke University Press, 2016.

Sharpe, Jenny. *Ghosts of Slavery: A Literary Archeology of Black Women's Lives*. Minneapolis: University of Minnesota Press, 2002.

Sheller, Mimi. *Consuming the Caribbean: From Arawaks to Zombies*. London: Routledge, 2003.

Shepherd, Verene A. "Indian Women and Labor Migration to the Caribbean: An Overview." In *Engendering Caribbean History: Cross-Cultural Perspectives*, edited by Verene Shepherd, 553–586. Kingston: Ian Randle, 2011.

———. *Maharani's Misery: Narratives of a Passage from India to the Caribbean*. Mona: University of the West Indies Press, 2002.

Siemsen, Thora. "On Working with Archives: An Interview with Writer Saidiya Hartman." *Creative Independent*, April 18, 2018. https://thecreativeindependent.com/people/saidiya-hartman-on-working-with-archives/.

Simmonds, Doig. "A Note on the Excavations in Cape Coast Castle." *Transactions of the Historical Society of Ghana* 14, no. 2 (1973): 267–269.

Singer, Natalia Rachel. "Life Experiences through Hybrid Memoirs." *Chronical Higher Education*, October 22, 2004. https://www.chronicle.com/article/The-Most-Influential-Books/6356.

Smith, Faith. "Introduction: Sexing the Citizen." In *Sex and the Citizen: Interrogating the Caribbean*, edited by Faith Smith, 1–18. Charlottesville: University of Virginia Press, 2011.

Smith, Sidonie. "Narratives and Rights: 'Zlata's Diary' and the Circulation of Stories of Ethnic Suffering." In *The Global and the Intimate: Feminism in Our Time*, edited by Geraldine Pratt and Victoria Rosner, 168–185. New York: Columbia University, 2012.

———. *Subjectivity, Identity, and the Body: Women's Autobiographical Practices in the Twentieth Century*. Bloomington: Indiana University Press, 1993.

Smith, Sidonie, and Julia Watson. *Reading Autobiography: A Guide for Interpreting Life Narratives*. 2nd ed. Minneapolis: University of Minnesota Press, 2010.

Spillers, Hortense J. "Mama's Baby, Papa's Maybe: An American Grammar Book." *Diacritics* 17, no. 2 (1987): 64–81.

Spivak, Gayatri Chakravorty. "Three Women's Texts and Circumfession." In *Postcolonialism & Autobiography: Michelle Cliff, David Dabydeen, Opal Palmer Adisa*, edited by Alfred Horung and Ernstpeter Ruhe, 7–22. Amsterdam: Rodopi, 1998.

Spurr, David. *The Rhetoric of Empire: Colonial Discourse in Journalism, Travel Writing, and Imperial Administration*. Durham, NC: Duke University Press, 1993.

Steedman, Carolyn. *Dust: The Archive and Cultural History.* New Brunswick, NJ: Rutgers University Press, 2002.

Stephens, Michelle. "What Is an Island? Caribbean Studies and the Contemporary Visual Artist." *Small Axe* 41 (2013): 8–57.

Stitt, Jocelyn Fenton. "The Aftereffects of Slavery: A Black Feminist Genealogy." *Meridians* 17, no. 1 (2018): 150–162.

———. "Disciplining the Unruly (National) Body in Staceyann Chin's *The Other Side of Paradise.*" *Small Axe* 45 (2014): 1–17.

———. "Gendered Legacies of Romantic Nationalism in the Works of Michelle Cliff." *Small Axe* 24 (2007): 52–72.

Stratchan-Innerarity, Racquel. "Preserving Archival Collections in the 21st Century: The Caribbean Experience." In *Decolonizing the Caribbean Record: An Archives Reader*, edited by Jeannette A. Bastian, John A. Aarons, and Stanley H. Griffin, 363–410. Sacramento, CA: Litwin Books, 2018.

Stuart, Andrea. *Sugar in the Blood: A Family's Story of History and Empire.* London: Portobello Books, 2012.

Tancons, Claire. "Women in the Whirlwind: Withholding Guadeloupe's Archipelagic History." *Small Axe* 16, no. 3 (2012): 143–165.

Thomas, Bonnie. *Connecting Histories: Francophone Caribbean Writers Interrogating Their Past.* Jackson: University of Mississippi Press, 2017.

———. "The Cook and the Writer: Maryse Condé's Journey of Self-Discovery." *PORTAL* 10, no. 2 (2013): 1–12.

Thomas, Deborah. "Caribbean Studies, Archive Building, and the Problem of Violence." *Small Axe* 41 (2013): 27–42.

Thompson, Krista. "The Evidence of Things Not Photographed: Slavery and Historical Memory in the British West Indies." *Representations* 113, no. 1 (2011): 39–71.

———. *An Eye for the Tropics: Tourism, Photography and Framing the Caribbean Picturesque.* Durham, NC: Duke University Press, 2006.

Tiffin, Helen. "Rites of Resistance: Counter-Discourse and West Indian Biography." *Journal of West Indian Literature* 3, no. 1 (1989): 28–46.

Tinsley, Omise'eke Natasha. "Black Atlantic, Queer Atlantic: Queer Imaginings of the Middle Passage." *GLQ* 14 (2008): 191–215.

———. *Ezili's Mirrors: Imagining Black Queer Gender.* Durham, NC: Duke University Press, 2018.

———. *Thiefing Sugar: Eroticism between Women in Caribbean Literature.* Durham, NC: Duke University Press, 2010.

Trotz, D. Alissa. "The Caribbean Family?" In *A Companion to Gender Studies*, edited by Philomena Essed, David Theo Goldberg, and Audrey Kobayashi, 370–380. Malden, MA: Blackwell Publishing, 2005.

Trouillot, Michel-Rolph. *Silencing the Past: Power and the Production of History.* New York: Beacon, 1995.

Tuck, Eve, and K. Wayne Yang. "R-Words: Refusing Research." In *Humanizing Research: Decolonizing Qualitative Inquiry with Youth and Communities*, edited by Django Paris and Maisha T. Winn, 223–248. Thousand Oaks, CA: Sage, 2014.

Twitty, Michael W. *The Cooking Gene: A Journey through African American History in the Old South.* New York: Amistad, 2017.

Vergés, François. "Cartographies of Memory, Politics of Emancipation." In *At the Limits of Memory: Legacies of Slavery in the Francophone World*, edited by Nicola Frith and Kate Hodgson, 229–248. Liverpool: Liverpool University Press, 2015.

Vilar, Irene. *The Ladies' Gallery: A Memoir of Family Secrets*. Translated by Gregory Rabassa. 1996. Reprint, New York: Other Press, 2009.

Wahab, Amar, and Dwaine Plaza. "Queerness in the Transnational Caribbean-Canadian Diaspora." *Caribbean Review of Gender Studies* 3 (2009): 1–34.

Wainwright, Leon. "Solving Caribbean Mysteries: Art, Embodiment and an Eye for the Tropics." *Small Axe* 12, no. 1 (2008): 133–144.

Walcott, Derek. "The Antilles: Fragments of Epic Memory." In *Caribbean Art at the Crossroads of the World*, edited by Deborah Cullen and Elvis Fuentes, 1–34. New Haven, CT: Yale University Press, 2012.

Wall, Cheryl. *Worrying the Line: Black Women Writers, Lineage, and Literary Tradition*. Chapel Hill: University of North Carolina Press, 2005.

Watson, Julia. "Ordering the Family: Genealogy as Autobiographical Pedigree (1996)." In *Life Writing in the Long Run: A Smith and Watson Autobiography Studies Reader*, edited by Sidonie Smith and Julia Watson. Ann Arbor: Michigan Publishing, 2017. http://dx.doi.org/10.3998/mpub.9739969.

Whitlock, Gillian. *Postcolonial Life Narratives: Testimonial Transactions*. Oxford: Oxford University Press, 2015.

———. *Soft Weapons: Autobiography in Transit*. Chicago: University of Chicago Press, 2012.

Williams, Heather Andrea. *Help Me to Find My People: The African American Search for Family Lost in Slavery*. Chapel Hill: University of North Carolina Press, 2012.

Williams, James. *Narrative of Events, since the First of August, 1834, by James Williams an Apprenticed Labourer in Jamaica*. Durham, NC: Duke University Press, 2001.

Winks, Christopher. "From Harvey River: A Memoir of My Mother and Her Island." *Review: Literature and Arts of the Americas* 42, no. 1 (2009): 138–140.

Wolff, Rebecca. "Maryse Condé." *Bomb*, July 1, 1999. https://bombmagazine.org/articles/maryse-condé/.

Wynter, Sylvia. "Novel and History, Plot and Plantation." *Savacou* 5 (1971): 95–102.

Yaeger, Patricia. "Ghosts and Shattered Bodies, or What Does It Mean to Still Be Haunted by Southern Literature?" *South Central Review* 22, no. 1 (2005): 87–108.

Yager, Jordy. "A Former Plantation Begins to Tell as Fuller of Slavery in America." National Public Radio, December 9, 2018. https://www.npr.org/2018/12/09/672349672/a-former-plantation-begins-to-tell-a-fuller-story-of-slavery-in-america.

Yuval-Davis, Nira. "Belonging and the Politics of Belonging." *Patterns of Prejudice* 40, no. 3 (2006): 197–214.

Index

About the Author

Jocelyn Fenton Stitt is division chair of social sciences, associate professor of women's studies, and affiliated faculty in critical studies of race and ethnicity, at St. Catherine University. Previously she was director of faculty research development at the Institute for Research on Women and Gender, University of Michigan. She coedited *Mothers Who Deliver: Feminist Interventions in Public and Interpersonal Discourse* (2010) and *Before Windrush: Recovering a Black and Asian Literary Heritage within Britain* (2008).

Available titles in the Critical Caribbean Studies series:

Giselle Anatol, *The Things That Fly in the Night: Female Vampires in Literature of the Circum-Caribbean and African Diaspora*

Alaí Reyes-Santos, *Our Caribbean Kin: Race and Nation in the Neoliberal Antilles*

Milagros Ricourt, *The Dominican Racial Imaginary: Surveying the Landscape of Race and Nation in Hispaniola*

Katherine A. Zien, *Sovereign Acts: Performing Race, Space, and Belonging in Panama and the Canal Zone*

Frances R. Botkin, *Thieving Three-Fingered Jack: Transatlantic Tales of a Jamaican Outlaw, 1780–2015*

Melissa A. Johnson, *Becoming Creole: Nature and Race in Belize*

Carlos Garrido Castellano, *Beyond Representation in Contemporary Caribbean Art: Space, Politics, and the Public Sphere*

Njelle W. Hamilton, *Phonographic Memories: Popular Music and the Contemporary Caribbean Novel*

Lia T. Bascomb, *In Plenty and in Time of Need: Popular Culture and the Remapping of Barbadian Identity*

Aliyah Khan, *Far from Mecca: Globalizing the Muslim Caribbean*

Rafael Ocasio, *Race and Nation in Puerto Rican Folklore: Franz Boas and John Alden Mason in Porto Rico*

Ana-Maurine Lara, *Streetwalking: LGBTQ Lives and Protest in the Dominican Republic*

Anke Birkenmaier, ed., *Caribbean Migrations: The Legacies of Colonialism*

Sherina Feliciano-Santos, *A Contested Caribbean Indigeneity: Language, Social Practice, and Identity within Puerto Rican Taíno Activism*

H. Adlai Murdoch, ed., *The Struggle of Non-Sovereign Caribbean Territories: Neoliberalism since the French Antillean Uprisings of 2009*

Robert Fatton Jr., *The Guise of Exceptionalism: Unmasking the National Narratives of Haiti and the United States*

Rafael Ocasio, *Folk Stories from the Hills of Puerto Rico/Cuentos folklóricos de las montañas de Puerto Rico*

Yveline Alexis, *Haiti Fights Back: The Life and Legacy of Charlemagne Péralte*

Katerina Gonzalez Seligmann, *Writing the Caribbean in Magazine Time*

Jocelyn Fenton Stitt, *Dreams of Archives Unfolded: Absence and Caribbean Life Writing*

